Practical Insight into CMMI®

Tim Kasse

Artech House
Boston • London
www.artechhouse.com

Library of Congress Cataloging-in-Publication Data
A catalog record for this book is available from the U.S. Library of Congress.

British Library Cataloguing in Publication Data
Kasse, Tim
   Practical insight into CMMI.—(Artech House computing library)
   1. Capability Maturity Model (Computer software)
   I. Title
   005.1'0685

ISBN 1-58053-625-5

Cover design by Yekaterina Ratner

International Standard Book Number: 1-58053-625-5

10 9 8 7 6 5 4 3 2 1

Practical Insight into CMMI®

For a listing of recent titles in the *Artech House Computing Library*,
turn to the back of this book.

To the process improvement and quality management professionals who toil in their respective companies to positively influence the development and delivery of the highest possible product and service quality that their projects can produce

Contents

6 The Evolutionary Differences Between CMM for Software and CMMI 69

8 Enabling the Project Leader to Better Manage and Control Through Risk Management 99

9 Enabling the Project Leader to Better Manage and Control Through Quality Management 107

Foreword by Bob Rassa

One thing that users of the new Capability Maturity Model–Integrated (CMMI®) have needed is a solid, easily understood practical guide to CMMI® adoption. CMMI® is still relatively new; users are still feeling their way along the path to success, and on that path they are realizing that solid interpretative guidance is hard to come by. This new book certainly satisfies that need for the process improvement community. As more and more organizations, commercial and defense, firm up their CMMI® adoption plans, they can count on this book as the most comprehensive and practical CMMI® implementation guide to date.

Based on his (and his colleagues') extensive background with the predecessor models, and his in-depth knowledge of systems engineering and software process methodologies, Tim Kasse has generated an extremely insightful and absolutely essential treatise on CMMI®. Long on background to provide a solid foundation of understanding, this guide provides clear and appropriate interpretations of CMMI® requirements and deployment concepts, with heavy emphasis on practical application and understanding.

Mr. Kasse also hits home on several essential elements of CMMI®. If one examines the CMMI® Continuous Representation, one can recognize that there is some increased focus on Project Management over the predecessor models, but the true significance of this doesn't always resonate. Mr. Kasse provides extremely powerful discussions, with real-world examples, that clarify the essential Project Management roles and responsibilities in CMMI®, roles that if not adequately fulfilled can lead to less than successful CMMI® implementation. This book also clearly articulates the increased emphasis on systems engineering, and helps clarify that CMMI® is not merely a maturity model that integrates stovepipe discipline-based models, but is rather a model for process improvement that causes exceptional systems engineering content to appear in the design environment of adopting organizations. And this, in fact, may be the single greatest advantage that CMMI® has over any other model set for process improvement.

Another major strength is the in-depth discussion on what CMMI® really means to the organization, and how to go about building the business case for adoption. Of particular significance is the discussion on achieving CMMI® Levels 4 and 5, wherein the real benefits and return-on-investment of continuous process improvement are felt. Level 5 is where the two representations of CMMI®, staged and continuous, tend to merge with only slight differences, and this book provides an outstanding discussion of both the similarities and the differences, thus giving the reader enough information to make the right intelligent decision about which representation to adopt.

Without question, this book is essential reading for the key members of any organization either contemplating, or in the process of, CMMI® adoption. It provides sufficient insight to answer most of the questions that have arisen relative to CMMI® interpretation, and will certainly be viewed as the definitive bible on CMMI® for many years to come.

Bob Rassa, Raytheon
CMMI® Steering Group Chair (Industry)

Foreword by Mike Phillips

As I write this foreword to Tim Kasse's book, we are nearing the third anniversary of the CMMI® Product Suite Version 1.1. Process improvement professionals like Mr. Kasse have trained over 10,000 people in this model, and appraisal teams have benchmarked nearly 200 organizations against this standard for developmental excellence. Our Web site at the SEI is now being accessed over a million times a month, by product developing organizations around the world. Though its origins are in the software and systems engineering communities, organizations are discovering its value in projects throughout today's complex enterprises. They are improving processes and practices, products and services, technical and business approaches.

Because progress along the model's improvement paths has often become a requirement for selection as a supplier, the CMMI® framework is often known for its maturity and capability levels. But the real value of the effort to understand and improve the organization's processes is NOT to "reach a level." Rather, it is in the direct result on the product—and the professional competence and agility of the organization to address the changes in a dynamic, high technology marketplace—that real "return on investment" is realized.

As we have expanded the coverage of these practices to more and more elements of the organization, it was time for a book like this one. The CMMI® framework captures hundreds of practices for organizations to consider to perform "better and better." But what are the ways that leaders can use the results of these efforts? How can they stimulate—champion—the "maturing" of the organization?

Mr. Kasse brings his years of experience in development, and in aiding others on their process improvement journey, to you in this "workbook." His "fire in the belly" is evident when he addresses audiences around the world to encourage them to get on board—and enjoy the ride toward better products and services delivered from workplaces that are also becoming more enriching environments.

It is my hope that you will earmark pages that assist you in making a difference on the projects and products that you lead or guide—whether they are developing software intensive systems, or in parts of the enterprise we have just begun to consider!

Mike Phillips, CMMI® Program Manager, Software Engineering Institute,
Carnegie Mellon University, Pittsburgh, Pennsylvania

Preface

For years, while offering training, mentoring, coaching, and general process improvement consultancy based upon CMM® for Software, I have frequently heard comments like the following:

- "We understand and appreciate what you are saying, but our management..."

- "Our management does not understand what CMM® is all about. All they care about is the Maturity Level 3 rating."

- "The problem is not the senior management team, but the middle managers. They don't understand how CMM® is going to help the organization!"

- "How is this going to help our business?"

- "The senior management team is totally committed to process improvement. We have supported CMM® training and assessment. Yes, we want to see measurable business results...not just get a level."

- "The middle managers are not the biggest problem. Believe it or not, the practitioners are the ones complaining about this process improvement effort...because they are under a lot of pressure and they feel this is only going to add to it!"

- "Our project managers believe in quality, but they are under pressure to get the product delivered better, faster, and cheaper, with emphasis on faster. They would like to improve and make it easier for their developers, but do not believe that using a model like CMM® is practical."

In other words, there was some complaint at each level of management and from practitioners about their understanding about the model and/or their willingness to support its full implementation and their ability to get any kind of real business value out of it. The unknowns were always too great from their point of view, and the return on investment was not well understood or believed.

Some leading companies did use CMM® for Software as a guide for excellence. They were the ones that realized not only the achievement of a higher maturity level, but also the promised accompanying business results.

With the release of the CMM® Integration^SM (CMMI®) Reference Model, the complaints and the resistance have started all over again. A few of the comments are different this time because of the increased content and the enlarged scope of the CMMI®. However, the basic reaction is yet another déjà vu knee-jerk response similar to the same one given about CMM® more than a decade earlier. What I soon realized was that very few people in any organization had the background, ability, and the desire to read through all of the details offered in CMMI®, much less digest them and share them in a convincing way with their management team and colleagues throughout the organization or business.

Almost all of CMMI® V1.1 Reference Model trainings in which I have personally participated have resulted in the participants expressing thanks for the excellent insight that was given on CMMI®, along with the added input that an additional course should be offered to the senior and middle managers to "get them to understand."

In 1998, I was asked to coach a senior and middle management team on the "essence" of CMM®. CMM® concepts were presented as "The Look and Feel of CMM®." Senior and middle management teams wanted to know what they should see and what they should expect to feel when their projects were developing products from processes based on the guidance of CMM®. This was not an easy task. However, I set upon a course of action to develop just such a course that would enable expectations to be realistically set for both the senior and middle managers regarding what their role and responsibilities should be to support their organization in this use of CMM® guidance.

Since November 1999, I have been deeply involved with CMMI®. This involvement ranges from comments for improvement to the SEI, to development of the intermediate CMMI® Workshop for Lead Appraisers and Process Group Managers, and to other trainings, appraisals, and process improvement consultancy. Applying my personal experience, I began to coach both senior and middle management teams in "The Look and Feel of CMMI®."

Practical Insight into CMMI® provides an understanding of the engineering, project management, process management, and quality management principles behind the specific and generic goals and practices of CMMI®. It does so without listing the specific goals and practices in their technical entirety. It offers clear interpretations that are based upon my long experience with the definition and the use of CMMI®. It borrows examples from the Kasse Initiatives Systems/Software Engineering Workshops in order to provide practical insight into those principles behind CMMI®. It integrates my experience with the concepts presented in CMMI®. This book presents complicated engineering concepts in a manner that will enable both higher-level managers and practitioners to visualize what it would be like to work in an organization that fully understood and embraced the best concepts of the CMMI® Reference Model. In addition, this book explains how to use process areas in more than one context or category, so that the power that can be tapped through its guidance for systems and software engineering development can be effectively utilized. Thus, it provides a bridge to the integrated systems/software world for developers, quality engineers, process improvement specialists, and managers whose previous experience was previously focused upon the predecessor model, CMM® for Software.

This book is designed for and will benefit:

- DoD organizations and contracting firms that are directed to accept and comply with CMMI® Reference Model guidelines;
- Organizations that are engaged in SW-CMM®–based process improvement and are trying to make a decision on whether to transition to CMMI®;
- Organizations that are in the process of mapping between CMM® for Software and CMMI®;
- Organizations that are just beginning to develop a process improvement initiative and want to utilize the most complete and robust model available in the world today;
- Organizations that desire more engineering discipline for their managers and developers;
- Systems engineering–oriented firms that are leaning toward staying with the existing SE CMM® or EIA–731 or are deciding whether they actually want all that CMMI® is offering or are willing to migrate their workforce in that direction;
- Hardware- or manufacturing-oriented companies that do develop software, but have stopped short of embracing CMM® for Software or the Systems Engineering CMM®;
- Organizations that routinely use multidisciplined teams to develop complex systems;
- Organizations that focus predominantly upon hardware engineering, systems engineering, and manufacturing;
- Universities that offer a systems engineering curriculum.

You are invited to read and apply the concepts found in *Practical Insight into CMMI®*. Some of the ideas will be useful immediately. Some will need to be discussed and perhaps tailored to address the concerns and focus of your particular organization and culture. Your improvement suggestions are always highly welcomed.

Success!

Acknowledgments

I would like to express my sincere thankfulness and gratitude to Pamelia S. Rost, who worked exhaustively behind the scenes as a reviewer, graphics designer, researcher, editor, copier, interface to the publisher, and nonstop supporter of this undertaking. Most importantly, she never stopped being a friend.

I would also like to thank Karyn Tegtmeier, who has contributed untold hours to many of my workshops, papers, and now this book. Karyn, along with Pamelia, reviewed each chapter, offering technical and grammatical support to ensure the highest quality possible before the book was sent to Artech House for their review.

Special thanks are offered to Mike Konrad and Mike Phillips of the Software Engineering Institute, and to Bob Rassa of Raytheon who served as the CMMI® Steering Group Chair (Industry), for their personal and political support of my efforts to write a slightly different book about the CMMI®.

I also want to say thanks to Tim Pitts, Artech House Commissioning Editor, for his very welcome support, which has been unwavering through two books so far. Lastly, I would like to give thanks to Ingo Tegtmeier, my friend, who does anything and everything he can to help me in dealing with daily events wherever I am in the world, so that I have a few moments of extra time to put my ideas into book form.

This book provides the reader with an insight into which an activities an organization would be engaged and what the role of each level of management and the practitioners would be if their systems and software engineering processes were based on CMM® Integration^{SM}. It captures the essence of each of the process areas by presenting them in a practical context without the technical structure of CMMI® masking the valuable nuggets of information.

Chapter 1—Engineering Systems Think

The merger of Systems Engineering and Software Engineering CMM® and process improvement ideas has resulted in the development of CMMI®. This chapter provides a brief overview of the systems engineering and software engineering sources that were merged to develop Integrated CMM® or CMMI®. In addition, it stresses or recaptures the focus on engineering systems think that seems to have gotten lost over the years where the focus has strictly been on artistic side of software engineering.

Chapter 2—Oriented-to-Business Results

The software industry has long criticized the CMM® model for its lack of focus on business results. Other total quality management models such as Malcolm Baldridge and the European Foundation for Quality Management place heavy emphasis on business results and not just the documentation of the process to gain industry certification. CMMI® clearly and repeatedly states the need for all process improvement activities to measurably support the organization's business objectives.

Chapter 3—Process Improvement Based on CMMI

CMMI® was developed to provide a single model to be used by organizations pursuing enterprise-wide process improvement. It provides needed guidance for integrating systems and software development activities. It supports the coordination of multidisciplined activities that are or may be required to successfully build a project. It is also being discovered that these CMMI®-based processes are able to be translated into business processes for other organizational departments such as human resources, finance, marketing, computer services, and contract management.

Chapter 4—CMMI Speak

This chapter intends to provide the reader with some of the more critical vocabulary that is used throughout CMMI®. While an organization is certainly not required to strictly adopt CMMI® terms in order to show compliance to its principles and guidance, some knowledge of the most important terms starts the journey of getting the look and feel of what it would be like to implement CMMI® concepts in an organization.

Chapter 5—Roles and Responsibilities

This chapter provides the reader with some ideas of the roles and responsibilities of the various levels of management and practitioners. It includes:

- Senior management;
- Middle management;
- Project leaders;
- Practitioners;
- Engineering process group;
- Quality assurance;
- Configuration Management;
- Testing;
- Measurement;
- Stakeholders.

Chapter 6—The Evolutionary Differences Between CMM for Software and CMMI

This chapter illustrates the evolutionary differences between CMM® for Software and CMMI® and presents an incremental approach for organizations interested in moving or evolving from a strict CMM® for Software process improvement focus to the integrated focus offered by CMMI®.

Chapter 7—Enabling the Project Leader to Better Manage and Control Through Project Planning and Project Monitoring and Control

Chapter 7 is the first of five chapters (Chapters 7 through 11) that focus on the inclusive topics of project management. It introduces my philosophy regarding the contributing components of project management. The beginning of this chapter includes a short introduction to risk management, quality management including quality assurance and Configuration Management, supplier management, and integrated project management. The topics of project planning and project monitoring and control are the focus of the look and feel description of this chapter following the general project management introduction.

Chapter 8—Enabling the Project Leader to Better Manage and Control Through Risk Management

Risk management has been placed in CMMI® as a separate process area to call attention to its importance in managing successful projects and successful businesses. The basic risk management functions of risk identification, risk analysis to determine probability, impact and time frame, risk prioritization, determining a risk management strategy, developing a risk mitigation plan, determining and evaluating contingency plans, and proactively tracking and managing the risks are all included in this chapter with direct links to the overall umbrella of project management.

Chapter 9—Enabling the Project Leader to Better Manage and Control Through Quality Management

While the continuous representation of CMMI® chose a categorization scheme that placed CM and QA in the category of support, it is my experience that effective use of the engineering principles of CM and QA are best realized by thinking of them as project management functions. The quality management process areas of process and product quality assurance and Configuration Management are described in this chapter as project management functions that provide input to a project manager to help him or her better manage and control and not simply go through the motions to satisfy audit or assessment criteria. The project's quality plan is emphasized in the section on process and product quality assurance. The section on Configuration Management describes in sufficient detail the Configuration Management functions of identification, baselining, change control, status accounting, interface control, supplier control, configuration auditing, and the Configuration Management system.

Chapter 10—Enabling the Project Leader to Better Manage and Control Through Supplier Management

Subcontracting or working with suppliers is becoming a common, but perhaps uncomfortable, fact of life. Companies that insisted they would not use subcontractors 1 year ago are suddenly finding themselves in a position of trying to decide how to select a qualified subcontractor or supplier. While there is much written on management of suppliers, it is believed by many that effective supplier management means that a project and/or business unit must have effective requirements engineering, project management, and quality management processes established and maintained for their own use to be able to properly and effectively apply them to their suppliers. This chapter takes this approach as it examines the process areas of Supplier Agreement Management and Integrated Supplier Management.

Chapter 11—Enabling the Project Leader to Better Manage and Control Through Integrated Project Management

Integrated Project Management takes project management to another dimension as it describes the project management function discussed in Chapters 7 through 10 based on the organization's set of standard processes. This chapter also serves as the conclusion to the overall discussion of project management.

Chapter 12—The Recursive Nature of Requirements Engineering

Collecting and understanding requirements is the necessary but not necessarily sufficient start of a successful project. While certainly not true in all cases, the requirements phase for many software-oriented projects has been largely restricted to requirements gathering. In probably far too many cases, design and even coding were started before requirements were known or stabilized to a sufficient point. This chapter presents the *recursive* nature of the total requirements gathering and analysis process from initial identification of stakeholders to deriving requirements to validating requirements at all stages. CMMI® process areas covered in this chapter will be Requirements Development and Requirements Management. Topics covered will include:

▸ Identifying stakeholders;

▸ Eliciting requirements;

▸ Documenting customer requirements;

▸ Translating customer requirements into product and product components;

- Identifying interface requirements;
- Developing operational concepts;
- Developing operational scenarios;
- Deriving requirements;
- Performing functional analysis;
- Discovering additional requirements;
- Analyzing and validating requirements at all stages.

Chapter 13—Alternative Solutions

This chapter presents the concepts and guidelines that CMMI® has to offer on establishing criteria and selecting product or product component solutions from alternative solutions. It includes the concepts of decision analysis and resolution for more formal decision making. Critical insight is provided that shows that alternative solutions are not only different ways of addressing the same requirements but that they also reflect a different allocation of requirements among the product components comprising the solution set. This chapter will also focus on the design and implementation of the product or product component.

Topics covered will include:

- Developing operational concepts;
- Developing operational scenarios;
- Deriving requirements;
- Developing alternative designs;
- Discovering additional requirements;
- Decision analysis and resolution.

Chapter 14—From Components to Products: Gluing the Pieces Together

This chapter presents CMMI® process areas of Product Integration, Verification, and Validation as a "mathematical triple" and shows how their use guides projects from the building blocks developed during technical solution to an integrated, verified, and validated set of product components that are then ready for packaging and delivery.

Chapter 15—Improving Processes at the Organizational Level

This chapter describes the organizational components necessary to establish and keep the organization on a path of continuous process improvement. It includes CMMI® process areas of Organizational Process Focus and Organizational Process Development. The description of the Organizational Process Development process area will emphasize the various components that must be in place before an organization can claim compliance to the requirements and guidance provided by this process area. It will distinguish between a product life cycle and a process description. It will clearly show the importance of establishing and enforcing tailoring guidelines for project use of organizational processes and it will show the importance of collecting, advertising, and using good examples for project uniformity and success.

Chapter 16—The Knowledge and Skills Base

This chapter provides the reader with an underlying understanding of an Organizational Training Program that takes into consideration:

- What business the organization is in;
- What core competencies must be developed or acquired to support that business;
- The knowledge and skills currently available in the organization's workforce;
- The training, mentoring, and coaching needed to develop or enhance the workforce knowledge and skills to accomplish individual, project, and organizational goals.

Chapter 17—Integrated Teams

An Integrated Team, also known as an Integrated Product Team, is composed of members who are collectively responsible for delivering the work product. Team members include empowered representatives from both the technical disciplines and business functional organizations involved with the product and have a stake in the success of the work products produced. Within defined boundaries, these representatives have decision-making authority and the responsibility to act for their representative organizations. These integrated teams may be viewed as a microversion of the company or business unit itself.

This chapter describes the conditions under which integrated teams are considered, built, and managed. It includes CMMI® process areas of Integrated Project Management, Integrated Teams, and Organizational Environment for Integration.

Chapter 18—Reducing Variation

This chapter presents an evolutionary path within CMMI® model that illustrates how process improvement steps taken to move from an individual focus, to a project focus, to a measurement-oriented organizational focus to a quantitative management focus can be thought of as successive steps in reducing variation in an organization's processes and business results. The process areas of Project Planning, Project Monitoring and Control, Measurement and Analysis, Organizational Process Definition, Integrated Project Management, Organizational Process Performance, and Quantitative Project Management will be used to support this chapter's concepts.

Chapter 19—Techniques for Establishing a Measurement Program

This chapter illustrates the strong measurement focus that can be found and utilized from CMMI®. Starting with basic project management measures and an understanding of getting a measurement program started through the implementation of the concepts found in the Measurement and Analysis process area, it guides the reader to the establishment of an Organizational Measurement Repository, the collection of peer review and test data, and the evolution of the organizational process measures that provide the building blocks for statistical process control and quantitative project management. CMMI® process areas of Organizational Process Performance and Quantitative Project Management will be examined in detail.

Chapter 20—Beyond Stability

This chapter describes the causal analysis and process innovations that can be built upon the quantitative and predictable knowledge of an organization's processes to solve business needs that otherwise could not be solved simply through hard work and management concern. CMMI® process areas of Causal Analysis and Resolution and Organizational Innovation and Deployment will be presented.

Chapter 21—Repeatable, Effective, and Long-Lasting

This chapter examines the specific and generic goals and their associated specific and generic practices from both the staged and continuous representations' points of view to help the reader more easily the concept of institutionalization of the process areas. The theme of implementing a process area or collection of process areas so that they are repeatable, effective, and long-lasting is emphasized.

Chapter 22—The Constagedeous Approach to Process Improvement

This chapter makes the case for the understanding and application of the principles of both the staged and continuous representations of CMMI® in supporting an organization's process improvement initiative.

Contents

Engineering Systems Think

The merger of Systems Engineering and Software Engineering CMM® and process improvement ideas has resulted in the development of CMMI®. This chapter provides a brief overview of the systems engineering and software engineering sources that were merged to develop CMM® Integration or CMMI®. In addition, this chapter stresses the importance of engineering systems think, which seems to have gotten lost over the years when the industry focus has predominantly been on the artistic side of software engineering.

CMM for Software

Establishment of the SEI

In the mid-1980s it became apparent to the United States Department of Defense (DoD) that the myriad of systems that were being developed for defense applications were becoming software intensive, were not meeting the established requirements, and were rapidly becoming cost-prohibitive.

The Software Engineering Institute (SEI), as a part of Carnegie Mellon University, was established in 1984 as a federally funded research and development center (FFRDC) with the mission to provide leadership in advancing the state of the practice of software engineering to improve the quality of systems that are dependent on software.

CMM v1.0 to CMMv1.1

Early questionnaires and model beginnings focused predominantly on software engineering processes. Capability Maturity Model (CMM®) for Software v1.0, released in August 1991, strongly referenced the link to the overall system and the requirements from which the software developers were

1

supposed to work. These requirements were referred to as "systems engineering requirements allocated to software." As CMM® for Software started to grow in popularity in the early 1990s, the parts of the industry that were more information technology–oriented protested the reference to systems engineering, and CMM® v1.1, released in 1993, no longer maintained that reference.

Software Product Engineering

The software life-cycle functions that coincided with the descriptions found in ISO 9001:1994 were placed all together in a Key Process Area (KPA) called Software Product Engineering.

Many debates took place in the hallowed halls of the SEI during the development of CMM® v1.0 regarding the need for a more detailed description of those life-cycle functions versus the containment of the size of CMM® and the number of key process areas that were being developed for CMM® Maturity Level 3. In the end, it was decided to keep only one KPA that described the "engineering" activities or functions and to reduce the content of that KPA to keep it compatible with the rest of the KPAs in CMM®. For many, including the CMM® authors, the engineering part of CMM® was reduced or de-emphasized for the sake of spreading its usage.

The need for a systems engineering CMM

While the use of CMM® for Software grew rapidly worldwide, it became very clear, very quickly, that the strict focus on software engineering did not satisfy the business or systems needs of the companies that were developing the software intensive systems. Assessments conducted by Jeff Perdue of the Institute of Software Process Improvement (ISPI) showed that the need for systems engineering process improvement and a systems CMM® was immediate. Following the final presentation of one of these software process assessments led by Mr. Perdue, one senior manager stood up and commented that if he had changed each reference from software engineering to systems engineering, the results would have been just as accurate. Comments like the one above led to the development of a systems engineering CMM® by the Software Engineering Institute, even though its original charter and government-provided guidance was restricted to software. Eventually, various CMM® models were developed for a myriad of disciplines other than software and systems engineering. These included models for software acquisition, workforce management and development, and integrated product and process development.

Although these models proved useful to many organizations, the use of multiple models also became problematic. Organizations desiring to focus their improvement efforts across the disciplines within their organizations ran into difficulties. The differences among the discipline-specific models, including their architectures, contents, and approaches, limited these organizations' abilities to focus their process improvements efforts successfully. In addition, the application of multiple models that were not consistently integrated within and across an organization resulted in higher costs in terms of training, appraisals, and improvement activities.

The need for an integrated model

CMM® Integration project was formed to sort out the problem of using multiple CMM®s. CMMI® Product Team's mission was to combine three source models—(1) Capability Maturity Model for Software (SW-CMM®) v2.0 draft C, (2) Electronic Industries Alliance Interim Standard (EIA/IS) 731, and (3) Integrated Product Development Capability Maturity Model (IPD-CMM®) v0.98—into a single improvement framework for use by organizations pursuing enterprise-wide process improvement.

Systems engineering

Systems engineering covers the development of total systems, which may or may not include software. Systems engineers focus on transforming customer needs, expectations, and constraints into product solutions and supporting these product solutions throughout the entire lifecycle of the product.

Software engineering

Software engineering covers the development of software systems. Software engineers focus on the application of systematic, disciplined, and quantifiable approaches to the development, operation, and maintenance of software.

Integrated Product and Process Development

Integrated Product and Process Development (IPPD) is a systematic approach that achieves a timely collaboration of relevant stakeholders throughout the life of the product to better satisfy customer needs, expectations, and requirements. The processes to support an IPPD approach are integrated with the other processes in the organization. The IPPD process areas, specific goals, and specific practices alone cannot achieve IPPD. If a project or organization chooses IPPD, it performs the IPPD-specific practices concurrently with other specific practices used to produce products (e.g., the engineering process areas), that is, if an organization or project wishes to use IPPD, it chooses a model with one or more other disciplines in addition to selecting IPPD.

The need for the integrated model became more apparent as CMMI® evolved into the set of models it represents today. In her work on software engineering at Carnegie Mellon University, Dr. Mary Shaw indicated that software engineering is still not considered to be an engineering discipline throughout the world, especially when it is compared to electrical engineering, mechanical engineering, and civil engineering. Leading companies that have software as a part of their products still face cost overruns, schedule slippage, poor performance, and unsatisfied customers.

A number of companies have set a precedent with their belief and approach to systems, software, and business goals. They have integrated all three using a unified quality management approach in their process improvement initiatives. Among those are Motorola, whose Microsystems business unit started developing "product life cycles" in 1985 that included systems, software, hardware, marketing, and manufacturing. In 1990, AT&T realized an increase in productivity and product quality by creating integrated teams that forced marketing, systems, software, and hardware representatives to work together and to be accountable as a team for the delivery of the product.

Integrating systems engineering and software engineering activities enabled Ford Aerospace from 1989 to 1992 to regain its competitive position in the command and control marketplace and reach CMM® Maturity Level 3 at the same time.

Systems engineering and systems management

We must first discuss the topics of what systems engineering and systems management are and what some of the commonly accepted functions of a systems engineer are in order to properly talk about engineering systems think.

The precise definition of systems engineering is not commonly agreed upon throughout the industry or with the major companies that employ systems engineers. This has led to a great deal of confusion and long hours of wasted debates. Some of the common and not-so-common names for systems engineering include:

- Systems engineers;
- Systems architects;
- Systems integrators;
- Systems management engineers;
- Systems quality assurance engineers;
- Systems theorists;
- Systems reengineers;
- Operations research (closely related profession);
- Management science (closely related profession).

We will try to clarify the confusion. First, let us take a look at the engineering of systems. Systems engineering is concerned with the engineering of systems. Systems management is concerned with strategic-level management of systems engineering. Systems engineering efforts therefore should involve:

- Systems management;
- Systems process;
- Systems engineering method and tools or technologies.

These three levels of systems engineering are illustrated in Figure 1.1.

Systems engineering can be viewed as a management technology. If we break management technology down into its components, we will be able to derive a clearer understanding of systems engineering.

Technology

Technology is the organization, application, and delivery of scientific knowledge, as well as other forms of knowledge for the betterment of a client group. Technology can be viewed fundamentally as a human activity.

Management

Management involves the interaction of the organization with the environment. The purpose of management is to enable organizations to better cope with their environments in order to achieve purposeful goals and objectives.

Management of technology

The management of technology (Figure 1.2) involves the interaction of:

- Technology;
- Organizations that are collections of people concerned with the evolution and use of technologies;
- Environment.

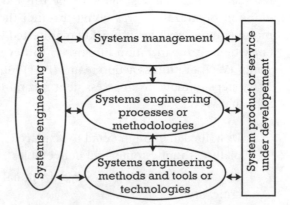

Figure 1.1   Three levels of systems engineering. (*From:* [1]. © 1999 John Wiley & Sons, Inc. Reprinted with permission.)

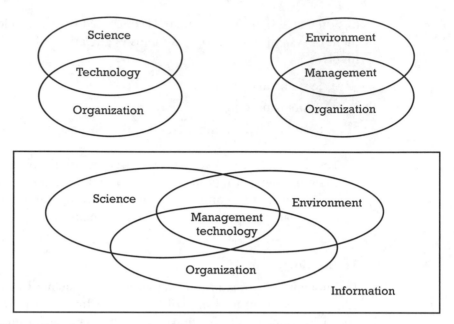

Figure 1.2   Management technology. (*From:* [1]. © 1999 John Wiley & Sons, Inc. Reprinted with permission.)

Systems engineering definition

Thus, if we combine all of the definition pieces we have just presented, we can define systems engineering to be the management technology that controls a total system life-cycle process, which evolves and results in the *definition, development,* and *deployment* of a system that is high quality, cost-effective, and on schedule in order to meet the user's needs.

Engineering systems thinking

Over the past 7–10 years, I have worked with a large number of companies that did not have a strong engineering discipline among its software systems developers or its management. While this did not seem to pose a problem when an organization was going through the initial phases of its process improvement initiative, it quickly manifested itself into a deep-seated problem when an organization attempted to develop its action plan. Working groups (WG) or process action teams (PAT) found it difficult to take the necessary steps to move from assessment recommendations to implementation tasks that were:

- Described in enough detail to be placed into a project-level plan (complete with milestones and deliverables);
- Prioritized according to organizational business need and project criticality;

‣ Scheduled for implementation according to defined increments;

‣ Able to be implemented within the financial and resource constraints of the organization.

Guidance for Action Planning

The author developed a method for successfully helping an organization make the transition from process assessment to action planning and implementation—Guidance for Action Planning^{SM} (GAP).

The concepts behind GAP come from the application of the engineering principle of decomposition of high-level system descriptions into more manageable subsystems and modules. In other words, this is the application of basic engineering principles to process improvement tasks. However, if an organization does not have both a management team and a workforce that embraces basic systems engineering thinking, it can prove to be painfully hard, if not impossible, to develop actionable process improvement plans.

The GAP provides a starter kit for the development of the action plan or plans for individual focus areas. It provides the vital intermediate details to get the organization going in the right direction, thus enabling it to implement and to complete its action planning within a reasonable time frame. It provides direction for the organization's senior management team and the process improvement champions to ensure that coordinated action will result from the assessment effort, and that this effort will support the organization's business objectives.

The GAP provides senior management with a big picture of the requirements for process improvement by showing what needs to be done, who needs to be involved, and what it might take to accomplish true and lasting improvement. This analysis provides a process improvement road map to support management decision making by clarifying how process improvement priorities can map to the corporate vision and business environment.

The GAP also provides important information for the Software/Systems Engineering Process Group (SEPG) and others involved in the development of the action plan as it defines the initial steps in the development of the focus area sections of the action plan. These steps are direct transitions from the assessment results (see Figure 1.3). The GAP assists the SEPG's facilitation of the development and implementation of the action plans that will support the process improvement needs of the organization the most.

The Guidance for Action Planning^{SM} provides the bridge between the assessment results and the activities necessary to develop actionable plans for improvement.

Systems thinking

Systems thinking is a discipline for seeing the whole. It is a framework for understanding interrelationships and repeated events rather than seeing things in isolation. Systems thinking is about seeing patterns of change

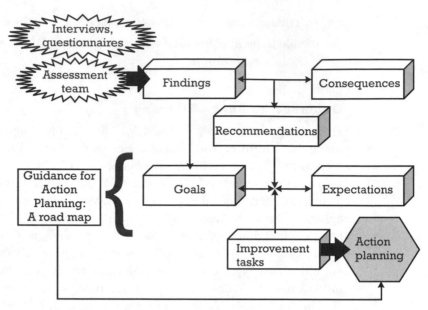

Figure 1.3 Guidance for Action Planning^{SM} road map.

rather than static snapshots. Systems thinking embodies the idea that the interrelationship among the parts relative to a common purpose of a system is what is important. Systems thinking is necessary for successful product development and process improvement.

The Fifth Discipline

Peter Senge led a team of authors to write a book, *The Fifth Discipline: The Art and Practice of the Learning Organization,* to describe a path for the "learning organization." According to Mr. Senge, systems thinking is the fifth discipline" and is the catalyst and cornerstone of the learning organization that enables success through the other four disciplines" [2]:

1. Personal mastery through proficiency and commitment to lifelong learning;
2. Shared mental models or the organization markets and competitors;
3. Shared vision for the future of the organization;
4. Team learning.

Mr. Senge describes certain truths or laws about the fifth discipline. A few of them are included here to support the concepts of engineering systems thinking.

   ▸ Short-term improvements often lead to long-term difficulties. When organizations only focus on the "low-hanging fruit," they frequently do not establish the basics functions necessary to continue long-term future growth.

- The easy solution may be no solution at all.

- Quick solutions, especially at the level of the symptoms, often lead to more problems than existed initially.

- Cause and effect are not necessarily closely related, either in time or in space. Sometimes solutions implemented here and now will have impacts far away at a much later time.

- *The entire system, comprised of the organization and its environment, must be considered together.*

Laws of engineering systems thinking

Engineering systems thinking is not merely a slogan; it is composed of basic "laws" that can and should be applied to everyday business life. Here is a summary of some of the more important engineering systems thinking laws according to my educational background and professional experience. Process areas that have been defined in CMM® Integration (CMMI®) appear in brackets and parentheses as indicators of the effort undertaken in the development of CMMI® in order to incorporate engineering systems thinking.

1. In all of the project's phases/stages, and along the system's life, the systems engineer has to take into account [Requirements Development (RD)]:

    - The customer's organization vision, goals, and tasks;

    - The customer's requirements and preferences;

    - The problem to be solved by the system and the customer's needs.

2. The whole has to be seen, as well as the interaction between the system's elements. Iterative or recursive thinking must replace the traditional linear thinking [RD–Technical Solution (TS)].

3. Project members should always look for the synergy and the relative advantages from the integration of subsystems [TS–Product Integration (PI)].

4. The solution is not always an engineering one. Remember to take into account:

    - Business and economic costs;

    - Reuse or utilization of products and infrastructure already developed;

    - Organizational, managerial, political, and personal considerations.

5. The systems engineer should consider as many different perspectives as possible.

6. Systems engineers and project mangers should always take into account (RD–TS):

    ‣ Electrical considerations;

    ‣ Mechanical considerations;

    ‣ Environmental considerations;

    ‣ Quality assurance considerations;

    ‣ Quality factors such as reliability, maintainability, expandability, and testability.

7. Future logistic requirements should be evaluated in all development phases including (RD–TS):

    ‣ Spare parts;

    ‣ Maintenance infrastructure;

    ‣ Support;

    ‣ Service;

    ‣ Maintenance levels;

    ‣ Technical documentation.

8. When a need arises to carry out a modification to the system, always take into account (RD–TS–Requirements Management):

    ‣ The engineering and nonengineering implications;

    ‣ The effects on the form, fit, and function;

    ‣ The system's response to the changes;

    ‣ The needs, difficulties, and attitudes of those who must live with the modification.

9. Each problem may have more than one possible working solution (TS):

    ‣ All possible alternatives should be examined and compared to each other by quantitative and qualitative measurements.

    ‣ Engineering trade-offs and cost-effectiveness should be considered at every stage.

10. Systems engineers should be encouraged to look for the changes that might introduce significant improvements with minimum effort.

11. Processes that result in slow or gradual results should be taken seriously [Organizational Innovation and Deployment (OID)].

12. A known solution is not always suitable for the current problem. Each available solution should be considered along with the risks, dependencies, and constraints inherent in the evolving system [Generic Practice (GP) 2.2].

13. Development risks must be taken into account throughout the entire product development cycle [Project Planning–Risk Management (RSKM)].

14. It is impossible to run a project without [PP–Project Management and Control (PMC)–Configuration Management (CM)–Generic Practices]:

  ‣ Control;
  ‣ Configuration Management;
  ‣ Milestones;
  ‣ Management;
  ‣ Scheduling methods.

15. The end user must be considered as a major part of the system (RD–PP).

16. Engineering systems thinking requires the integration of expertise from different disciplines and requires the examination of different perspectives, calling for teamwork to cover those perspectives [Integrated Project Management, Integrated Product and Process Development, Integrated Teaming (IPM–IPPD–IT)].

17. Selecting partners and subcontractors is critical. Do not enter into a partnership unless the partner is willing to share your risks as well as your successes and profits [Supplier Agreement Management (SAM)].

18. Limit the responsibility assigned to an external factor, since this increases the dependency on it [SAM–Commercial Off the Shelf Software (COTS)].

19. Take the shelf life into consideration when selecting components for production.

20. Engineering systems thinking includes probability and statistics both when defining the systems specifications and when determining the project targets such as cost and performance [Decision Analysis and Resolution (DAR)].

Summary

One of the most prominent problems observed in software and software/systems organizations today is the lack of engineering discipline, cited by mangers at all management levels. CMM® for Software was developed to encourage organizations to develop processes to guide its software development. CMM® Integration recognizes that engineering systems thinking is an important asset for building systems and has put the "engineering" back into process improvement.

References

[1] Sage, A. P., and W. B. Rouse, *Handbook of Systems Engineering and Management*, New York: John Wiley & Sons, 1999.

[2] Senge, P. M., et al., *The Fifth Discipline: The Art and Practice of the Learning Organization*, New York: Doubleday, 1990.

Oriented-to-Business Results

The software industry has long criticized the CMM® model for its lack of focus on business results. Other total quality management models, such as Malcolm Baldridge and the European Foundation for Quality Management, place heavy emphasis on business results and not just documenting the process to gain industry certification. CMMI® clearly and repeatedly states the need for all process improvement activities to measurably support the organization's business objectives.

State of the practice for software engineering

Today's situation in software systems

In [1], two key ideas were presented concerning organizations engaging in process improvement initiatives: (1) "The median annual cost per engineer of software process improvement using the CMM® for Software was $1,375..." and (2) "...The savings to organizations were about 5 times this amount—$6,875 per software engineer." This statistic alone should have companies that build software systems scrambling around the world to become involved with their own process improvement initiatives based on CMM® or now its enhanced and integrated big brother, CMM® Integration.

Examples of software systems problems

If the statistics reported by the Software Engineering Institute are not motivating enough, the following examples that have occurred in the past 10 years should cause most of us to pause and think:

‣ A bank in the United Kingdom transferred $3 billion to other banks because of a design flaw.

> ‣ A major airline lost $50 million in bookings due to a design error.
> ‣ A misplaced decimal point in software supporting rocket launching for the U.S. Air Force resulted in a $3 billion loss and a nationwide investigation.
> ‣ Late delivery and poor quality software resulted in a $240 million penalty for a telecommunications company in Europe.
> ‣ A high-speed train collision killed hundreds—a high price to pay for software errors.

Engineering competency

During the past 8 years, my process improvement consultancy activities with engineering firms, financial institutions, insurance companies, IT companies and business units, and government software/systems developers have revealed a significant lack of engineering competency. Overall, there appears to be an inability to manage the engineering processes. In many cases, organizational process definitions are poor to nonexistent. In others, the processes appear to be very well developed but are not trained, supported, or enforced and, as a result, are not uniformly used or kept "living." A common complaint among managers at all levels is that there is a lack of engineering discipline. A systems approach to problem solving appears to be for the other guy. The comment we hear often is: "...but my project has such great pressures that we don't have time to think of alternatives and do things in a systems way."

Quality management and the underlying quality functions are misunderstood and are poorly implemented throughout the life cycle. Quality assurance is still reported to be the testing group. The difference between quality control (evaluates the products and life-cycle work products —peer reviews and testing) and quality assurance (evaluates the processes—evaluations and assessments) is rarely understood. Measurement programs are implemented late and are poorly oriented. Too often, I am told that a business unit's focus is on hours spent on reviews but not the result of those reviews. In addition, even if processes exist and attempts are made to follow them, efficiency and effectiveness measurements are rarely implemented.

An example will serve to illustrate this critical lack of understanding and use of measurements. A quality assurance manager in a large IT department routinely reported on the number of audits and reviews that he and his staff participated in each month. When confronted with the question So What?, he replied that often the quality engineers had spent more than 50 hours per week on those activities. It was then suggested that for his quality group's activities to be considered effective, he might concentrate on how many serious noncompliances were uncovered by these quality assurance activities, and how many his staff had helped the projects to fix.

The reporting of numbers of audits and hours of work certainly represents "status." The result of following the quality assurance processes and producing results such as the elimination of noncompliances in a given reporting period and increasing the probability of producing a high quality product indicates effectiveness.

Another engineering competency weakness that we have seen is that people are most often hired to satisfy a particular project need. There is little evidence that the people are hired because of an organizational understanding of the core competencies needed to support business objectives. Indeed, the facts seem to indicate that people are routinely hired without an acceptable percentage of core competency skills and, even worse, they are hired without a demonstrable ability to learn and master core competency skills.

Support for the organization's business objectives

In order for a focus on process improvement to be successful, it must be tied to the organization's business objectives. CMM® for Software did not place such a great emphasis on the process improvement effort supporting business objectives, although one could argue that it was certainly implied. The SEI did not allow this important notion to slip by when CMMI® was being developed. Understanding and supporting the business objectives play an important role in the definition of critical process areas such as Organizational Process Focus, Organizational Process Definition, Organizational Training, Organizational Process Performance, Organizational Innovation and Deployment, Risk Management, Integrated Teaming, Organizational Environment for Integration, Quantitative Project Management, Requirements Development, Technical Solution, Measurement and Analysis, and Decision Analysis and Resolution.

To get an understanding of the organization's business objectives, there are a few questions that can be presented to the senior management team:

- What are the organization's highest priorities?
- What business consequences have resulted from weak or ineffective processes?
- What action is being taken to correct the cause?
- How can a focus on process improvement support the organization's business objectives?

Business objectives should be able to be stated in everyday terms. An example of a business objective would be to reduce system errors that are discovered by customers. This business objective may have been derived from the statistics of the last two or three releases in which large numbers of errors were being reported by the customers. Having the organization's business objectives clearly stated and documented assists, if not ensures, that the process improvement effort will be aligned with those business objectives and will result in desired business results. The following are a few generic business objectives that are commonly stated in brainstorming sessions with senior management teams:

- Improve predictability of development cycle length, delivery time, and costs.

- Find and fix each problem once.

- Reduce system errors that are discovered by customers.

- Increase control of suppliers.

- Increase quality of products.

- Always work with the correct version of a module or life-cycle work product.

Support for senior management's vision

A vision is a guiding image of success formed in terms of a contribution to society. A mission statement answers the questions: Why does our organization exist? What business are we in? What values will guide us? A vision, however, is more encompassing. It answers the question: What will success look like? It is the pursuit of this image of success that really motivates people to work together.

The concept of visioning is not yet a comfortable concept for many senior managers, especially as it relates to process improvement. However, in recent years, visioning has become recognized as a major process improvement factor. If the process improvement initiative does not support management's vision, then the probability is very low that management will support process improvement over the long term.

In today's highly competitive world, organizations are merging and/or downsizing. Employees of these evolving organizations want to know how their efforts can contribute to the health and well-being of their organization. Some senior managers have a strong vision, but often it is not communicated to the practitioners. Some practitioners have a fuzzy idea of what the vision must be but are not able to articulate it. Some senior management teams express great disagreement as to what the common vision should be.

Visioning is such an important concept for today's business that its value cannot be overemphasized. The following questions may help an organization to define its vision.

- Where does senior management think the organization will be in the next year and in the next 2 to 5 years?

- What products will be in the mainstream?

- Who will the competitors be?

- Will there be collaborators or strategic alliance partners?

- What technology changes are expected and/or will be required to support the vision?

- What does the organizational structure have to be to support this vision?

> • Who will the organization's suppliers be?
> • What must the organizational culture be to support this vision?
> • How will a process improvement initiative support this vision?

Support for project leaders to better manage and control

Clearly if the CMMI®-based process improvement initiative is to support achieving business results, an organization must be able to show what measurable value will be brought to the project leaders who bear the line responsibility for product delivery. Today's project leaders are under ever-increasing pressure to deliver products that meet or improve the schedule, for less than the budget allows, and with higher quality and certainly no less functionality. It seems only reasonable that if they are willing to support a process improvement initiative they should be able to expect some or all of the suggested results:

> • More accurate schedules;
> • Higher productivity of developers;
> • Better quality products;
> • Traceable requirements;
> • Controlled configuration items;
> • Reviews focused on critical components;
> • Better control of suppliers;
> • Reduction of potential risks.

End-to-end quality

While the CMMI® model is oriented to supporting organization's process improvement efforts in technical disciplines such as systems and software engineering, it is being proven that its concepts can be readily transferred to the definition and control of an organization's business processes. Developing integrated systems are only one part of the organization's value chain that strives to provide end-to-end quality to its customers.

It can be argued that it is not sufficient for an organization to have high maturity technical and project management processes, but an organization must strive to have a set of integrated business processes for all of its departments and functions.

As each organization sets up its process improvement initiative, it should periodically assess its overall business process improvement efforts using questions like these:

> • What business are you in?

- How does each department contribute to the business's success?
- How do these departments interact with each other to maximize company profit and achieve business goals?
- What business processes exist in each department to optimize its product quality and minimize interface conflicts?
- What standards and models are being used to accomplish daily tasks?
- What personal processes are being used for each person to optimize his or her performance?
- Does each person understand his or her role in supporting the organization's business quality goals?

Summary

We conclude this chapter with a look at the Deming quality chain illustrated in Figure 2.1. Dr. W. Edwards Deming always advocated focusing on quality first. His belief was that if an organization continually focused on improving its product and service quality, it would in turn decrease costs, see improved productivity, be able to decrease prices, increase market share, stay in business, provide more jobs, and, as a final result, see the much sought-after return on investment (ROI).

It is my opinion that CMMI® provides more guidance in its description of the process areas, goals, practices, and examples to support Dr. Deming's ideas of quality than any other model of its kind in the world.

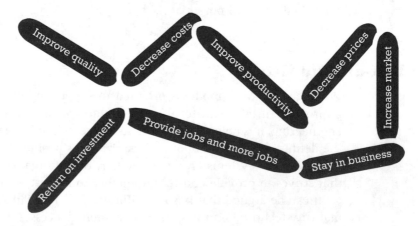

Figure 2.1 The Deming quality chain. (*After:* [2].)

References

[1]   Software Engineering Institute, *Software Engineering Institute, Annual Report 2001*, Pittsburgh, PA: Software Engineering Institute, 2002.

[2]   Deming, W. E., *Out of the Crisis*, Cambridge, MA: MIT Center for Advanced Engineering, 1986.

Contents

Process Improvement Based on CMMI

CMMI® was developed to provide a single model to be used by organizations pursuing enterprise-wide process improvement. It provides needed guidance for integrating systems and software development activities. It supports the coordination of multidisciplined activities that are or may be required to successfully build a project. It is also being discovered that these CMMI®-based processes can be translated into business processes for other organizational departments such as human resources, finance, marketing, computer services, and contract management.

The resulting quagmire of standards and models developed to govern the systems/software engineering processes

Since the late 1960s and early 1970s, various standards governing the processes of developing products or product components have existed. There were government standards, industry standards, corporate standards, business unit standards, and project standards. Interface standards were established to ensure that suppliers developing open systems product lines would indeed develop compatible product components. As software intensive systems grew in size and complexity and as the demands on system performance rose in general, meeting customer requirements became more difficult. Nowhere was this seen more clearly than in the United States Department of Defense (DoD).

Large defense contractors built systems that did not meet either some or all of the specifications or even the intended use of the product. The defense contractors offered to improve the systems they had developed and delivered in exchange for a long-standing maintenance contract. This put the DoD in a difficult position. Either it had to contract out to maintain the large volume of different hardware and software systems that it had purchased or try to maintain them itself. Both options were risky at best. In an attempt for the government to gain some semblance of control, individual armed forces standards gave way to DoD standards such as DoD-Std-2167 and DoD-Std-2168 on software development and software quality assurance planning. DoD contractors reacted with dismay at the bureaucracy being levied on them but offered no real enforceable solution themselves. IEEE standards were also being produced on software development and quality management focus areas to support the commercial world's need for process and quality.

The development and quality standards of the 1970s and 1980s evolved into ISO standards such as ISO 9001 and ISO 9000-3 for product development and a software interpretation of ISO 9001 respectively. ISO 9001 was developed to ensure a minimum level of quality for products that were being exchanged between European and Asian countries. Its application to software products and services was quite controversial because a company with an ISO 9001 certificate did not always translate into a guaranteed level of quality, product or product performance.

Through the need of the DoD to determine the capability of its contractors before contract award, the Software Engineering Institute was conceived. Through the leadership of Watts Humphrey, techniques for capability evaluation and assessment were developed and the Capability Maturity Model for Software was created and released in August 1991. The model was intended to help buyers select the appropriate suppliers with the required process capability and to guide an organization's process improvement efforts.

During that same time frame, the European Commission sponsored a project called BOOTSTRAP. The mission of the BOOTSTRAP methodology was to study investments in technology upgrades and generally lay the groundwork for European technology transfer standards and common practices. The main goal was to speed up the application of software engineering technology in the European software industry. The project took the SEI CMM® reference model as the basic reference and included guidelines for a company-wide quality system.

Based on the success of CMM® for Software in the United States and the BOOTSTRAP methodology in Europe, as well as demands from other disciplines and interests, a plethora of CMM®s were developed. These included:

- People CMM® v1.0—September 1995;
- Systems Engineering CMM® v1.1—November 1995;
- Integrated Product Development v1.0—February 1996;
- Software Acquisition CMM® v1.02—December 1996.

In addition, specialized CMM®s were developed for topics such as software quality assurance [1] and measurement [2]. Many organizations found these various CMM®s to be useful, but they also found them to be overlapping, contradicting, lacking standardization, and being at great varying levels of detail. However, more were developed.

The FAA developed an integrated CMM® reference model—FAA-iCMM® (Dr. Linda Ibrahim, project leader)—and released v1.0 in November 1997. Bellcore led a group of telecommunications experts and developed Trillium, a CMM®-based model focused, modified, and adapted for the telecommunications community.

Turning our attention to ISO, IEC, IEEE, and EIA standards efforts, we find the International Organization for Standardization (ISO) and the International Electrotechnical Commission (IEC) established a Joint Technical Committee (JTC1) on Information Technology in June 1989. The JTC1 initiated the development of an international standard ISO/IEC on software development processes to provide a uniform framework for managing and engineering software. This effort resulted in an international standard being published in August 1995.

CMM® for Software also influenced an international collaborative effort to produce a standard for software process assessment that resulted in the development of the Software Process Improvement and Capability dEtermination (SPICE–ISO 15504).

This initiative of the ISO/IEC/JTC1/SC7/WG10 set out to develop an assessment method that provided a measurement scale, criteria for evaluation against the scale, a set of standards, best practices, and industry norms, and a clear mechanism for representing the results. This standard focused on developing process areas with basic practices and a path to increase the capability levels of those process areas in contrast to the CMM® for Software approach, which focused on maturity levels of a predetermined set of process areas that could only be achieved by an organization.

During the same time frame, DoD-Std-2167A-1988 evolved into Mil-Std-498, which was influenced by ISO/IEC 12207. This, in turn, influenced IEEE/EIA 12207-1997 for worldwide acceptance.

Which standard, model, or method was the right one to choose? Which one would give an organization a clear path to care about process improvement, quality management, and its business objectives without an overwhelming amount of overhead? Simple questions like these were on many people's minds and were expressed verbally and sometimes heatedly in offices, hallways, and bars and at process improvement conferences.

Eventually, it became clear that organizations did not ever have to do any real work such as design and produce a product; they needed only to conduct an assessment or evaluation based on the model or standard of the month and then apply what was learned to their ongoing process improvement efforts. Of course, they also had the option of going out of business.

In the midst of this frameworks quagmire, Sarah Sheard of the Software Productivity Consortium reported [3] (Figure 3.1), the CMM® Integration project was formed to develop a single process improvement framework for

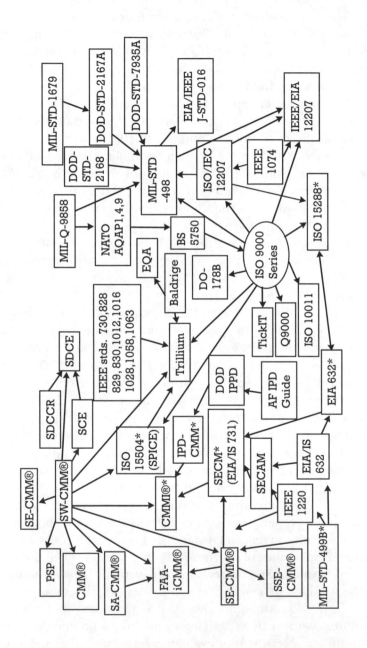

Figure 3.1 The frameworks quagmire. (*From:* [3]. © 2003 Software Productivity Consortium. Reprinted with permission.)

use by organizations pursuing enterprise-wide process improvement. The CMMI® Product Team developed a new framework that not only accommodated multiple disciplines but also was made flexible enough to support two different representations: the staged representation made popular by CMM® for Software and the continuous representation used by Systems Engineering CMM® and SPICE. Furthermore, the CMMI® Product Team ensured that all of the products developed were consistent and compatible with the ISO/IEC 15504 Technical Report for Software Process Assessment.

CMMI and ISO 9001:2000

Soon after CMM® for Software v1.1 was released by the SEI, individuals who were involved with ISO 9001:1994 started to compare that ISO standard with the contents of CMM®. In 1999, Arnold Das developed an ISO 9001 to CMM® correlation graphic to show the differences (see Figure 3.2) [4].

ISO 9001	SEI CMM®
4.1 Management responsibility	▬▬▬▬
4.2 Quality system	▬▬▬▬
4.3 Contract review	• • • • • • • • • •
4.4 Design control	▬▬▬▬
4.5 Document and data control	▬▬▬▬
4.6 Purchasing	▬▬▬▬
4.7 Control of customer supplied product	··················
4.8 Product identification and traceability	▬▬▬▬
4.9 Process control	▬▬▬▬
4.10 Inspection and testing	▬▬▬▬
4.11 Control of inspection, measuring, and test equipment	··················
4.12 Inspection and test status	▬▬▬▬
4.13 Control of nonconforming product	▬▬▬▬
4.14 Corrective and preventive action	▬▬▬▬
4.15 Handling, storage, packaging, preservation, and delivery	··················
4.16 Control and quality records	▬▬▬▬
4.17 Internal quality audits	▬▬▬▬
4.18 Training	▬▬▬▬
4.19 Servicing	··················
4.20 Statistical techniques	▬▬▬▬

Strong correlation	▬▬▬▬
Weak correlation	• • • • • • • • •
No correlation	··················

Figure 3.2   ISO 9001 to CMM® correlation. (*After:* [4].)

The correlations ran from strong to weak to no correlation at all. It was concluded by ISO 9001 advocates that CMM® offered more detail and guidance but was not broad enough to satisfy the ISO 9001 breadth. Advocates of CMM® for Software showed that while some of CMM® Level 2 key process areas were covered by ISO 9001:1994, they were not covered in full and Level 3 key process areas were not covered well at all, with the exception of the Software Product Engineering key process area. The battle lines were drawn.

Over the past 8 years CMM® for Software has evolved and expanded into CMM® Integration. The ISO 9001:1994 standard has also evolved into ISO 9001:2000, being influenced by the BOOTSTRAP Assessment Methodology, the development of ISO 15504, and CMM® for Software v2.0 Rev C.

With the SEI CMMI® Product Team evolving CMMI® in conjunction with ISO 15504, it can be seen today that the correlation between ISO 9001:2000 and CMMI® is significantly higher than ISO 9001:1994 and CMM® for Software. A brief summary of this correlation was provided by Boris Mutafelija to the author. The source of this comparison can be seen in [5].

ISO 9001:2000 to CMMI correlation

There are no explicit requirements for:

- Institutionalization;
- Creating and maintaining organizational process assets:
  - Organizational Measurement Repository;
  - Database of good and best practices;
- Missing details for the following process areas:
  - Organizational Training;
  - Risk Management;
  - Decision Analysis and Resolution;
  - Organization Process Performance;
  - Quantitative Project Management;
  - Organization Innovation and Deployment;
  - Causal Analysis.

CMMI to ISO 9001:2000 correlation

There are no explicit requirements for:

- Customer focus and satisfaction;
- Management representative responsible for quality management;
- Infrastructure (buildings, workspace, equipment, and so forth);
- Customer property;
- Control of monitoring and measuring devices (weak correlation).

Process improvement for software, systems, and business based on CMMI

Why base your organization's process improvement success on CMMI®? This indeed may be the question in your mind if you are thinking about all of the models, standards, and methods that have been produced so far and are still in existence. First and foremost, the emphasis of CMMI® is to support the development processes and changing of cultures to show a measurable benefit for the organization's business objectives and vision. CMMI® provides a framework from which to organize and prioritize engineering, people, and business activities. It supports the coordination of multidisciplined activities that are or may be required to successfully build a project. As CMMI® is becoming used as the basis for improving an organization's software/systems processes, it is also being discovered that these processes are able to be translated into other organizational departments such as human factors, finance, marketing, computer services, and contract management.

CMMI® provides the basis for an organization to develop and control its own project management and engineering processes so that it can, in turn, manage the results of its supplier's processes. It ensures identification and control of an organization's "core competencies" and it enables an organization to competitively "posture" itself in today's fast-changing world.

A frequently overlooked advantage of CMMI® is the aspect that CMMI® captures *lessons learned* from the use of CMM® for Software and other models, methods, and standards over the past 10 years. These lessons learned can be found in many of CMMI®'s process areas, including:

- Engineering process areas of Requirements Development, Technical Solution, Requirements Management, and Product Integration;
- Project Planning and Project Monitoring and Control;
- Supplier Agreement Management;
- Measurement and Analysis;
- Risk Management;
- Integrated Teaming;
- Organizational Process Performance;
- Quantitative Project Management;
- Organizational Innovation and Deployment.

CMMI and engineering systems thinking

Because CMMI® has integrated the concepts of Systems Engineering CMM® and CMM® for Software, it returns the concept of engineering systems thinking to projects and organizations where it has been sorely lacking for more than a decade.

The laws of engineering systems thinking, presented in Chapter 1, can be encapsulated in a few key ideas here:

- In all of the project's phases and stages, and along the system's life, the systems engineer has to take into account:
  - The customer's organizational vision, goals, and tasks;
  - The customer's requirements and preferences;
  - The problem to be solved by the system and the customer's needs.
  - The whole has to be seen as well as the interaction between the system's elements. Iterative or recursive thinking must replace the traditional linear thinking.

- The solution is not always an engineering one. We must remember to always take into account:
  - Business and economic costs;
  - Reuse or utilization of products and infrastructure already developed;
  - Organizational, managerial, political, and personal considerations.

Consider these benefits of a CMMI®-based process improvement initiative:

- Increased control of costs and ability to predict development cycle length and costs of multidisciplined product and product components;
- The ability to remove defects early and efficiently from the life-cycle work products;
- Reduced rework leading to reduced development cycle time;
- Increased predictability and control of product quality;
- Enhanced ability to make cost-benefit trade-offs of development methodologies, technologies, and processes;
- Increased capability to select and manage qualified suppliers;
- Enhanced ability to make risk management decisions based on quantitative data;
- More time available for top innovators to spend on problems and challenges requiring creative energy;
- Knowledge retention and expansion;
- Satisfied customers.

It is CMMI® and only CMMI® that has successfully combined the tried-and-true ideas presented by CMM for Software and embraced engineering systems thinking at the same time.

Summary

Why base your organization's process improvement initiative on CMMI®? CMMI® represents integration of multiple military, ISO, IEEE, and commercial standards and procedures that cover all aspects of building systems. It is closely linked to ISO 9001:2000. The emphasis of CMMI® is to support the development processes and changing of cultures to show a measurable benefit for the organization's business objectives and vision. CMMI® provides a framework from which to organize and prioritize engineering, people, and business activities. It supports the coordination of multidisciplined activities that are or may be required to successfully build a project and it returns the concept of engineering systems thinking to project development.

References

[1]   Bush, M., "The SEI Capability Maturity Model: One Day Overview," invited seminar for OPL Benelus, Brussels, Belgium, January 1995, *Modern Software Assurance and a Five-Level Model of Software Assurance Maturity, High Integrity Systems*, 1.2, 1994, pp. 157–169.

[2]   Daskalantonakis, M., "A Practical View of Software Measurement and Implementation Experience with Motorola," *IEEE Software*, Vol. 18, No. 11, 1992, pp. 998–1010.

[3]   Sheard, S., *The Frameworks Quagmire*, Herndon, VA: Software Productivity Consortium, 2003, http://www.software.org/quagmire.

[4]   Das, A. M., *High Level Comparison of ISO 9001 and SEI Capability Maturity Model for Software*, presentation, 1999.

[5]   Mutafelija, B., and H. Stromberg, *Systematic Process Improvements Using ISO 9001:2000 and CMMI®*, Norwood, MA: Artech House, 2003.

CMMI Speak

This chapter intends to provide the reader with some of the more critical vocabulary that is used throughout CMMI®. While an organization is certainly not required to strictly adopt CMMI® terms in order to show compliance to its principles and guidance, some knowledge of the most important terms starts the journey of getting the look and feel of what it is like to implement CMMI® concepts in an organization.

The SEI has chosen to use definitions from *Webster's Dictionary* when those definitions suffice. Some of the terms used in CMMI® have meanings attached to them that differ from their everyday use. These are some of the phrases, word groupings, and terms that will be emphasized in this chapter. Many of the terms are taken from Chapter 3. Other terms are taken from the CMMI® Glossary and Acronyms Section. Examples taken from industry experience of the authors are also added to provide a context to help the reader interpret the terms for their organization.

Model

A *model* is a structured collection of elements that describes characteristics of effective processes. A model is used to help set process improvement objectives and priorities and improve processes. A model is used to help ensure that the processes we put in place throughout our organizations will be stable, capable, and mature. A model is intended to be used as a guide for the improvement of project and organizational processes. A model provides:

- A place to start;
- The benefit of an industry's prior experiences;
- A common language;

- A shared vision;
- A framework for prioritizing actions;
- A way to define what improvement means for your organization.

Model options

With respect to CMMI®, there are a number of model options. These currently include:

- Systems Engineering + Software Engineering (CMMI®-SE/SW v1.1);
- Systems Engineering + Software Engineering + Integrated Product and Process Development (IPPD) (CMMI®-SE/SW/IPPD v1.1);
- Systems Engineering + Software Engineering + Integrated Product and Process Development (IPPD) + Supplier Sourcing (SS) (CMMI®-SE/SW/ IPPD/SS v1.1);
- Systems Engineering + Software Engineering + Supplier Sourcing (SS) (CMMI®-SE/SW/SS v1.1).

The ability for an organization to achieve a common process improvement language is especially important for companies that have multiple sites in multiple countries and maintain operations in a cross-cultural environment. The Dutch-based company ING Group has more than 100 companies worldwide under its umbrella. In 1998, at the European SEPG conference held in London, it was reported that the single most important success that ING achieved as a result of its CMM®-based process improvement program was increased beneficial communication from Argentina to the Netherlands and from Poland to Des Moines, Iowa.

Disciplines

The term *discipline* usually refers to a structured and systematic approach to a task, such as an approach to training for a sport or an engineering process to solving problems. CMMI® provides strong support for developing and institutionalizing engineering discipline among its workforce.

Within CMMI®, discipline refers to a body of knowledge, developed skill sets, and sequence of processes that are related to product or process development. Software engineering, systems engineering, integrated product and process development, and supplier sourcing are all considered disciplines.

When we talk about engineering disciplines to which requirements may be allocated for development, or may be needed on a project, we typically think of software engineering, systems engineering, hardware engineering, electrical engineering, mechanical engineering, and manufacturing.

Adequate, appropriate, as needed

Adequate, appropriate, and as needed appear in CMMI® to allow managers at all levels and practitioners to interpret the specific and generic goals and practices in light of the organization's business objectives.

For example, Generic Practice 2.3 for the process area of Risk Management states: "Provide adequate resources for performing the risk management process, developing the work products, and providing the services of the process." Adequate could be satisfied by:

- Numbers of people;
- Skills of the people carrying out the risk management process;
- The extent to which the risk mitigation activities are defined;
- Any tools that might be used to support the risk mitigation activities;
- People who must monitor the risks;
- People who ensure that the Top 10 Risk List is current.

Establish and maintain

Establish and maintain includes making sure a process is used as well as documented. This should include proof such as minutes of meetings, audit reports, peer review data, measurement data, proof of use, and so forth. For example, establish and maintain the strategy to be used for risk management. The risk management strategy must be developed and contain content such as:

- Scope of the risk management effort;
- Methods and tools to be used for risk identification, risk analysis, risk mitigation, risk monitoring, and communication;
- How these risks are to be organized, categorized, compared, and consolidated;
- Risk mitigation techniques to be used, such as prototyping, simulation, alternative designs, or evolutionary development.

The procedures and templates to develop a risk management strategy should be documented, trained, and able to be coached. Each project would have its risk management strategy defined along with a risk management plan. A risk management plan may be incorporated into a project management plan as a section. It does not need to be a stand-alone document. The project monitoring and control activities would show that the risk management strategy is followed if risks cross established risk thresholds and/or become problems.

Customer

A *customer* is the individual, project, organization, group, and so forth that is responsible for accepting the product or for authorizing payment. The customer is *external* to the project but not necessarily external to the organization. The term *customer* also serves as a variable when we discuss requirements gathering or elicitation.

The customer requirements represent the stakeholders' needs (Figure 4.1) (see the following definition of a stakeholder), expectations, constraints, and interfaces that have been collected and consolidated, had conflicts resolved, and have been translated into customer requirements. These "customer requirements" will be evolved into technical or product/product component requirements.

Policy

A *policy* or an organizational policy as it is used in CMMI® is defined as a guiding principle, typically established by senior management that is adopted by the organization to influence and determine decisions. The organizational policy defines the organizational expectations for the process and makes these expectations visible to those in the organization who are affected.

Another related view of policy is that it is supposed to be a "behavior expectation–setting document." The policy should describe how organizational employees should go about doing their daily work. The policy should describe how the employees are supposed to behave or act and what values they are supposed to live each working day. For example, a policy on peer reviews may state that all projects must plan and carry out peer reviews on

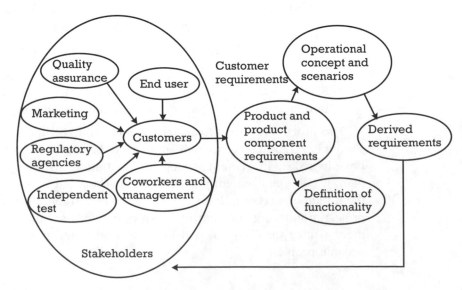

Figure 4.1 Customer, product, and product component requirements.

critical product components or subsystems or even modules. If an evaluation were to be carried out by an independent evaluator, he or she could
read the policy on peer reviews and then interview project managers and
project members to find out if they have identified *critical product components*
and if they have conducted or plan to conduct peer reviews on the life-cycle
work products defining those product components. Finding out how the
peer reviews are conducted, what type of training reviewers receive, and
what analysis is conducted on defects that are found would be an issue for
determining the process of conducting the reviews. The policy, if implemented, would ensure that the peer reviews were conducted.

Stakeholder

A *stakeholder* is a group or individual that is affected by the outcome of a
project or can affect the activities or output of the project.

Stakeholders can include:

> Customers;

> End users;

> Developers;

> Producers;

> Testers;

> Quality assurance;

> Database;

> Configuration Management;

> Suppliers;

> Marketers;

> Maintainers;

> Safety regulation agencies;

> Managers.

Relevant stakeholder

A *relevant stakeholder* is used to designate a stakeholder that is identified for
involvement in specified activities and is included in an appropriate plan
such as the project plan. The chief financial officer (CFO) could be a relevant
stakeholder for a project that is operating under a fixed-price budget and is
critical to the organization's business success. The CFO might be involved at
the beginning of the project when the budget is first established and before
the contract is signed. He or she might be involved at milestone reviews to
ensure that the project is progressing within the budget constraints.

Project manager

A *project manager* is the person responsible for planning, directing, controlling, structuring, and motivating the project. He or she may provide both technical and administrative direction and control to those performing project tasks or activities within his or her area of responsibility. The project manager is ultimately responsible to the customer. The project manager takes on different roles and responsibilities as the size, diversity, and complexity of the project changes:

- Small project;
- Large integrated project consisting of systems, software, mechanical, electrical, and plastics engineering components.

Senior manager

The term *senior manager* as it is used in CMMI® refers to a management role at a high enough level in an organization that the primary focus of the person is the long-term health and success of the organization rather than the short-term project and contractual concerns and pressures. A senior manager may be responsible for the oversight of a program that may contain many projects that are managed by project managers. He or she must be aware of the critical dependencies between projects. The senior manager normally establishes the business objectives and ensures that his or her vision is presented to and understood by all levels of management and practitioners. A senior manager has the authority to direct the allocation or reallocation of resources in support of the organization's process improvement initiative.

It is also typical for the senior manager to have profit and loss responsibility. Synonyms for senior manage include executive and top-level manager and may even be the head or CEO of the organization.

Organization

An *organization* is a structure in which people collectively manage one or more projects as a whole and whose projects share a senior manager and operate under the same policies. An organization is:

- A unit within an enterprise or company, agency, or service;
- Most often within a single geographical site;
- Increasingly defined over multiple sites, multiple countries, and multiple cultures;
- Normally self-contained.

An organization operates within a defined set of business objectives and according to the senior manager's vision. An organization can also be a major product line within a business unit. Some attributes of organizations include:

- Common management;
- Common business focus;
- Desire to have a common process improvement focus;
- Profit and loss requirements.

Enterprise

Enterprise is used to refer to very large companies that consist of many organizations in many different locations with different customers.

Development

Development, as it is used throughout CMMI®, implies maintenance activities as well as development activities. Experience has shown that best practices should be applied to both development and maintenance projects if an organization is in pursuit of engineering excellence.

Product

A *product* may be thought of as any tangible output or service that is the result of following a process and is intended for delivery to a customer or end user. A product can also be any work product that is delivered to the customer according to contract.

Product component

Product components are generally lower-level components of the product and are integrated to "build" the product. Product components may be a part of the product delivered to the customer or serve in the manufacture or use of the product. For example, for those companies that manufacture mobile phone batteries, the mobile phone battery is a product. For those companies that build and deliver mobile phones, the battery is a product component.

Work product: Life-cycle work product

A *work product* is any artifact produced by a life-cycle process (Figure 4.2) and can also be referred to as a *life-cycle work product*. Life-cycle work products can include:

- Requirements specifications;

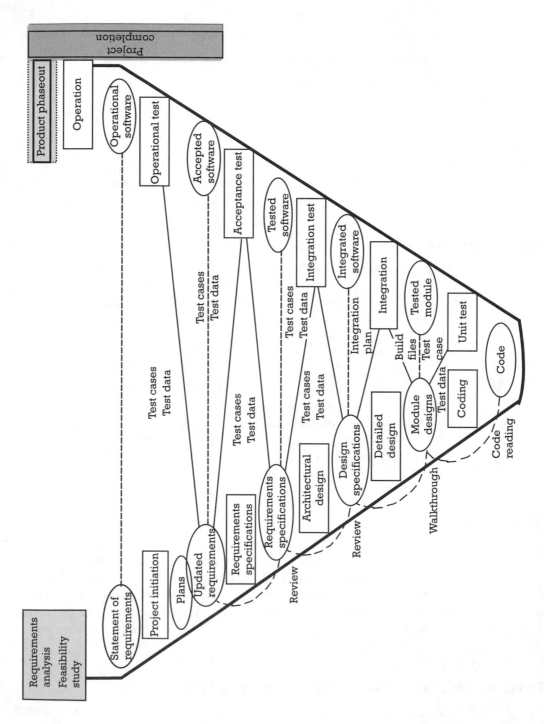

Figure 4.2 V-Model software development life cycle.

> Interface specifications;
> Architecture specifications;
> Project plans;
> Design documents;
> Unit test plans;
> Integration and system test plans;
> A process such as a manufacturing product assembly process.

Project

A *project* is a managed set of interrelated resources that delivers one or more products to a customer or end user. The set of resources has a definite beginning and end and operates according to a plan. Such a plan typically specifies:

> Product to be delivered or implemented;
> Resources and funds used;
> Work to be done;
> Schedule for doing the work.

Appraisal

An *appraisal* is an examination of one or more processes by a trained team of professionals using an appraisal reference model as the basis for determining strengths and weaknesses.

Assessment

An *assessment* is an appraisal that an organization conducts for itself for the purposes of process improvement.

Tailoring guidelines

Tailoring a process makes, alters, or adapts process descriptions, normally described at the organizational level, for use on a particular project. For most organizations, one organizational process definition cannot or will not be followed 100% for all of the projects. Some adaptation is normally needed. Tailoring guidelines then describe what can and cannot be modified and identify process components that are allowable candidates for modification. Tailoring guidelines can cover:

> Selecting a standard process;

> ▸ Selecting an approved product life cycle;
> ▸ Tailoring the selected standard process and life cycle to fit the project's needs.

Verification

Verification includes verification of the product and intermediate work products against all selected requirements, including customer, product, and product component requirements. Verification is inherently an incremental process. It begins with the verification of the requirements, progresses through the verification of the evolving work products, and culminates in the verification of the completed product.

Verification addresses whether the work product properly reflects the specified requirements. Verification assures "You built it right."

Validation

Validation demonstrates that the product, as provided, (or as it will be provided) will fulfill its intended use in the operational environment. Validation assures that "You built the right thing."

Goal

A *goal* is a required CMMI® component that can be either a *generic* goal or a *specific* goal. The word *goal* as used in CMMI® always refers to a model component.

Objective

The term *objective* is used in CMMI® in the common everyday sense; this is our objective or goal to be accomplished.

Document

A *document* is a collection of data, regardless of the medium on which it is recorded. It generally has permanence and can be read by humans or machines. Documents include both paper and electronic documents.

Quality and process performance objectives

The phrase *quality and process-performance objectives* covers objectives and requirements for:

> ‣ Product quality;

> ‣ Service quality;

> ‣ Process performance.

Process capability is defined to be the range of expected results that can be achieved by following a process. The maturity of an organization as defined by the staged representation of CMMI® and previously of CMM® was supposed to be used only as an indicator of that process capability.

If an organization was assessed at CMMI® Maturity Level 2, a project of similar size, complexity, and application domain should be able to be contracted to an organization and the customer should be able to expect similar results in terms of product and service quality and process performance.

Process performance is a measure of the actual results achieved by following a process. It is characterized by both process measures (e.g., effort, cycle time, and defect removal efficiency) and product measure s (e.g., reliability, defect density, and response time).

Operational concept and operational environment

Operational concept is a general description of how the system is envisioned to operate, where in the operating environment the system will reside or be distributed, how long the system must operate, and how effective the system's performance must be. Operational concepts evolve during the requirements engineering and development activities to facilitate the selection of product-component solutions that, when implemented, will satisfy the intended use of the product. Operational environment is the intended use environment. This is the environment the product or product component will reside in for operating, support, maintenance, and training functions including its physical surroundings and people interactions.

Operational scenarios

An *operational scenario* is a sequence of events that might occur which includes the interaction of the product with its environment and users, as well as the interaction among its product components. Operational scenarios are often created by defining a possible state and asking what-if questions. Operational scenarios are used in eliciting requirements from stakeholders (end users, management, regulatory agencies, testing, and so forth) as a way to help the customers to better understand their requirements and understand what it will really take to implement those requirements. Operational scenarios are used effectively to understand and refine requirements elicited from the customers.

Systems engineering

CMMI® defines systems engineering as the interdisciplinary approach governing the total technical and managerial effort required to transform a set of customer needs, expectations, and constraints into a product solution and support that solution throughout the product's life. This definition includes the definition of technical performance measures, the integration of engineering specialties towards the establishment of a product architecture, and the definition of supporting life-cycle processes that balance cost, performance, and schedule objectives.

From [1] (Figure 4.3), we have additional insights into systems engineering:

- Systems engineering is concerned with the engineering of systems.
- Systems management is concerned with *strategic level* systems engineering.
- Systems engineering efforts involve:
  - Systems engineering methods and tools or technologies;
  - Systems process;
  - Systems management.

The term *systems engineering* is not as commonly accepted throughout the world as one might expect. Some common and not-so-common names for systems engineering include:

- Systems engineers;
- Systems architects;
- Systems integrators;
- Systems management engineers;

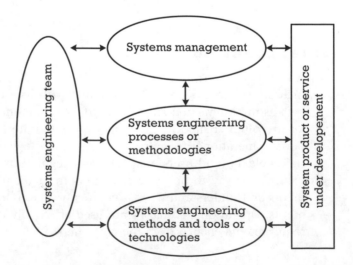

Figure 4.3 Three levels of systems engineering. (*From:* [1]. © 1999 John Wiley & Sons, Inc. Reprinted with permission.)

▶ Systems quality assurance engineers;

▶ Systems theorists;

▶ Systems reengineers;

▶ Operations research (related);

▶ Management science (related).

Summary

One of the important benefits to an organization that chooses CMMI® is the development of a consistent engineering, quality management, and project management vocabulary across its business units. This chapter was written to provide the reader with some of the more critical vocabulary that is used throughout CMMI®. The reader is encouraged to thoroughly study CMMI®, which is available on the SEI Web site and in [2].

References

[1]   Sage, A. P., and W. B. Rouse, *Handbook of Systems Engineering and Management*, New York: John Wiley & Sons, 1999.

[2]   Kulpa, M. K., and K. A. Johnson, *Interpreting the CMMI: A Process Improvement Approach*, Boca Raton, FL: Auerbach Publications, 2003.

Roles and Responsibilities

This chapter provides the reader with a short description of the roles and responsibilities of the various levels of management and practitioners. Descriptions of the various roles and responsibilities can be found embedded in various places throughout CMMI®, including the front material, the process areas, and the generic practices. These ideas will be combined with my own ideas and interpretations to provide the widest and most flexible but usable definitions.

- ▶ Senior management;
- ▶ Middle management;
- ▶ Project leaders;
- ▶ Practitioners;
- ▶ Process group;
- ▶ Quality assurance;
- ▶ Configuration Management;
- ▶ Integration and system testing;
- ▶ Measurement team;
- ▶ Systems engineering.

Senior management

Establish policies

The term *senior manager* was defined in Chapter 4 as a management role at a high enough level in an organization that the primary focus of the senior manager is the long-term health and success of the organization rather than the short-term project and contractual concerns and pressures.

The senior manager normally establishes the business objectives and ensures that his vision is presented to and understood by all levels of management and practitioners. Together with the authority to establish the business objectives and sharing his vision with the organization, comes the responsibility of caring for the profit and loss of the organization.

Senior management is responsible for defining policy in line with the vision and business objectives. As previously defined, a policy is a "behavior expectation setting document" that describes how the organization's employees should go about their daily work. It makes the senior manager's expectations visible and provides high-level guidance for the development of more detailed processes, procedures, guidelines, templates, and checklists.

Allocate or reallocate resources

A senior manager has the authority to direct the allocation or reallocation of resources in support of the organization's process improvement initiative. This can involve the allocation of people, computers, telecommunications equipment, funding, training, and even physical space to groups or activities such as:

- Systems/Software Engineering Process Group (SEPG);
- Quality assurance group;
- Integration and test group;
- Configuration Management group that utilizes a CM tool such as PVCS or Clearcase.

Establish authority and responsibility

Project managers and other responsible persons and groups not only have the responsibility for carrying out a process such as requirements engineering but also have the authority to do so. It is quite common to hear that project managers or project leaders have the responsibility to lead their project to successful completion within the given budget and time constraints without being given the authority to make decisions that may even involve replanning and renegotiation with the customer. Projects that are designated as critical are often not only watched closely by higher-level management but are also virtually run by them. Senior managers must take greater time to choose their project leaders carefully and to train, coach, and then give them the responsibility they need to successfully manage and control their projects.

Authorize training

Training budgets and training capabilities need the visible support of the senior manager, regardless of whether it is training at the organizational level in order to support the organization's strategic business direction the set of organizational processes, or it is providing training to address common project needs. Training may take the form of in-house training, e-learning through local or on-line universities, training, mentoring, and coaching from in-house experts or provided by vendors, and on-the-job training. Frequently human resources are tasked with establishing an organization-wide training program. Any endeavor at this level requires the support of senior management.

Provide visible support

The activities that we have discussed so far and others are part of the set of what is required of senior management to provide necessary visible management support. Some of these senior management activities include:

- Ensuring effective bidirectional communication from senior management to the developer;
- Developing or overseeing the development of management and technical policies;
- Establishing a Software Engineering Process Group (SEPG) if one does not exist along with the SEPG chairman role;
- Setting up a Software Quality Assurance Group (SQA) program at the organizational and project levels;
- Ensuring that the software Configuration Management function is established and operating on all projects;
- Ensuring that the necessary funding and time is allocated to support the defined process improvement activities;
- Ensuring that necessary training, mentoring, and coaching are provided to support the process improvement initiative throughout the organization;
- Ensuring that all other resources that are required to support the process improvement initiative are available;
- Participating in the review of all commitments that are being made on behalf of the organization to ensure that all commitments that have been made before, and including this one, can be honored;
- Making sure that all levels of management and practitioners understand the vision and business objectives of the organization;
- Ensuring that the process improvement initiative addresses the business objectives of the organization;
- Letting the organization know on a continuous basis the importance of the process improvement initiative from the senior management point of view.

It is important to add that sending out memos and e-mails and conducting annual general assembly speeches espousing care for process improvement and quality are not sufficient. Visible management support means "walking the talk" in the activities in which the senior manager participates to show by example. It means ensuring that a discussion on processes and quality is part of the monthly senior management progress meeting as well as focusing on cost, schedule and risk.

Approve organizational commitments

Mr. Watts Humphrey established the Commitment Process and Senior Management Oversight Review meetings as the pillars of CMM® and CMMI®. There is often a misunderstanding of indicating commitment for process improvement on the part of senior management and the "commitment process." A high-level view of the commitment process includes these steps:

- Work breakdown structure is defined.
- An initial estimate is made of the magnitude of the commitment.
- The disciplines involved participate in developing the implementation plan including estimating the size, effort, and schedule.
- An independent review of the plan is held.
- Agreement is reached on the commitment through negotiation.
- Senior management approves the commitment.
- A mechanism is provided to renegotiate the commitment in the event of a requirements change.
- A postimplementation review is held to discover what went right and what went wrong to learn how to improve future commitments and to compare actual performance with original estimates.

Of course, project teams and supporting teams must have confidence that the work can be performed within cost, schedule, and performance constraints. Senior management's involvement with the commitment process comes in its support of the proper execution of the commitment process and in its own visible participation. There was a misunderstanding that this involvement meant that the senior manager was to engage in a technical review of the commitment being proposed. Actually, the need for senior managers to review internal and external commitments, or recommitments, is to ensure necessary support for these commitments together with all of the other existing and pending commitments that have been made throughout the organization. In other words, it is a business commitment review on the part of the senior manager, not a technical one.

Senior management oversight

Mr. Humphrey's vision was that senior manager should conduct senior management oversight reviews for each of the projects on a periodic basis. These senior management oversight reviews should include an understanding of the processes that are being used on the projects, their efficiency, their effectiveness, and the resulting product quality that is being reached when they are followed.

Middle management

Corporate bridge

Middle management provides the corporate bridge between the programs and projects and the senior management team. It is middle management who must truly understand the organization's strategic direction and the senior manager's vision. This understanding of strategic direction and vision must be communicated to all other levels of management and practitioners, so that the daily project management, development, or maintenance activities can support them. It is middle management that must emphasize these policies and procedures to the project managers and practitioners in support of the vision and business objectives. Middle management may not know all of the small technical details of the processes and procedures that their people should be following, but they should be keenly aware of what is expected of their project members and what processes, methods, standards, guidelines, templates, checklists, and tools with which those project members are supposed to be in compliance.

Risk management decision making

Middle management should receive project and process management information. This information, combined with the knowledge of the organization's strategic direction and vision, allows them to make sound risk management decisions to guide the organization's daily operations. Thus, middle management is expected to be the advocate of a strong organizational measurement program that provides deeper insight into product and service quality along with process performance.

Process improvement steering committee

Without senior management involvement, the process improvement initiative may flounder and not be oriented toward supporting the organization's business objectives. Without middle management involvement, the critical process improvement resources and other individuals that are needed to work on specific focus area improvements will probably not be made available. Middle management must be "on board" to ensure the "right" people are provided where they are needed for as long as they are needed [1].

If individuals are to devote 25% of their time to a process improvement working group, that 25% must be made as important to them as the 75% they are being asked to devote to project work. They must be evaluated for their contributions to the process improvement effort in the same manner they are evaluated for their development efforts. In addition, if an individual is asked to devote 25% time to process improvement, this must not be 25% above the 120% they are already working. It is *middle management* who owns these resources and who must balance their work to accomplish business goals set by the senior management team. It is *middle management* who must "protect" the time allocated and spent on the process improvement working groups or the entire process improvement effort will be in danger from day one to the next.

Middle managers normally serve on the process improvement steering committee and should be involved in the following activities:

- Ensuring that the software process improvement activities are in line with the vision and business objectives that have been established by the senior management advisory board:
  - Reviewing the proposed budget for the improvement effort;
  - Making recommendations to the senior management advisory board regarding program direction, budget, and program risks.
- Ensuring that the necessary resources for the working groups and SEPG are available in a timely fashion:
  - Establishing the working groups to concentrate on prioritized focus areas (e.g., commitment process, estimation procedures, and testing methods);
  - Supporting, where needed, negotiations for people's dedicated time to the process improvement effort.
- Conducting process improvement program oversight reviews on a periodic basis (recommended once per month):
  - Ensuring that software process improvement activities progress in line with documented budgets and plans;
  - Performing reviews and approval of working group deliverables.
- Providing visible support for the SEPG and working groups.

Process owner

While the term *process owner* has different implications in different organizations and different process improvement initiatives, I think it is important for middle managers to take on the role of the process owner. For the purposes of this discussion, *process owner* means the person responsible for all of the activities surrounding a process focus area. The process owner may simply be the sponsor of a working group that is facilitated by an engineering process group member, or the process owner may be a middle manager that has significant knowledge and a desire to actually participate in the development of new processes or the revision of existing ones. As the process owner, the middle manager must participate in the periodic senior management oversight meeting and report the progress on his or her process focus area.

In this way middle management is forced to be involved with the process improvement initiative and forced to know exactly what progress has been made, what activity is being worked on, what measurable benefits have been realized, what issues have been logged, and what risks have been identified. Armed with that knowledge, the middle manager can provide additional resources and support of his or her process focus area, can report true progress to the senior management team, and can participate much more proactively in discussions and actions that ensure the process improvement initiative is achieving business results. In addition, the middle manager can provide stronger direction to the project managers and practitioners who work under his or her control.

When middle managers serve as a process owners, they also find themselves with the ability to more easily relate to process improvement and quality management questions such as these:

- Would you please describe your role (as you currently see it and live it) in process improvement and change?
  - How do you encourage and show your support for process improvement efforts in your organization?
  - Do you feel you must change anything about your attitude, commitment, or skill base to support process improvement and change in the future?
- What change rate to you think can be realistically expected and supported for the organization worldwide?
- How will current stress on the organization affect the process improvement plans and expectations?
- How will quality management and process improvement make the senior management vision come alive?
- What level of coaching skills do the senior management and middle management need to support the process improvement needs of the organization in the coming years?
- Where do training, mentoring, and coaching fit in with on-the-job experience? How does it work today? What are the plans for tomorrow?
- How will you help lead the organization to stay abreast of the ever-changing state of the art in technology?
- What are the organization's current ideas for integrating cultures in the near-term future and mid-term future?
- What skill sets in quality management, process improvement, and change management do you think the process group, quality group, and change management group will need in order to support improvement worldwide, now and in the mid-term future?
- What is the organization's greatest process improvement achievement so far?

> ▸ How does the organization recognize and reward its process improvement champions?

Project manager

Definition of project management

Project management is the combination of people, processes, techniques, and technologies necessary to bring the project (or program) to successful completion. Measures of success depend on the particular project. However, most projects are measured on what may now be considered the quadruple constraint of:

- ▸ Time (schedules);
- ▸ Cost (on or over budget);
- ▸ Performance (based on specifications);
- ▸ Quality (meeting or exceeding customer expectations in the intended use environment).

The old project management role

Historically, the project manager's role was to plan, control, organize, and direct the work of several individuals or departments so the project could succeed.

The new skills required of a project manager

Today the project manager is expected to be:

- ▸ Better educated;
- ▸ Open, friendly, and people-oriented;
- ▸ A better listener;
- ▸ Quality conscious;
- ▸ Receptive to new ideas;
- ▸ More participative;
- ▸ Facilitators;
- ▸ Skilled at group process and group dynamics;
- ▸ Encouraging to others to participate in plans and decisions;
- ▸ Understanding in how to coach, inspire, and motivate;
- ▸ Able to span boundaries;
- ▸ Able to provide and apply integrative management techniques to unique, complex organizational ventures characterized by interdependent efforts, a variety of specialists, over multiple sites, multiple languages, and multiple cultures.

The process areas of CMMI® certainly expound on the project planning and project monitoring and control functions that make up the basics of project management, but the concerns of the project manager are scattered among many process areas in multiple categories in CMMI®. We will examine a reasonable subset of them here.

Estimation

Estimation is still a critical component of project management, and the project manager is responsible for making sure the following estimates are made and used in the project planning.

First, the project manager needs to work with his or her lead engineers and estimate the scope of the project by establishing a top-level work breakdown structure (WBS). The WBS defines the work or tasks to be performed and is the primary planning and analysis tool used in almost all projects. It should answer two questions: (1) What is to be accomplished? and (2) What are the necessary hierarchical relationships of the work effort? The WBS process also serves the project manager as a tool by:

- Providing a complete list of the software, hardware, services, and information technology work tasks that must be completed during the development and production of a product;
- Defining the responsibility, personnel, cost, duration, risk, and precedence of each work task;
- Providing an easy-to-follow numbering system to allow a hierarchical tracking of the progress.

From the WBS, the project manger can direct his or her project members to develop work packages that describe what must be performed, by whom, and in what time duration and start to establish project control.

The project manager is responsible to ensure that standard estimations are made by those who will be responsible for the development and testing of the product or product components. These standard estimations include:

- Size and complexity;
- Effort and cost;
- Schedule;
- Risks;
- Knowledge and skills;
- Stakeholder involvement;
- Critical computer resources;
- Technical activities;
- Quality.

Project planning

Of course, the project manager must oversee the development of the project plan as the basis for managing the project to completion. The project plan is accompanied by a number of "supporting" plans or "plans that affect" the project. These plans may be incorporated into one physical or logical document called the *project plan*, or they may be separate plans that are referenced within the project plan itself. Some of these supporting plans may be developed together with representatives of the supporting groups such as quality assurance or Configuration Management, but the project manager is responsible for these supporting plans' content and for ensuring that all of the supporting plans fit together to support the project's successful completion. If asked about the contents and direction of the project's quality plan, the project manager should never answer, "Go ask the quality engineer," even though the quality engineer assigned to support the project may have had a strong hand in developing the project quality plan along with other project members, including the project manager. Plans that affect the project plan, which are typically developed together with the project plan, include:

- Project quality plan;
- Project Configuration Management plan;
- Risk management plan;
- Knowledge and skills plan;
- Stakeholder involvement plan;
- Data management plan;
- Integration strategy;
- Verification strategy;
- Validation strategy.

Before the project plan and all other plans that affect the project are solidified, the project manager is responsible to ensure that all supporting groups or disciplines are committed to the concepts, budget, and schedule that are contained in the total project planning package. This may involve several rounds of negotiation until total agreement is reached and the project manager is confident that all relevant stakeholders are committed to the project's success.

Criticality

The project manager should assume responsibility for working with the customer, the organization's senior management team, and outside groups such as regulatory agencies to determine which product components or subsystems should be treated as critical. Criticality definitions must be defined up-front at the organizational level. These criticality definitions are then translated into quality functions such as peer reviews, tests, and audits for each level of criticality. Using the concept of criticality, the project manager can better direct the use of the project's resources and focus the application of the project's activities including the quality functions on the project's critical components that will help optimize the factors of cost, schedule, performance, and quality.

Monitoring and controlling

Once the project plan has been developed and committed to, a major portion of project management is *monitoring and controlling*. The project manager is responsible for seeing that these monitoring and control activities are carried out and the results are used to manage and control the project's activities in the future. These activities include:

- Tracking actual results against the planned estimates;
- Conducting weekly or periodic project meetings with project members and other representatives such as quality assurance and test;
- Participating in milestone meetings to report on progress against major milestones and resetting the project direction as needed;
- Attending senior management oversight meetings on a periodic basis to discuss project progress, processes, and resulting product quality;
- Taking corrective action as necessary to keep the project on track according to plan or making adjustments to the plan and establishing a new commitment from all relevant stakeholders.

Requirements validation, functional architecture, and alternative solutions

While the initial requirements elicitation may be carried out with a multiple disciplined team that may or may not include the project manager, the project manager is responsible for the evolution of those requirements and their validation with the customer and/or end users. This also means that the project manager must have the authority to interface with the customer with or without other organizational representation. Staying with this theme, the project manager is responsible for his or her team to develop the functional architecture to guide the construction and testing of the product or product component and for ensuring that alternative technical solutions are considered according to predefined selection criteria before the final set of requirements are established and the technical solution is implemented.

Peer reviews and unit testing

It is also the responsibility of the project manager to ensure that peer reviews and unit tests are planned on the life-cycle work products that are identified from the product life cycle chosen for the project. For peer reviews this means that the project manager is responsible for ensuring that:

- Peer reviews are planned, especially for critical components.
- Peer reviews are led by trained moderators.
- Peer reviews are conduct by trained review team members that have the right level of knowledge and skills, the right application domain experience, and the right level of project knowledge to provide useful and effective input to help detect and remove major defects.
- Peer reviews are not considered complete until defect analysis and correction has taken place according to the exit criteria established by the peer review moderator.
- Peer review data is placed into a database and analyzed for different categories of defects and trends per life-cycle phase.
- Peer reviews are used to improve product and life-cycle work product quality and for process improvement and not for employee evaluation.

For unit testing the project manager is responsible for ensuring that:

- Unit tests are planned.
- Unit tests follow project or organizational standards and templates for unit tests.
- Each unit test contains a section describing expected results that are to be compared against actual results and corrective action is taken as necessary.
- A sampling of unit tests is observed and evaluated by quality assurance.
- Unit test results are taken into consideration as part of the transition criteria from the project environment to the integration and systems testing environment.

Configuration Management (CM)

The project manager is responsible for ensuring that developmental Configuration Management is carried out on the project. Whether this is supported by a centralized CM group or is a collaboration of the project's CM specialists working together with the organization's CM engineers, it is the responsibility of the project manager to ensure that the basic CM functions of identification, baselining, configuration control, status accounting, and configuration auditing are carried out according to the standards and guidelines developed for the organization. This responsibility includes:

- Ensuring that modules or product components are baselined only after they have been peer reviewed and unit tested with documented results;

- Ensuring that communication and cooperation exists between the project's CM specialists and the CM group engineers that are assigned to support the project's CM needs;
- Serving as the head of the project level change control board (CCB), perhaps along with the quality engineer and testing representative, in analyzing change requests that do not affect the agreed upon requirements;
- Ensuring that all life-cycle work products and associated plans are updated, if necessary, whenever a change request is approved at the project or organizational level (especially critical when it is the requirements that are changed; this ensures systems integrity);
- Using the information provided by the function of CM status accounting to manage and control the project better.

Quality assurance

Besides working with quality engineers to develop the project's quality plan, the project manager is responsible for reviewing and responding to noncompliance reports that are the result of objective evaluations carried out on the processes, procedures, standards, guidelines, templates, and checklists that have been identified to be followed in the project's quality plan. The project manager should also support the escalation procedure that a quality engineer may follow if the project does not respond to the noncompliance reports in a timely fashion.

Supplier management

Project managers who manage suppliers must be involved with:

- Supplier selection criteria;
- Developing the requirements to a sufficient level to determine which requirements would or should be designed and implemented by a supplier;
- Developing the project plan to a sufficient level to determine if the supplier's estimations are in line with project expectations;
- Helping to develop the Request for Proposal (RFP);
- Helping to select the supplier based on the supplier selection criteria;
- Leading the orientation meeting with the supplier's team to ensure complete understanding of what is expected and who is responsible for what part of the development;
- Managing the supplier through specialized project management activities that keep track of the supplier's progress and performance;
- Ensuring that the supplier's capability level is maintained through periodic review.

Practitioners

Practitioners is a general term for those project members who participate in the life-cycle activities including requirements gathering, architecture definition, detailed design, coding or construction, unit testing, integration and systems testing, and acceptance testing and delivery. They also include members of groups such as quality assurance, Configuration Management, engineering process group, measurement, database, and so forth. Practitioners do not normally serve as project managers, although they may serve as a lead engineer for their project.

Practitioners are not only expected to do, but they are also expected to participate in a variety of project activities including:

- Requirements analysis;
- Estimation;
- Making commitments;
- Development;
- Tracking daily work progress;
- Developing status reports;
- Participating in project meetings and milestone meetings as required;
- Identifying risks;
- Carrying out risk mitigation activities;
- Participating in objective evaluations for process compliance;
- Participating in training, mentoring, and coaching;
- Providing training, mentoring, and coaching for other project members in their areas of expertise;
- Conducting peer reviews;
- Conducting unit tests;
- Following Configuration Management guidelines, especially at the developmental control level;
- Providing inputs for process improvement;
- Understanding and implementing the senior manager's vision;
- Understanding and supporting the organization's business objectives;
- Embracing changes in technical processes and organizational development and helping colleagues to deal with the changes as well;
- Aligning personal career development goals with those of the project and organization;
- Studying and acquiring knowledge and skills that will increase individual competence levels that support the organization's business objectives.

Process group

Organizational focus

Organizational process improvement should be based on a complete understanding of an organization's strengths and weaknesses of its set of standard
processes and the project's defined processes that are tailored from them.
Process improvement occurs within the context of the organization's business objectives, but process improvement does not happen by itself or
because the senior management team issues a memo proclaiming to
happen.

Facilitating the organization's process improvement activities

The responsibility for facilitating and managing the organization's process
improvement activities is normally assigned to a process group. Figure 5.1
shows a sample process improvement infrastructure needed by an organization for successful process improvement along with the relative position of
the process group (i.e., SEPG). This process group is normally seen as the
focal group for action planning, process improvement, technology insertion,
training, and awareness and expectation setting. Process groups are frequently viewed as a channel for institutionalizing the organization's knowledge of process methods, practices, and technology. Process groups are the
organization's champion of change and its members are change agents.

Collectively the members of the process group need to be able to demonstrate their ability to manage, develop, coach, and guide process improvement and its accompanying cultural changes. First and foremost, they need
to understand senior management's vision and the organization's business
objectives to be able to efficiently and effectively guide the process

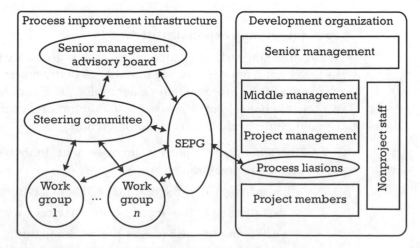

Figure 5.1   Sample process improvement infrastructure.

improvement effort. Without this explicit knowledge, the organization's process improvement effort may demonstrate compliance to a model such as CMMI® but not be supportive of the organization's business objectives at all.

Engineering background

Process group members should have a solid engineering background. They should have a general knowledge of the organization's application domains and knowledge of modern engineering techniques and methods. They must be up-to-date on accepted engineering standards (DoD, MoD, IEEE, ISO, IEC ESA, NASA, and so forth). They must also have a good understanding of the project management support functions such as quality assurance and Configuration Management. The managers and engineers alike must respect them. They must have a strong knowledge and good experience in project management and a working knowledge of metrics to help the project managers manage and control their projects better.

Process group members must be people oriented with superior communication skills and willing to perform most of their work in the project developers' offices not their own. They should always be ready to provide hand-holding support for the managers and practitioners on the various projects where the process ideas are being introduced.

Organizational development skill

While process group members must have the technical background to maintain credibility with the product or product component developers, they must also be knowledgeable in the organizational development skills as well (i.e., managing technological change, team building, collaborative consulting) to effect successful technology transition.

Process group responsibilities

While the many tasks attributed to the process group are important ones for its members, it must be stressed that the job of the process group is to be the champion of the process improvement effort. It is expected to facilitate the process of change, *not be responsible* for the process change. Process group responsibilities include but are not limited to:

▸ Coordinating the process improvement initiative up, down, and across the organization:

   ▹ Participating in the senior management advisory board reviews;

   ▹ Participating in the steering committee reviews;

   ▹ Facilitating the activities of the working groups: staying on top of what is going on, what difficulties are being encountered, and what successes are being realized;

- Promoting technical awareness and education about process improvement.
- Managing/facilitating the process improvement initiative:
  - Facilitating the definition/improvement of the technical and managerial processes, methods, techniques, and tools for developing and maintaining product and product components;
  - Assisting in the evaluation of new tools and techniques based on their understanding of the existing processes;
  - Facilitating the definition and maintenance of organization policies and standards for processes and products;
  - Discovering good practices, getting them adapted for general use on the projects throughout the organization, and baselining them as best practices;
  - Overseeing and facilitating pilot projects and implementation of improvements into the projects and across the organization;
  - Directing the definition of process metrics, initiating the collection of data, and assisting the working groups and projects in the analysis and use of the resulting information.
- Ensuring that the processes are "living":
  - Maintaining a dialogue with project personnel regarding the application and performance of developing processes:

    Sharing good ideas from other parts of the organization;

    Listening to issues/ideas from the practitioners.
  - Initiating periodic process improvement progress checks and reassessments;
  - Initiating practitioner-driven review of specific processes.
- Maintaining a library of process assets:
  - Overseeing the process database (process asset library) for product and process assets used across the organization;
  - Facilitating the development and retention of tailoring guidelines for specific use of the assets in the process asset library.

Process group manager

Each process improvement infrastructure should have an identified process group manager. This individual is a senior person with most of the attributes listed in the section on what process group members should know. The process group manager is responsible for coordinating all of the process improvement activities throughout the organization. He or she has direct access to the senior manager. He or she serves as the link among the senior management advisory board, the steering committee, and the working groups. The process group manager serves as the link between the organization's process improvement initiative and the organization's line, function, and project management.

In order to ensure that a process improvement program moves forward, The process group manager must function as a project manager for the process program. This means that he or she must utilize basic project planning and tracking tools. He or she must set milestones, hold meetings with agendas, record minutes, track action items, and so forth. Without strong project management skills and follow-through, the initiative will lack leadership and will not progress in a timely fashion.

The process group manager is also the spokesperson for the process improvement initiative. This involves continuous oral and written communication about the process improvement effort, its successes, and its failures. The process group manager must be willing to give a presentation on any aspect of the process improvement initiative many times before the rest of the organization starts to accept that message that he or she is giving. The process group manager is the lead organizational champion for the process improvement effort.

Quality assurance

The classic responsibility of quality assurance is to provide visibility into the processes being followed on the projects for the management team at all levels and to determine if they are efficient and effective and producing the necessary product quality to satisfy customer, competitor, organization, or project quality goals. Figure 5.2 shows SQA participating in three distinct but related directions. The first direction is to management, as just described. The second direction is to the developers. This responsibility is inadequately executed worldwide based on my experience of assessments and process improvement consulting.

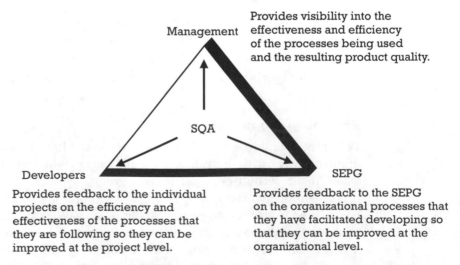

Figure 5.2 SQA: Agent for process improvement.

Quality assurance engineering or responsibles should provide feedback to the individual projects and project members on the efficiency and effectiveness of the processes that the project members are required to follow so that they can be improved at the project level as necessary. The third direction is when the quality assurance engineers find that project members are indeed faithfully following the organizational processes but they are not efficient or effective and/or they are not producing the required product quality. In this case the quality assurance engineers are responsible for providing this feedback to the process group so that these processes can be improved at the organizational level.

In addition to the process compliance and process improvement aspect of quality assurance, some basic quality assurance roles and responsibilities include:

- Assisting the project manager in developing quality goals;
- Assisting the project manager in creating the project's quality plan;
- Supporting the project in selecting an adequate set of standards, practices, and procedures;
- Identifying all deviations for the agreed-upon processes as early as possible;
- Ensuring that all identified deviations are recorded, corrected, or escalated to the appropriate level of management, up to and including the senior manager;
- Negotiating criticality levels for the product components and subsystems, with the various engineering disciplines;
- Ensuring that all detailed technical activity plans are made available and reviewed for conformance with process definitions;
- Performing ad hoc process compliance evaluations to ensure the quality functions are being implemented along with the normal technical project activities;
- Interfacing with the appropriate customer representatives on process and/or product quality problems;
- Evaluating the supplier's quality plan and resulting implementation to ensure that any required policies and procedures are being adhered to;
- Evaluating the supplier's quality assurance activities to ensure that the supplier product or product component will not downgrade the product quality required for the integrated system or subsystem;
- Evaluating the projects and organization's Configuration Management activities to ensure the integrity and consistency of the work products and the bidirectional traceability of those life-cycle work products back to the requirements;
- Ensuring that the customer receives a complete and correct description of the delivered product or product components and accompanying documentation;

▸ Ensuring that the development tools and utilities used to develop and test the product or product components fit the development process;

▸ Serving as the internal customer representative to keep that point of view in front of the development team.

Configuration Management

Those individuals who participate in the Configuration Management function either at the project, organizational, test, or release levels are responsible for helping the projects to preserve the results of the hard work that has been done while at the same time providing for a controlled, systematic way of making necessary changes.

As will be described in detail in Chapter 7, Configuration Management engineers and managers and other individuals such as the project manager, the quality assurance engineer, and the test manager work together to enable the proper execution of the basic Configuration Management functions including:

▸ Identification;

▸ Baselining;

▸ Change control;

▸ Configuration Management status accounting;

▸ Configuration auditing;

▸ Managing the Configuration Management system;

▸ Interface control (both technical and organizational);

▸ CM tool support;

▸ Supplier control;

▸ Migration from developmental change control to organizational change control.

The organizational change control board (CCB) is responsible for controlling any and all changes to the requirements that represent the agreement or contract with the customer. In that capacity, the organizational-level CCB takes on the responsibility of representing the interests of all groups and disciplines that may be affected by the proposed changes to existing baselines. Some organizations have also established a requirements CCB (RCCB) that includes the chief architect. All requirements and requirements changes, including those that originate from trouble reports, are first funneled to this RCCB to determine if the requested change would have an impact on the established architecture and strategic business direction. If it is determined that no significant impact would be realized to the architecture or strategic business direction, the requirements change request would be passed on to the standard CCB.

The CCB at the organizational level authorizes the establishment of organizational-level baselines such as the functional, allocated, or product baselines, authorizes changes to those baselines, and authorizes the creation and release of products and product components from the product baseline.

As described in the roles and responsibilities for the project manager section, the project-level CCB is responsible for the change control activities for all developmental baselines that are under the control of the project manager. The basic Configuration Management functions must be performed, but may be done so with slightly less formality than if those functions were focused on customer requirements. Project-level change control, together with organizational change control, is responsible for the smooth transition from developmental or project control to formal or organizational control as the product components move through the product life-cycle stages to an integrated, verified, and validated product.

Integration and system testing

In order to have clear and obvious objectivity during the integration and systems testing phase of the product life cycle, many organizations establish an independent test team that focuses on those functions. Such a testing group is expected to have application knowledge and understanding, a test methodology, testing experience, knowledge of the test environment, and test team members that exhibit creativity, insight, determination, and analytical ability.

While it is often not the fault of the integration and systems test group, integration and systems testing engineers are not involved enough in the early life-cycle phases of the product life cycle. Independent test representatives from the integration and systems test group should be involved in peer reviews of product or systems requirements specifications and the engineering discipline–allocated requirements specifications such as the software requirements specification or the hardware requirements specification.

Independent test representatives should be involved in peer reviews of interface specifications and architecture specifications. Experienced test engineers can best answer questions such as: Is this requirement testable? Even before the various specifications are developed, independent test representatives can be very effective by participating on multidisciplined requirements elicitation teams together with systems engineers, software engineers, marketing, program management, design experts, and so forth to help the stakeholders understand better what the testing implications are of their wants, needs, constraints, and interface requirements.

To support integrated project management, test group representatives should work with the project manager and lead designers to develop an integration strategy and determine the integration sequence and testing environment that will support the project's needs.

During the actual integration and systems testing activities, the integration and systems test group is responsible for implementing:

▶ Stress, load, and boundary testing;

▶ Functional testing;

▶ Quality factor testing such as reliability, maintainability, portability, and so forth;

▶ Documentation testing to ensure that the user and maintenance documentation matches the system to be delivered.

Prior to the implementation of the integration and systems testing, the integration and systems test group may work closely together with Configuration Management to ensure the verified and validated product components are indeed ready to be integrated and tested.

When the project uses suppliers, the integration and systems test group is responsible for developing the acceptance tests and implementing all necessary acceptance testing activities to confirm that the supplier's confidence in the delivered system was justified.

In many IT shops, the customer expects the development organization to provide a partial or full test team to work together with that organization's test team to carry out acceptance testing. While not normally considered the development organization's responsibility, it is often a good means to understand more of the customer's capabilities for future design, development, and testing of deliverable systems.

Measurement team

Most organizations have at least one person who has an interest in and an ability to understand metrics and measurements. Few organizations have a designated measurement group. While it may not seem worthwhile for an organization to form a separate measurement group, it has been my experience that having a measurement expert or two supporting the organization's metrics needs is quite valuable. I have typically seen one of two scenarios:

1. The "metrics guru" collects a lot of data that is hidden in his or her desk on floppies and CD-ROMs and is not used or shared by anyone else.

2. The metrics guru collects data and sends out reports combined with awe-inspiring supporting graphics that few, if any, project managers or project members can understand, much less use.

CMMI® does not demand an organizational measurement group, but it is recommended that middle- and large-sized organizations designate a measurement team to facilitate and support the organization's measurement needs. Even small organizations are encouraged to have a team member with an interest in measurements, or they may hire an outside consultant from time to time to receive guidance on establishing a measurement program.

The measurement team is expected to support organizational measurement needs at every management and practitioner level. They are responsible for assisting the organization and its projects in defining measures based on business objectives. In addition, they are responsible for:

- Helping to determine data collection schemes;
- Helping to determine data storage and retrieval schemes;
- Determining appropriate analysis techniques in advance of the data collection and analysis;
- Analyzing the data based on the agreed-upon analysis techniques;
- Calculating derived measures;
- Providing information to the projects based on the analyzed measures;
- Coaching project managers to use measurement results to better manage and control the project;
- *Ensuring that stored measures also includes the information needed to understand and interpret the measures.*

In addition, the measurement team, in cooperation with quality assurance and the process group, helps to develop measures that will determine the effectiveness of the processes the projects are following.

Measurement is critical for every project's success. A measurement ream may prove quite useful to support that critical need.

Systems engineering

Systems engineering provides a cradle-to-grave view of the evolving system. Systems engineers help to define the total technical and managerial effort required to transform the set of customer needs, expectations, and constraints into a life-cycle balanced solution. This includes the definition of technical performance measures, the integration of engineering specialties towards the establishment of a product architecture, and the definition of supporting life-cycle processes that balance cost, schedule, performance, and quality objectives.

Specific systems engineering activities include:

- Serving on a multidisciplined team to elicit requirements from the identified stakeholders;
- Transforming those customer requirements into product and product component requirements that can be used by project members to refine and build the product;
- Allocating the technical requirements to the various disciplines such as software, hardware, mechanical engineering, hydraulics, manufacturing, people, and processes;

- Supporting the definition of the overall systems architecture and definition of functionality;
- Defining interfaces between systems components;
- Analyzing requirements change requests to ensure the chosen optimal alternative technical solution is not adversely affected;
- Supporting integration and systems testing;
- Supporting the project manager by providing a total systems view throughout the entire product life cycle.

Summary

Process improvement that supports business objectives requires the cooperation and coordination of all levels of management and practitioners. Short description of the roles and responsibilities of the various levels of management and practitioners have been provided from various places throughout CMMI® and were combined with my own ideas and interpretations to provide the widest and most flexible but usable definitions.

Reference

[1]   Kasse, T., "Action Focused Assessment for Software Process Improvement," Norwood, MA: Artech House, 2002.

The Evolutionary Differences Between CMM for Software and CMMI

This chapter illustrates the evolutionary differences between CMM® for Software and CMMI® and presents an incremental approach for organizations interested in moving or evolving from a strict CMM® for Software process improvement focus to the integrated focus offered by CMMI®. This incremental approach is also a compliant means by which organizations on the threshold of adapting a model can methodically embrace CMMI®.

Many individuals and companies have argued in the past and continue to argue today about whether it is reasonable or worth it to move from a process improvement initiative based on CMM® for Software to one that is based on CMM® Integration. Certainly for those companies whose products are predominantly software, it does not seem to make sense to disrupt what they already know. Besides, what if the company moves to CMMI® and it loses its maturity level?

I have a different point of view based on my experience in helping to develop CMMI® and in teaching, appraising, and consulting with companies throughout the United States, Europe, and Asia. CMMI® represents an upgrade to the concepts that were recorded in CMM® for Software more than 10 years ago. CMMI® represents 10 years of lessons learned from thousands of external and internal consultants, from CEOs, CIOs, presidents, and vice-presidents, and from project managers and practitioners whose organizations used CMM® for Software in many different applications, industries, sizes of companies, military, commercial, and so forth. It represents the continuous process improvement that was always the theme of any quality management effort. From my point of view, the question that must be answered is: Why would anyone want their organization's process improvement initiative to be based on 10-year-old thinking, when CMMI® is available and represents current thinking based on applying continuous process improvement to CMM® itself?

Before providing the overview of the upgrades, it must also be stated up front that the standard bar has been raised. CMMI® does expect an organization to know more and be willing to strive for a higher level of excellence, but that is what evolution is all about and what any focus on excellence demands.

This chapter intends to present the evolutionary differences between CMM® for Software and CMM® Integration to give the reader an insight into those lessons learned. Details will be presented in subsequent chapters, where categories of process areas are described.

An integrated approach

As described in Chapter 1, CMMI® was developed to support multidisciplined process improvement initiatives using an integrated model to eliminate, or at least drastically reduce, the need for multiple models and standards that were causing confusion and excessive costs for companies that were trying to satisfy them all. The highest degree of integration can be found in the CMMI® Model CMMI® for Systems Engineering, Software Engineering, Integrated Product and Process Development, and Supplier Sourcing (CMMI®-SE/SW/IPPD/SS, V1.1).

Two representations

CMMI® models support two representations, as shown in Figure 6.1. The staged representation represents the legacy of CMM® for Software and is used to guide the overall organizational process maturity level improvement approach. It organizes the process areas into five maturity levels to provide an incremental path for the organization's process improvement initiative as a whole. The continuous representation was adapted from the work on ISO

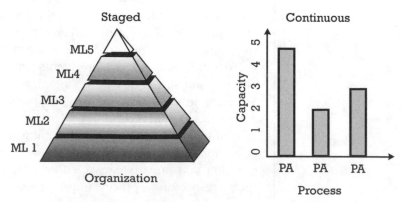

Figure 6.1   CMMI® model representations.

15504 (SPICE) and Systems Engineering CMM® and is used to support the individual process area capability level approach. It uses six capability levels, capability profiles, target staging, and equivalent staging as organizing principles for the model components. A description of how to combine the staged representation and the continuous representation into a "constagedeous" approach to process improvement is presented in Chapter 16.

CMMI process area contents

This book does not intend to provide a detailed description of the model structure for either of the representations. However, to be complete, it is important to note that information that is available for each process area described in CMMI® compared to CMM® for Software.

Each CMMI® process area is described by:

- Purpose statement;
- Introductory notes;
- Related process areas;
- Practice-to-goal relationship;
- Specific goals;
- Generic goals;
- Specific practices;
- Generic practices;
- Notes;
- Work products;
- Subpractices;
- Discipline amplifications;
- Generic practice elaborations,

Purpose statement

The purpose statement is the first statement that the reader sees following the name of the process area in CMMI®. This was true of CMM® for Software as well, but in CMMI® the purpose statement is now highlighted by a boldface title. In CMM® for Software, the purpose statement was simply the first statement in the descriptive paragraph that followed the name of the key process area.

Introductory notes

The introductory notes in CMMI® fulfill the same purpose as the descriptive paragraph in CMM® for Software but with two distinctive differences: (1) This section of the process area description is delineated by a boldface section head titled "Introductory Notes"; and (2) the descriptions found for most of the process areas are more extensive and more explanatory.

Frequently, the introductory notes section provides a context and additional explanation of the details found in the specific goals and specific practices that follow. It is my opinion that this significantly contributes to a faster understanding of the process area content.

Listing of specific and generic goals

This is simply a listing of the specific and generic goals to provide the reader with an immediate understanding of the intent of the process area.

Practice-to-goal relationship

The specific goals and generic goals are also listed along with the tags of the specific practices and generic practices to provide a high-level overview of the process area and what it would take to institutionalize the practices at various capability levels.

Specific goals

Specific goals apply to only one process area and address the unique characteristics that describe what must be implemented to satisfy the purpose of the process area. Specific goals are listed along with their associated specific practices so that there is no room for misinterpretation of what must take place for the specific goal to be satisfied. In CMM® for Software, a similar mapping was only found in a separate appendix. In addition, key practices could be mapped to more than one goal, and even if the practice was mapped to a single goal, subpractices could contribute to achieving another goal. In CMMI® there is a clear distinction made between the mapping of specific practices to specific goals and generic practices to generic goals. Subpractices map to one specific practice.

Generic goals

Generic goals apply to more than one process area. Achievement of each of these goals relative to a process area signifies *improved control* in performing the process. Achievement of each of these goals in relationship to each process area enables the institutionalization that will ensure the process is repeatable and lasting. Institutionalization will be described in detail in Chapter 15.

Specific practices

A specific practice is an activity that is considered important in achieving the specific goal that is mapped to a process area. The description of specific practices directly follows the specific goal to which they contribute.

Generic practices

Generic practices are practices that apply to any process area because, in principle, they can improve the performance and control of any process. The description of generic practices directly follows the generic goal to which they contribute.

Notes

Notes are normally short additional descriptions of a specific goal or a specific practice that provides additional insight into the meaning or intent of that specific goal or specific practices. Notes augment the details found in the introductory notes section.

Work products

Typical work products provide examples of methods, tools, techniques, and so forth that may be used to support the implementation of a practice.

Subpractices

Subpractices are suggested courses of action that correspond to practices and provide additional insight into the practices.

Discipline amplifications

Amplifications contain information that is relevant to a particular discipline, such as hardware or software, and is associated with specific practices.

Generic practice elaborations

Generic practice elaborations explain how to apply a generic practice in the context of the process area.

Process area upgrades and additions

Both the staged and continuous representations of CMMI® offer categories of process areas that have been developed by authors and contributors of CMMI®. For purposes of this book, I have decided to place the process areas into slightly different categories. The categories are:

- Project management concepts;
- Engineering concepts;
- Process management concepts;
- Integrated teaming concepts;

- Quantitative management concepts;
- Optimizing concepts.

We will continue with the description of the evolutionary differences between CMM® for Software and CMMI® by first looking at the project management concepts process areas.

Project management concepts process areas

Project Planning

The Project Planning process area basically follows the concepts found in the corresponding CMM® for Software Project Planning key process area (KPA); however, there have been some upgrades and some additions:

- There is a heavier emphasis on having a detailed work breakdown structure (WBS).
- Estimation focuses on size and complexity.
- Effort and cost are determined based on the size and complexity estimations.
- Schedule is established based on the size and complexity estimations.
- Project planning now includes a focus on the project team members having the necessary knowledge and skills to carry out the project according to the estimations and plans.
- Data management, or the planning and maintaining of project data items and their contents, has been added to the list of project management concerns.
- The identification and involvement of stakeholders are an important evolution of the "all affected groups" statement that appeared frequently in CMM® for Software.
- The "commitment process" is now explicitly defined in Specific Practice 3.3-1 continuous representation or simply SP 3.3 in the staged representation. This represents an important recognition of the fact that the message of the commitment process was buried in the Common Feature Commitment to Perform in CMM® for Software.

Project Monitoring and Control

Project Monitoring and Control takes on the same flavor as Project Tracking and Oversight from CMM® for Software. Monitoring commitments has been elevated to the specific practice level (SP 1.2). Monitoring is also more strongly emphasized in CMMI®. Monitoring stakeholder involvement is explicitly brought out and enables the Generic Practice GP 2.6—Identify and Involve Relevant Stakeholders.

Risk Management

The concepts inherent to Risk Management finally made it to process area status. Risk Management is a critical function of project management and should be handled within the boundaries of project planning and project monitoring and control. Risk Management covers:

- Risk identification;
- Risk assessment;
- Risk analysis;
- Risk prioritization;
- Risk mitigation;
- Risk contingency planning.

Process and Product Quality Assurance

This process area stresses the objective evaluation of products as well as processes. The evaluation criteria must be established based on business objectives and answer the following questions: What will be evaluated? When or how often will a process be evaluated? How will the evaluation be conducted? Who must be involved in the evaluation?

Configuration Management

As the title for this process area suggests, the practices apply to other disciplines and artifacts as well as software. The more encompassing Configuration Management system, which includes the storage media, the procedures, and the tools for accessing the Configuration Management system, has replaced the idea of a software library.

Supplier Agreement Management

Supplier Agreement Management is one of the most significantly updated process areas in my opinion. It replaces the initial ideas found in software subcontract management. Supplier Agreement Management focuses on controlling sources of products or product components that are built or acquired outside of the project's boundaries.

Integrated Supplier Management

Integrated Supplier Management builds on the concepts established in the Supplier Agreement Management PA by adding practices that emphasize a cooperative and coordinated relationship with suppliers.

Measurement and Analysis

This process area is a new addition and was motivated by the many organizations that struggled with setting up a measurement program and properly executing it while evolving the organizational maturity. Many organizations reported achieving a CMM® Maturity Level 3 only to find out that their path to CMM® Maturity Level 4 was blocked because their process database held the wrong type of data to support quantitative project management.

Measurement and Analysis assists an organization in evolving its measurement program from basic project management measures to those based on the organization's set of standard processes to statistical control of selected subprocesses according to the organization's business needs. An organization that barely passed the Measurement and Analysis common feature requirements of CMM® for Software would not pass the measurement requirements of CMMI®.

Engineering concepts process areas

The information found in the engineering process areas of CMMI® are contained in six to seven process areas if you count Decision Analysis and Resolution along with the other engineering process areas, as I am inclined to do. This is in contrast to the key process area of software product engineering that provided an overview of all of the software life-cycle phases in just that one KPA. I believe that the strongest difference between CMM® for Software and CMMI® is the description found in the engineering process areas. These process areas were brought from the Systems Engineering CMM® and are the contributors of the engineering systems think described in Chapter 1.

Requirements Development

The concepts presented in Requirements Development are consistent with the latest publications on Requirements Engineering. There is a clear need defined for identification and management of the stakeholders who have wants, needs, constraints, and interface requirements. The Requirements Development PA includes a strong focus on *interface requirements* reflecting the importance of managing and controlling interfaces that is becoming evident to most organizations throughout the world. This is especially true for large international companies that attempt to manage multisite, multicountry, and multicultural projects. It is also true for many large companies that have made the decision to predominantly use suppliers rather than build up development capability in-house. It also suggests the use of models, simulations, and prototyping to perform risk assessments to reduce the cost and risk of product development.

The Requirements Development PA includes a description of developing an operational concept and operational scenarios to refine and discover new requirements, needs, and constraints. This tightly couples Requirements Development to the Technical Solution process area.

Requirements Development, together with Technical Solution, truly shows the recursive nature of developing requirements as illustrated in Figure 6.2.

Requirements Development emphasizes the idea of starting the process of *requirements validation* very early in the product life cycle and continuing it until the technical solution is chosen.

Technical Solution

The Technical Solution PA provides the matching bookend for Requirements Development focusing on the refinement of the operational concepts and operational scenarios started during the Requirements Development activities. Technical Solution represents a different way of thinking by stressing the need for developing alternative solutions before the final selection of requirements that will be used to develop the product.

An upgrade and a raising of the standard bar also is evident in Technical Solution as the quality factors (e.g., maintainability, expandability, reliability) that were discussed in CMM® for Software Maturity Level 4 KPA of Software Quality Management are now brought forth in a CMMI® Maturity Level 3 PA.

Requirements Management

The Requirements Management PA was also brought over from the systems engineering process area. It covers much of the same concepts as the Requirements Management KPA found in CMM® for Software. There are two concepts that are either new or upgrades:

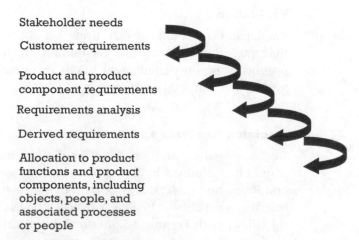

Requirements Development together with Technical Solution truly shows the recursive and iterative nature of developing requirements:

Stakeholder needs

Customer requirements

Product and product component requirements

Requirements analysis

Derived requirements

Allocation to product functions and product components, including objects, people, and associated processes or people

Figure 6.2 Requirements Development.

- Bidirectional traceability is now explicitly requested. From a maturity level point of view, traceability was a CMM® Maturity Level 3 concept and is a CMMI® Maturity Level 2 concept.

- Requirements Management is expected to operate in parallel with Requirements Development and Technical Solution and offer support as new requirements are discovered and requirements change requests are made.

Product Integration

Product Integration presents the concepts to achieve complete product integration throgh progressive assembly of product components in incremental stages according to a defined integration sequence. Product Integration:

- Points out the need to establish and maintain the environment required to support the integration of product components;

- Presents the idea of applying Product Integration, Verification, and Validation in successive triplets until the product is ready for packaging and delivery;

- Stresses the effective management of all interfaces;

- Describes the activities of packaging and delivery, a concept that CMM® for Software has long been criticized for not having.

Verification

Verification ("You built it right"), as it was defined in Chapter 3, is used to assure that selected work products meet their specified requirements. Verification expects a verification strategy that addresses the specific actions, resources, and environments that will be required for work product verification to be developed.

Validation

Validation ("You built the right thing") is distinguished from Verification in that validation methods and techniques are used to demonstrate that a product or product component fulfills its intended use when placed in its intended operational environment.

Decision Analysis and Resolution

Decision Analysis and Resolution is used to help determine which issues should be examined by formal decision analysis. While Decision Analysis and Resolution can certainly be used in a large number of situations such as selecting a supplier or making a critical strategic business decision, its natural affinity with Technical Solution makes it easier to explain when associated with the engineering process areas.

Decision Analysis and Resolution is a new concept for the software world whose time has certainly come.

Process management concepts process areas

CMMI® process areas often taught in a category called process management include Organizational Process Focus, Organizational Process Definition, Organizational Training, and Integrated Project Management. The concepts found in Organizational Process Focus and Organizational Training are virtually the same in CMMI® as compared to CMM® for Software. We will only mention the other two.

Organizational Process Definition

The wording for this process area has changed subtly but significantly from that of CMM® for Software. "Establish and maintain a usable set of organizational process assets including the organization's set of standard processes" acknowledges that an organization may utilize more than one standard process to handle its product lines and business needs. The term *process database* has evolved into *organizational measurement repository*.

Integrated Project Management

Integrated Project Management takes on the aspects of Integrated Software Management and Intergroup Coordination that were found in CMM® for Software. It also emphasizes the need to proactively integrate all of the plans that affect the project with the project plan such as the Configuration Management plan and the risk management plan.

Integrated Teaming Concepts process areas

The Integrated Teaming Concepts process areas are new additions to the evolving chain of project management techniques found in CMM® for Software. The new process areas are:

- Integrated Project Management (IPPD);
- Organizational Environment for Integration;
- Integrated Teaming.

CMMI® defines integrated product and process development (IPPD) as a systematic approach that achieves a timely collaboration of relevant stakeholders throughout the life of the product to better satisfy customer needs. The processes to support an IPPD approach are integrated with the other processes in the organization. If an organization chooses IPPD, it performs the IPPD specific practices concurrently with other specific practices used to produce products.

Organizational Environment for Integration

Organizational Environment for Integration presents important characteristics of effective environments for integration which include:

- An organization's shared vision;
- People trained to utilize the collaborative environment through collaboration, integration, and leadership;
- A workplace that provides resources to maximize the productivity of the people assigned to the integrated teams.

Integrated Project Management (IPPD)

The Integrated Project Management PA has two specific goals added to it to emphasize the IPPD concepts. These specific goals:

- Create the shared vision for the project;
- Align the project's shared vision with the organization's shared vision and the integrated team's shared vision.

Integrated Teaming

The Integrated Teaming PA focuses on the team members and the concepts by which they are managed. An integrated team is defined to be composed of relevant stakeholders from critical disciplines and support groups who generate and implement decisions for the work products that they are developing.

Quantitative management concepts process areas

The description of quantitative management concepts can be found in two CMMI® process areas:

1. Quantitative Project Management;
2. Organizational Process Performance.

These two process areas represent one of the largest improvements over the concepts found in CMM® for Software. Lessons learned and a greater understanding of quantitative project management for software as well as other engineering disciplines can be found in Quantitative Project Management and Organizational Process Performance. Even companies that have achieved CMM® Maturity Level 3 should consider adopting the process areas from CMMI® Maturity Levels 4 and 5, if their business case demands, to take advantage of this advanced thinking.

Quantitative Project Management

The Quantitative Project Management process area combines the concepts found in Quantitative Process Management and Software Quality Management in CMM® for Software. Quantitative Project Management is not about using fishbone diagrams or bar charts and declaring Maturity Level 4 success. Quantitative Project Management must be tied to the organization's strategic goals for product quality, service quality, and process performance. When higher degrees of quality and performance are demanded, the organization and projects must determine if they have the ability to improve the necessary processes to satisfy the increased demands. Assuming the technical requirements can be met, the next decision facing the organization is to determine if it is cost-effective.

Organizational Process Performance

The Organizational Process Performance process area is a new process area that significantly strengthens the concepts of quantitative management found in CMM® for Software. Organizational Process Performance was developed to help organizations set the stage for quantitative process management. It stresses establishing an organizational process performance baseline for the organization.

Optimizing concepts process areas

Following the concepts found in CMM® for Software and building on the upgraded ideas found in Quantitative Project Management and Organizational Process Performance, CMMI® contains two process areas that constitute the Optimizing Maturity Level or CMMI® Maturity Level 5. CMMI® process areas that make up the Optimizing Level include:

- Causal Analysis and Resolution;
- Organizational Innovation and Deployment.

Causal Analysis and Resolution

The Causal Analysis and Resolution process area contains essentially the same concepts as its CMM® for Software counterpart Defect Prevention, but it is definitely more tightly coupled to the quantitative understanding of the organization's standard processes.

Organizational Innovation and Deployment

The Organizational Innovation and Deployment process area combines the concepts found in the two KPAs of CMM® for Software: Process Change Management and Technology Change Management. It suggests the selection and deployment of incremental and innovative technological improvements that can improve the organization's ability to meet its quality and process performance objectives.

The standard bar for process improvement and engineering excellence has been raised, but it has been raised in the spirit of continuous process improvement applied to the original concepts captured in CMM® for Software. It captures lessons learned over an 8-year period. I encourage individuals, projects, and organizations to embrace these updated concepts and apply them to achieve higher levels of engineering excellence that make measurable differences to business objectives.

An incremental path to move from CMM for Software to CMMI

The evolutionary differences between CMM® for Software and CMMI® have been presented, but many individuals and organizations may still be wondering how a transition from CMM® for Software to CMMI® could be made in a systematic, nonthreatening way. The following description provides one incremental path that was used to support an IT shop that first achieved a CMM® Maturity Level 3 rating but used CMMI® process areas to help them achieve that goal and place the organization in a position to continue with its process improvement initiative based on CMMI® and simultaneously satisfy the requirements of ISO 9001:2000 certification:

- Clearly map organizational business objectives to the CMM®.
- Clearly map ISO 9001:1994 capabilities to those demanded by ISO 9001:2000.
- Solidify CMM® Maturity Level 2 capability if a CMM® process improvement initiative is already in progress and that milestone has not yet been achieved.
- Perform a gap analysis between organizational capability and that demanded by ISO 9001:2000.
- Determine which CMMI® process areas will support the improvement needs to achieve the ISO 9001:2000 certification. Use CMMI® process areas to provide more guidance to the ISO 9001:2000 certification effort with an eye to process improvement.
- Adapt CMMI® process areas that represent significant improvements and additions to CMM® for Software key process areas, including:
  - Measurement and Analysis;
  - Supplier Agreement Management;
  - Risk Management;
  - Extensions to Project Planning and Project Monitoring and Control;
  - Implement bidirectional traceability to Requirements Management capabilities.

- Obtain ISO 9001:2000 certification.

- Work toward and obtain CMM® Maturity Level 3.

- Use CMM® Maturity Level 3 and ISO 9001:2000 capabilities to work towards CMMI® Maturity Level 3.

- Obtain a level of confidence that the organization has achieved CMMI® Maturity Level 2.

- Incorporate CMMI® engineering process areas.

- Incorporate Integrated Product and Process Development practices.

- Incorporate Integrated Supplier Management.

- Achieve CMMI® Maturity Level 3 rating.

- Use the quantitative management concepts found in CMMI® Maturity Level 4 process areas as business objectives demand more quantitative control.

An organization does not have to throw away any quality management progress that it has made to make use of CMMI®. Both ISO 9001:1994 and CMM® for Software provide some of the foundation needed immediately for ISO 9001:2000 and for the effective use of CMMI®. Many of the upgrades fought for in CMM® for Software are present in CMMI®. CMMI® provides the engineering systems think that CMM® for Software lacked. The CMMI® also demands more engineering discipline to be applied to product development but in a way that is always linked to the organization's business objectives.

Summary

The evolutionary differences between CMM® for Software and CMMI® illustrate an incremental approach for organizations interested in moving or evolving from a strict CMM® for Software process improvement focus to the integrated focus offered by the CMMI®.

Contents

Enabling the Project Leader to Better Manage and Control Through Project Planning and Project Monitoring and Control

Chapters 7 through 11 focus on the inclusive topic of project management. The topics of project planning and project monitoring and control will be covered in this chapter. This chapter also serves as the beginning of the description of project management. This scope of project management encompasses activities that help the project manager to better manage and control his or her project. It covers the traditional project management activities such as project planning and project monitoring and control. It will also cover risk management, quality assurance, Configuration Management, supplier management, and, finally, integrated project management.

Risk Management has been placed in CMMI® as a separate process area. Placing Risk Management in CMM® or CMMI® was debated for years. It was placed as a separate process area to call attention to its importance in managing successful projects and a successful business. However, in my opinion, Risk Management should not be implemented as a separate function but as a critical part of project management. Risk Management will be covered in Chapter 8.

While the continuous representation of CMMI® chose a categorization scheme that placed CM and QA in the category of support, it is my experience that effective use of the engineering principles of CM and QA are best realized by thinking of them as project management functions. As will be described in Chapter 9, quality assurance not only can ensure that defined and agreed-upon processes are being followed on projects, but quality managers or quality engineers can also and should act as advisors to the projects they support and provide quality reports that provide information on which project managers can take action.

Configuration Management, also described in Chapter 9, covers a full set of functions that provide a project manager with insight into the progress and quality of the evolving product or product component. For these reasons, they will be discussed as part of project management.

Supplier Agreement Management and Integrated Supplier Management cover the ever-increasing important topic of supplier management. While there is much written on the management of suppliers, it is believed by many that effective supplier management means that a project and/or business unit must have effective requirements engineering, project management, and quality management processes established and maintained for their own use to be able to properly and effectively apply them to their suppliers. Supplier management will be presented in Chapter 10.

Integrated Product Management combined Integrated Software Management and Intergroup Coordination from CMM® for Software as a base. It can be thought of as the implementation of the project management functions discussed in this chapter and Chapters 8 through 10 but based on the organization's set of standard processes. Integrated Project Management will be discussed in Chapter 11 and will also act as the conclusion to the overall discussion of project management.

Project planning

Project management can be defined as establishing and maintaining an environment that gets the work done. To effectively manage and control a project, the project leader must be able to identify the customer(s), define and manage the requirements, understand the system that must be built, establish the necessary project roles, understand the project factors that must be managed, establish the project management life cycle, and choose a product life cycle. These and more roles are defined in Figure 7.1.

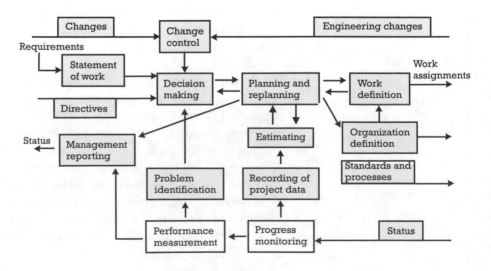

Figure 7.1   Project management.

The purpose of project planning is to establish and maintain plans that define project activities and activities of other relevant stakeholders that affect the project. This involves estimating, developing the project plan, interacting with the relevant stakeholders, resolving conflicts, obtaining a commitment to the plan, and maintaining it throughout the project management life cycle. The project plan will usually need to be revised as the project progresses. This is necessary to address changes in requirements, commitment changes, inaccurate estimates and assumptions, corrective actions, and process improvements. Plans should not be regarded as one-time events. It is my experience that this is too often the case. Even when necessary changes are acknowledged, the actual plan does not get changed. Figure 7.2 shows the iterative nature of planning.

In addition to the functional and nonfunctional requirements, the project planning is driven by system objectives, system overview, and system constraints. The system overview provides insight into why the system is being built: research and development; for a specific customer; to meet an existing or anticipated market need; or possibly to upgrade an existing system to a newer technology. Effective project planning should also provide the project with some insight into what problem is trying to be solved. Is the problem a known one? Is it an anticipated problem such as the loss of production support or support for existing technology? In addition, the system overview should describe the interactions between the proposed system and its environment. For example, it should describe the new system interfaces with other existing systems. It should mention the protocols that must be used to interface with them. It should list the anticipated users and in what manner they will use the system, and certainly the project planning should describe any change in the environment over its lifetime, including what is expected or anticipated.

Constraints

System constraints would include both design constraints and functional constraints. Functional constraints usually include:

Figure 7.2   Iterative nature of planning.

- Performance;
- Efficiency;
- Response times;
- Capacities;
- Safety;
- Security;
- Quality factors such as maintainability, expandability, reliability, and portability.

Design constraints usually include:

- Development standards and processes;
- Compilers;
- Operating systems;
- Operating environment.

The final deliverable is not necessarily the best solution to the customer's problem, but it is usually the one that optimizes the quadruple constraints of cost, schedule, performance, and quality, as illustrated in Figure 7.3.

Scope description

The *scope description* is a full description of what will be produced. It serves as a communication tool to ensure that what is being produced is what the customer and sponsor want the project to produce. It should describe the critical features and functions that are related to the final deliverable. The scope description includes:

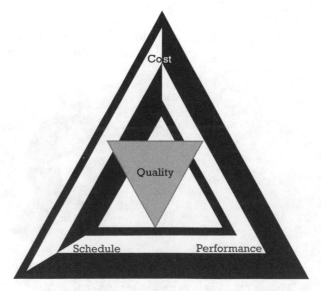

Figure 7.3   Quadruple constraint.

- The restated definition of the customer's needs;
- A detailed description of the final deliverable including its features and functions;
- The customer's criteria for acceptance in measurable terms;
- A description of the scope boundaries;
- A description of the end point for the final deliverable.

The scope description should be reviewed before it is finalized. A checklist such as this one will help:

- Have you identified the problem that the final deliverable is supposed to solve?
- Will the final deliverable help to resolve the problem that the customer is expecting in its intended environment?
- Does the scope description accurately describe what will be produced by the project?
- Is there a consensus on what will be produced by the project?
- Has the list of customer requirements been properly elicited?
- Are the customer's acceptance criteria written from the customer's point of view?
- Is the end point for the project clearly defined?
- Have all relevant stakeholders been identified that will be affected by the project or that can affect the project?
- Have any project overlaps been identified?
- Did the project team actively participate in defining the scope of the project?

Work breakdown structure

The *work breakdown structure* (WBS) serves to help estimate the total scope of the project. The WBS is developed and used to divide the overall project into an interconnected set of manageable components. It should then evolve with the project. The WBS is typically a product-oriented structure that helps to identify and organize the logical units of work to be managed ("work packages").

The WBS answers two questions: What is to be accomplished? What is the necessary hierarchical relationship of the work effort? The WBS is structured in accordance with the way the work will be performed and reflects the way in which the project costs and data will be summarized and eventually reported. The WBS is normally represented as a treelike structure. The most common WBS is the six-level indented structure shown in Figure 7.4.

The WBS normally contains:

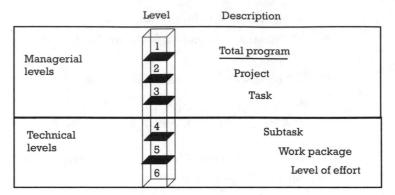

Figure 7.4   Work breakdown structure.

- ▶ Scope of work;
- ▶ Identified risks;
- ▶ Deliverables;
- ▶ Supporting activities and associated plans such as quality assurance and Configuration Management;
- ▶ Required skills and knowledge;
- ▶ Integration and life-cycle management of nondevelopmental items;
- ▶ Work products that will be externally acquired;
- ▶ Work products that will be reused.

Estimation

Some of the *factors* to consider when estimating project planning parameters include product requirements, identified tasks and work products, the technical approach chosen, the selected project life-cycle model, the size and complexity attributes of the work products, the models or historical data for converting the estimates into labor hours and costs, and the methodology used to determine needed materials, skills, labor hours, and costs.

The estimating *rationale* and supporting data should be documented for the review and commitment of stakeholders to the plan and for maintenance of the plan as the project progresses.

The life cycle

The life cycle consists of phases that are predefined or need to be defined depending on the scope and nature of the project. Larger projects may contain multiple life-cycle phases such as concept exploration, development, production, operations, and disposal. Development phases (for example, for software engineering) may include:

- ▶ Subphase descriptions for requirements analysis;

- Design and construction;
- Integration and verification.

Intermediate phases may require prototypes, increments of capability, or spiral model cycles.

Project life cycles with defined stages include:

- Evolutionary;
- Incremental;
- Spiral;
- V-Model;
- Waterfall;
- Overlapping waterfall.

Figure 7.5 provides an illustration of an incremental life-cycle model.

Size estimation

Size is the most commonly accepted attribute used to estimate effort, cost, and schedule. However, other attributes are also very important and some of them can and should be used with size to ensure greater success in

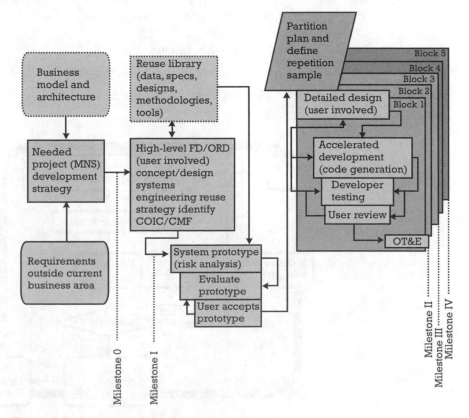

Figure 7.5 Incremental development processes.

estimation. These attributes include complexity, connectivity, and structure. The attribute of complexity is obvious when thought about but not often included in the equation. For example, a program could be very small in terms of lines of code but actually contain very complex algorithms that could result in lower-than-expected productivity if not taken into consideration. A relative level of difficulty or complexity should be assigned for each size attribute.

Examples of size measures include:

- Lines of code;
- Function points;
- Feature points;
- Number of classes and objects;
- Number of interfaces;
- Number of inputs and outputs.

One popular estimation technique is the Delphi estimation method illustrated in Figure 7.6.

The Delphi method includes recognizing that there is uncertainty in estimating. The Delphi method is focused upon utilizing the most knowledgeable people and asking those people to estimate the size of the project based on the current state with three estimates:

1. *Optimistic:* best case, smallest estimate;
2. *Expected:* most probable, middle estimate;
3. *Pessimistic:* worst case, largest estimate.

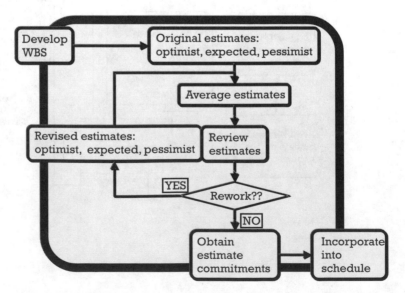

Figure 7.6   Delphi method.

$$\frac{Optimistic + 4(Expected) + Pessimistic}{6}$$

This formula takes into account the best guess and shifts in the direction corresponding to the more likely direction, considering the uncertainty of the estimate.

Effort and cost

Estimates of effort and cost are determined from the size and complexity estimates. Historical data and/or models are applied to the planning parameters to result in the estimates of effort and cost. Cost planning parameters include:

- Risks;
- Critical competencies;
- Allocated requirements;
- WBS;
- Cost of externally acquired work products;
- Knowledge and skills training, mentoring, and coaching needs;
- Capability of the tools in the engineering environment;
- Travel required;
- Level of security required.

Schedule

The project's schedule is also established and maintained based upon the size and complexity estimations. Some activities that are normally used to establish a project's schedule include:

- Determining the time phasing of the work activities;
- Determining the inch-pebbles and milestones to support progress measurement;
- Defining activities of appropriate duration;
- Availability of resources;
- Skill level of work team;
- Critical dependencies on suppliers of hardware and software;
- Defining milestones of appropriate time separation;
- Using historical data for schedule verification.

Risk

While risk management is a separate process area in CMMI®, risk management is an activity that in integral to successful project management. Risks can be identified starting with the WBS, developed during the estimation process, and should take into consideration the cost, resources, schedule, and technical aspects of the project. Risks should be analyzed to determine the impact, probability of occurrence, and time frame in which the problem(s) are likely to occur.

Data management

Data are various forms of documentation required to support a project in all of its areas. The data may exist in any medium, and distribution may take many forms including electronic files and e-mail. Data may be reports, manuals, engineering notebooks charts, drawings, files, e-mail, and project correspondence. E-mails are especially important to estimate and control as they are becoming increasingly used as legal documents. Data requirements for the project should be established for both the data items and their contents.

Knowledge and skills

The project team member's knowledge and skills need to be compared against the proposed or assumed knowledge and skills base used for estimation of effort, cost, and schedule. Too often projects are estimated based on an intermediate or high level of project team member skills and experience. Actual allocation of human resources frequently results in a project manager getting a large percentage of project members with less knowledge and skills. This should result in reestimation before the project plan is built. This is an area that must be examined from the risk management point of view.

Stakeholder involvement

For each major activity, the stakeholders that are affected by the activity and those who have expertise needed to conduct the activity should be identified.

The stakeholder list normally changes as the project moves through the product life cycle. Stakeholders in the later phases of the life cycle should have early input to the requirements and design decisions that affect them. Stakeholders may include:

- Senior managers;
- Project functional managers (e.g., systems engineering, software engineering, mechanics);
- Support management (e.g., quality assurance, Configuration Management, and so forth);
- Financial managers;
- Subcontractors/suppliers;
- Customers and end users;
- Project members.

Project resources

Project resources, including labor, machinery/equipment, materials, and methods and their required quantities, build on the initial estimates and provide additional information that can be used to expand the WBS.

Establishing the project plan

The plan generated for the project defines all aspects of the effort. It ties together project life-cycle considerations, technical and management tasks, budgets and schedules, milestones, data management, risk identification, resource and skill requirements, and stakeholder interaction.

Plans from other process areas may provide additional detailed guidance and should be compatible with the overall project plan in order to indicate who has the authority, responsibility, accountability, and control. These plans may be incorporated into the project plan as separate chapters or they may exist as stand-alone documents. Candidate plans that affect project success include:

- Quality assurance;
- Configuration Management;
- Data management;
- Risk management;
- Measurement and analysis;
- Knowledge and skills building (training);
- Stakeholder involvement;
- Integration strategy;
- Verification strategy;
- Validation strategy.

The plan for stakeholder interaction includes some or all of the following:

- List of all relevant stakeholders;
- Rationale for stakeholder involvement;
- Expected roles and responsibilities;
- Relationships between stakeholders;
- Relative importance of stakeholder to project success by phase;
- Resources needed to ensure relevant stakeholder interaction;
- Schedule for phasing of stakeholder interaction.

To obtain commitment from relevant stakeholders, differences between the estimates and resources must be negotiated and reconciled.

Project teams and supporting teams must have confidence that the work can be performed within cost, schedule, and performance constraints. Internal and external commitments or recommitments must be reviewed with senior management to ensure necessary support for this commitment together with all of the other existing and pending commitments that have been made throughout the organization.

Commitment Process Overview

The commitment process is a process that is established and maintained to ensure that commitments are made with the involvement and agreement of those who will do the work. This is a vastly different concept from what is normally stated by senior managers when they indicate they are "committed" to process improvement and product and service quality. The commitment process includes these steps presented in a high-level form here:

- Work breakdown structure is defined.
- An estimate is made of the magnitude of the commitment.
- The disciplines involved participate in developing the implementation plan, including estimating the size, effort, and schedule.
- An independent review of the plan is held.
- Agreement is reached on the commitment through negotiation.
- Senior management approves the commitment.
- A mechanism is provided to renegotiate the commitment in the event of a requirements change.
- A postimplementation review is held to discover what went right and what went wrong to learn how to improve future commitments and to compare actual performance with original estimates. Sometimes this is referred to as a postproject review where lessons learned are captured.

The commitment process is on the critical path for three process areas, as shown in Figure 7.7.

Project monitoring and control

The documented project plan is used as the basis for monitoring activities, communicating status, and taking corrective action. Recording actual project progress and performance must also include recording associated contextual information to help understand the measures. The purpose of project monitoring and control is to provide an understanding into the project's progress so that appropriate corrective action can be taken when the project's expected performance deviates significantly from the plan.

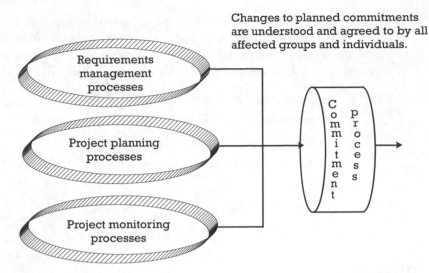

Figure 7.7 Commitment process.

Criteria must be established for determining just what does constitute a significant deviation from the project plan. The corrective actions may require replanning, which may even include revising the original plan and establishing a new agreement with the customer.

Actual values of the project planning parameters together with associated contextual information must be recorded including:

- Attributes of the work products:
    - Size;
    - Complexity;
    - Weight;
    - Form, fit, or function.
- Cost and expended effort;
- Schedule;
- Technical performance (completion of activities and milestones against the schedule);
- Staffing profiles;
- Resources:
    - Physical facilities;
    - Computers and peripherals;
    - Networks;
    - Security environment.
- Knowledge and skills acquisition of project personnel (training needs);
- Capture estimates and actuals in an organization-wide historical database for use by ongoing and future projects.

In addition, project monitoring and control must track commitments, risks, data management, and stakeholder involvement. When the actual values recorded deviate significantly from the estimated values, some corrective action must occur. Examples of potential actions include:

- Modifying the statement of work (SOW);
- Modifying the requirements;
- Revising estimates and plans;
- Renegotiating commitments;
- Adding resources;
- Revising understanding of project risks.

Summary

Project planning and project monitoring and control are the basic project management functions that must be understood and carried out on every project. In the next chapter, we will examine the details of risk management.

Enabling the Project Leader to Better Manage and Control Through Risk Management

Risk management

Risk as a science was born in the sixteenth-century Renaissance, a time of discovery. The work *risk* is derived from the early Italian *risicare* that means "to dare." Today, risk is defined as the possibility of loss. Unless there is a potential for loss, there is no risk.

Risks are future events with a probability of occurrence and a potential for loss. Many problems that arise in systems/software development efforts were first known as risks by someone on the project staff. Many organizations and projects worry about risks only during risk management season. At the beginning of a project or a new business year, management encourages the projects to identify all of the risks that they can. Risks are brainstormed regardless of type, probability, or potential loss, placed in a file, and promptly forgotten until the start of the next risk management season. Even when risks are identified in a brainstorming session and tracked on the project, many of the risks are not risks at all but known problems.

When a project manager knows that the number of people and their level of knowledge and skills are not sufficient to satisfy the goals of the project, this is not a risk—it is a problem. Problems must be dealt with. Problems are realized risks. Risks have the possibility of being managed.

Making decisions under conditions of uncertainty

Risk management is decision making under conditions of uncertainty. Robert Charette[1] described risk management as a project management activity that does not deal with future decisions, but with the future of present decisions.

Risk management (Figure 8.1) involves:

▶ Identifying potential problems before they occur;

▶ Analyzing their probability, potential impact, and time frame;

▶ Determining a risk management strategy;

▶ Planning risk-handling activities to mitigate adverse impacts on achieving project and organizational objectives;

▶ Determining and evaluating contingency plans;

▶ Proactively tracking and managing the risks.

Project managers *do* manage risks, but:

▶ Tend to manage the risks they see, and do not often see all of the risk or the critical risks;

▶ Tend to only manage risk for which they have domain expertise;

▶ Tend to really manage to cost and schedule—the symptoms;

▶ Are usually selected and rewarded for their crisis management skills.

Figure 8.1 Risk management cycle.

1. Robert N. Charette is a Cutter Consortium Fellow, the director of the Risk Management Intelligence Network, and a senior consultant with the Agile Software Development & Project Management Practice. With more than 25 years of experience in a wide variety of international technology and management positions, Dr. Charette is recognized as an international authority and pioneer regarding information systems, technology, and telecommunications risk management.

While risk management is a new process area found in CMMI®, risk management is certainly not a new topic and its benefits have long been documented. Those benefits include:

▸ Facilitating a closer look at *strategy* and decision-making criteria;

▸ Creating a shared product vision;

▸ Facilitating upward communication of risks;

▸ Facilitating downward communication of strategy and decision-making criteria;

▸ Helping project members to:

  ▸ Take a closer look at their plans, procedures, and processes compared to the business needs and possible problems;

  ▸ Think of alternative approaches to problem solving;

  ▸ Determine backup plans in the event of problems;

  ▸ Prevent problems before they occur.

To prepare for risk management, a project leader and his or her project members need to determine risk sources and categories or "bins" for collecting and organizing the risks, define risk parameters, and establish a risk management strategy.

Sources of risk

There are many sources of risks, both internal and external, to the project. Many of these sources of risk are just accepted without adequate planning to reduce the probability or impact of the risk. Typical sources of risks include:

▸ Poorly defined requirements;

▸ Unavailable technology;

▸ Unrealistic schedule estimates;

▸ Inadequate knowledge and skills of staff;

▸ Inadequate supplier capability.

Categorizing risks

It is important for the project team to have a clear understanding of the parameters used to categorize risks in order to develop a mitigation strategy and manage these risks throughout the project life cycle. Standard parameters for categorizing risks include:

▸ Likelihood or probability of occurrence;

▸ Consequence, impact, or potential loss;

▸ Time frame in which the risk might occur.

It is very important for any project to understand risk in terms of quantitative data. For example, it would be the best if we could determine that the probability of a risk occurring is 80% or the business impact is $2 million. It would also be great if we could say with certainty that the risk will occur in the sixth month of the project. Unfortunately, projects do not have such quantitative data when a risk management culture is being established throughout the organization. To get things started, it is recommended that relative terms be defined and used for those parameters.

Examples for likelihood are:

- Remote;
- Unlikely;
- Likely;
- Highly likely;
- Near certainty.

Examples for consequences are:

- Low, medium, high;
- Negligible, marginal, significant, critical, catastrophic.

Examples of time frames are:

- Short term;
- Medium term;
- Long term.

In addition, it is important for the project to define control points to trigger management actions. In other words, define the early warning signals that the risk is becoming serious.

Risk management strategy

A risk management strategy needs to be established and maintained to ensure that any risk mitigation activities that are put in place will be effective and support business objectives. The risk management strategy should include objectives, constraints, and alternatives. Two alternatives to mitigating a risk are: (1) avoiding the risk by changing the requirements, the product design, or the project's defined process; or (2) accepting the risk and dealing with the consequences if the risk occurs (becomes a problem). For those risks that exceed established thresholds for risk exposure, the project team needs to develop a set of activities to reduce the probability of the risk occurring and/or reduce the impact of the occurrence of the risk. Some risk mitigation activities include:

- Changing control mechanisms to monitor risk areas;

- Considering alternative designs;
- Providing additional training;
- Providing cross-training to ensure each function is backed up;
- Involving users such as focus groups more;
- Increasing peer reviews such as inspections and structured walkthroughs;
- Developing and using a traceability matrix;
- Increasing the level of testing and auditing testing results;
- Providing additional time and cost;
- Using prototyping;
- Using simulation;
- Searching for higher-performance hardware;
- Following an incremental development or evolutionary development approach.

The risk management strategy is necessary in order to support the project manager to determine risk mitigation activities that will:

- Provide the greatest reduction in risk;
- Require the fewest resources;
- Require available resources;
- Have the least impact on the schedule.

The question that requires an answer is: What set of strategies best manages the project's risk?

- *Acceptance:* Accept the consequences of the risk (do nothing). Make a conscious decision to live with the risk, having determined that the mitigation effort would be more expensive than the problem.
- *Avoidance:* Eliminate the risk altogether in order to avoid a lose-lose situation (e.g., decision not to bid on a request for proposal). Change or lower the requirements while still meeting the user's needs.
- *Reduction:* Decrease the risk through mitigation, prevention, and anticipation. Reduction can be applied to either the probability or the consequences.
- *Causal analysis:* Research further the root causes and determine the possible benefits.
- *Elimination:* Eliminate the risk completely whenever possible based on the cost of the problem and the cost of the solution.
- *Protection:* Employ redundancy to mitigate the risk (e.g., two systems backing up each other).

> *Reserves:* Use contingency funds and build in schedule slack to cover uncertainties.

> *Transfer:* Shift the risk to another person or group better able to act upon it.

Risk mitigation plan

Based on the risk management strategy adopted by the project and/or business unit, a risk mitigation plan should be developed for the most important risks to the project. Suggested risk plan content includes:

> Risk description or risk statement—why item is a risk;

> Source or cause of risk;

> Point of contact for details of identified risk;

> Date identified as a risk;

> Risk probability: probable, possible, unlikely;

> Consequence or impact—high, moderate, low:

> > Cost impact;

> > Schedule impact.

> Time frame: long, medium, short, immediate;

> Classification of risk:

> > Management, technical, process;

> > Other.

> Person or team assigned to handle risk;

> Recommended risk management choices;

> Risk triggers or thresholds;

> Modules and function points affected;

> Possible mitigating actions;

> Contingency plan;

> Reduction in scope if avoided.

Contingency plans are normally developed for selected critical risks in the event that if the risk cannot be mitigated with the techniques chosen, a plan B, or alternative course of action, must be taken.

Risk monitoring

Risk monitoring should be included with the other standard project management monitoring and control activities discussed in Chapter 7. It is imperative that the thresholds that define when a risk becomes unacceptable and triggers the execution of a risk mitigation plan or a contingency plan are determined and used during risk monitoring. Figure 8.2 illustrates

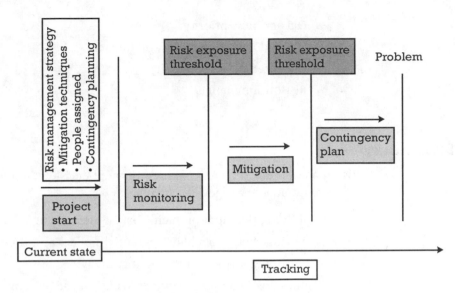

Figure 8.2 Establishing risk thresholds.

establishing the risk management strategy, risk identification, determination of risk mitigation techniques that will be used, the determination of contingency plans prior to the project's start, and risk monitoring using those established thresholds.

It should be noted that risk monitoring will probably result in the identification of new risks, setting of new thresholds, and challenges to the previously agreed to risk mitigation activities. It is my recommendation that a top 10 risk list be developed for each project that is constantly monitored and updated as necessary. As the project moves through the project life-cycle phases, this top 10 risk list should reflect the success or failure of the risk mitigation and contingency planning made so far and result in an updated set of risk items with adjusted priorities and possibly new risk mitigation and contingency planning techniques.

The risk status report may be a part of the standard project management status report or may be a separate reporting item. Suggested contents include:

- Top 10 risk items;
- New risk items since the last report;
- Number of resolved items that were successfully mitigated, avoided, or had their impact reduced to lower priority;
- Number of contingency plans that had to be invoked;
- Risks that became problems;
- Time histories of above;
- Status to *existing risks*:
  - Risk statement;

> ‣ Old and new priority;
> ‣ Old and new probability and impact;
> ‣ Old and new responsibility;
> ‣ Reason for change.

Summary

Risk management is about making informed decisions under conditions of uncertainty. Risk management involves:

- Identifying potential problems before they occur;
- Analyzing their probability, potential impact and time frame;
- Determining a risk management strategy;
- Planning risk-handling activities to mitigate adverse impacts on achieving project and organizational objectives;
- Determining and evaluating contingency plans;
- Proactively tracking and managing the risks.

Effective risk management depends on open communication with all of the project's relevant stakeholders throughout the project life cycle. It is an essential part of project management. The SEI has recognized this and provided it with the exposure in CMMI® Model that it deserves.

Enabling the Project Leader to Better Manage and Control Through Quality Management

As presented in Chapter 7, the concepts of project management are being presented in Chapters 7 through 11. The quality management process areas of Process and Product Quality Assurance and Configuration Management are now described in this chapter as project management functions that provide input to project managers to help them better manage and control and not simply go through the motions to satisfy audit or assessment criteria.

Process and Product Quality Assurance

While the continuous representation of CMMI® chose a categorization scheme that placed CM and QA in the category of support, it is my experience that effective use of the engineering principles of CM and QA are best realized by thinking of them as project management functions. This section of Chapter 9 focuses on the support that a project manager can and should expect from the functions of Process and Product Quality Assurance.

Quality control

Process and Product Quality Assurance is often misunderstood or purposefully equated to testing. Perhaps it is important to firstly distinguish between *quality control* and *quality assurance*. Quality control evaluates or checks the quality of the products and life-cycle work products. Quality control functions or activities help to determine if the product is within defined tolerances and of acceptable quality. Tools and techniques used for quality control include peer reviews such as inspections or structured walk-throughs and the different levels of testing. Peer reviews and most testing techniques are described in the process areas of Verification and Validation.

Quality assurance

Quality assurance in contrast evaluates or checks to see if the process is working. Is the process being followed? Are the quality control checks being applied with the proper rigor? Are the quality control checks efficient and effective? Is the process causing quality problems? Is the process working for the organization? Tools and techniques used by quality assurance responsibles include process audits or objective evaluations as they are referred to in CMMI® and assessments or appraisals such as a gap analysis or a SCAMPI[SM] appraisal.

The purpose of Process and Product Quality Assurance is to provide management at all levels and practitioners with objective insight into the processes that are in place and identified to be used on the projects. Objective evaluations are used to determine if the processes are indeed being followed on the projects, and if they are, answer the questions of if they are efficient and effective and if they are enabling the project members to produce the required product quality.

Quality functions

To be compliant with the requirements and guidelines of Process and Product Quality Assurance, each project is expected to develop a project quality plan to document the quality functions that will be needed to support the project throughout the life cycle. These quality functions include, but are not limited to:

- Setting quality goals for the project that support the organization's business objectives;
- Conducting peer reviews throughout the product life cycle;
- Performing multiple levels of testing such as unit testing, integration testing, systems testing, and acceptance testing;
- Designing in quality factors such as maintainability, expandability, and reliability;
- Conducting objective evaluations with respect to product quality;
- Conducting objective evaluations with respect to process quality;
- Conducting objective evaluations of customer and maintenance documentation;
- Conducting objective evaluations of Configuration Management activities;
- Providing visibility into the process and product quality for management and practitioners through quality reporting;

▸ Getting noncompliance issues resolved before the product is delivered to the customer.

These quality functions may be performed by:

▸ Project leaders and product and product component developers;

▸ Quality managers or quality responsibles;

▸ Organizational-level quality assurance group;

▸ Systems engineering;

▸ Integration and systems test;

▸ Documentation;

▸ Database;

▸ Others.

Project quality plan

Thus, in summary, given that a project development plan exists, a project quality plan must describe:

▸ What quality functions will be performed?

▸ Who will perform them?

▸ During what phase of the product life cycle will they be performed?

▸ Who has approval authority?

▸ How will conflicts over nonconformance be resolved?

Questions including the following should be asked and answered in the project quality plan:

▸ What peer reviews will take place and when?

▸ How will the data from the peer reviews be utilized?

▸ Which tests will be conducted and by whom?

▸ Which tests will a quality responsible observe?

▸ What objective evaluations will a quality responsible conduct?

▸ What metrics will be used for the capture and analysis of identified defects?

▸ How will the correction of the discrepancies be assured?

▸ What are the criteria for the acceptance of the product from a quality point of view?

As the project leader or project manager is ultimately responsible for the product quality produced by his or her project members, it is important that the project leader work with the quality responsibles supporting his or her project to develop and manage this project quality plan.

It should be pointed out that the project quality plan is *not the same* as the quality assurance plan that may be developed by the quality assurance group documenting how the quality responsibles will support the project with their advice and quality evaluations.

The consequences to a project and ultimately the business objectives of an organization, if projects do not develop and follow a project quality plan, are:

- Qualify functions may be left out.
- Quality criteria will be forgotten or ignored.
- Interfaces may not work together.
- Process steps may be ignored.
- The product or product component may not match the customer's requirements and expectations when it is delivered.
- Problems take a long time to discover and fix.
- The resulting rework is expensive.
- Development and production time lengthens.
- The delivery date is delayed.
- The business unit can incur financial penalties.
- There is risk of losing business and even the customer.

Quality assurance responsibles

The quality assurance responsibles should be providing consultation and an objective evaluation of the project's plans, processes, standards, procedures, guidelines, templates, and checklists with regard to:

- Compliance with the organizational policies;
- Compliance with externally imposed requirements, standards, and procedures required by the customers;
- Processes, standards, and procedures that are appropriate for use by the project;
- Required knowledge and skills of the staff;
- Training needs;
- Historical data.

Project leaders should be able to expect the following support from quality assurance to help them better manage and control their project:

- Knowledge about the software process;
- Input as to the efficiency of the software process being used by project members;
- Assistance in creating an executable and successful project plan;

- Assistance in creating the project's quality plan;
- Assistance in choosing the right standards for the project's needs;
- Assistance in tailoring the standards and processes for practical use by the project;
- Assistance in setting up peer reviews for the software life-cycle work products;
- Assistance in putting together the right quality plan to match the criticality of the life-cycle work products;
- Performing objective evaluations and traceability audits to ensure that the quality goals are being met and the system's integrity is maintained.

Objective evaluation

Objective evaluation in quality assurance evaluations is critical to the success of the project. Objective evaluation:

- Provides the quality responsibilities with the organizational freedom to be representatives of management on the project;
- Protects the quality responsibles from adverse actions by the project managers such as loss of job, pay, or position;
- Provides management with the confidence that the objective information about the activities and work products of the project is being accurately reported;
- Ensures that everyone performing the quality assurance activities are trained in quality assurance/quality management concepts;
- Ensures that those designated to perform the QA activities are separated from those directly involved in developing or maintaining the work products;
- Provides an independent reporting channel to the appropriate level of organizational management to allow noncompliance issues to be escalated to the appropriate levels of management as necessary.

Objective evaluation applied to performed processes as defined or referenced in the project plan against applicable process descriptions, standards, procedures, and so forth should be conducted based on clearly established and maintained criteria and business needs and answer the following questions:

- What will be evaluated?
- When or how often will a process be evaluated?
- How will the evaluation be conducted?
- Who must be involved in the evaluation?

Objective evaluation applied to the project's work products and services looks for compliance against the applicable process descriptions, standards, and procedures.

The purpose of these objective evaluations is to provide the project manager and project members with information that will help the project manager to look into process and product violations and implement corrective action as soon as possible to reduce the quality management and project management risks. Quality reports in the form of evaluation reports, corrective action reports, and quality trends should be tracked, openly communicated to all relevant stakeholders in a timely manner, and resolved. Noncompliance issues must be resolved at a level as close as possible to the source of the issue. Quality assurance loses perceived value almost immediately if the quality responsibles immediately report their noncompliance findings to higher-level management without giving the project members or project leader a chance to respond to the issues. Noncompliance issues should be analyzed to determine if there are any quality trends that should be discussed with the project leader that might motivate preventative actions being put in place.

To be complete, trends discovered from analysis of quality reports and documentation of the process and product quality assurance activities should be recorded in sufficient detail so that the results can be available and understood by all relevant stakeholders that are concerned with product quality.

Quality assurance group

There are many possibilities to setting up a quality assurance or quality management organization. One in particular that has proven popular for many different types of organizations and in many different countries is described here:

- A centralized quality management group is established at the organizational level and is headed by a middle-senior manager.

- The quality engineers that serve in this organizational quality management group are individuals that have between 10 and 20 years of experience, including development and project management experience.

- There are normally about 1.5–2% of these highly qualified quality engineers compared to the total development staff. One financial organization in the Netherlands had approximately eight senior quality engineers compared to 600 software developers.

- Each project of medium to large size is required to nominate at least one project quality assurance (PQA) coordinator. This person does in fact report to the project manager but is only responsible for ensuring the necessary quality functions for the project are carried out.

- The quality engineers mentor and coach the PQA coordinators on a regular basis.

- The quality engineers also support the quality directives of the organization by representing the independent and objective point of view on process and product quality.

- When necessary, the quality engineers will confront the project manager and escalate any serious noncompliances up to the highest management level in the organization.

- Once a month the quality engineers meet with all of the PQA coordinators to discuss quality processes and procedures. Presentations are made on a selected quality topic. Approaches to dealing with difficult project situations regarding quality are discussed. Expert consulting is brought in periodically to address this forum and provide CMMI® interpretation and quality management guidance.

- Once a month, the quality engineers meet with the project managers to discuss what quality support they need, the responsiveness of the PQA coordinators, and their own responsiveness and process improvements that could be made to assist the project in producing higher-quality products and services.

Configuration Management

The purpose of Configuration Management is to establish and maintain the integrity of the work products using configuration identification, configuration control, configuration status accounting, and configuration audits throughout the product life cycle.

Configuration Management is focused on the rigorous control of the managerial and technical aspects of the work products, including the delivered system.

Webster's Dictionary defines integrity to be "the quality of state of being unimpaired; wholeness, completeness, constancy, not fragmented."

Integrity

To more completely understand the concept of integrity with regards to Configuration Management, let us explore further. If a system exhibits integrity, we can expect to see the following things happen:

- Changes to any configuration item within the system are only made according to an established and maintained process.

- The system is secure from misdirected developers who seek to circumvent the rules.

- The system is secure from hostile attacks that threaten to damage the contents of the configuration items.

- Life-cycle work products are kept consistent when requirements change requests are approved and the requirements specification is modified. All related life-cycle work products are reviewed to determine if accompanying changes to them are necessary as well.

▸ Periodic audits are made on the contents of the system to ensure that changes made to product components are complete and correct.

▸ Regression testing is conducted to ensure that defects are corrected and existing functionality remains.

The need for Configuration Management of software components can be used to illustrate the importance of this project management support function. The most frustrating software problems are often caused by poor Configuration Management such as:

▸ The latest version of source code cannot be found.

▸ A difficult bug that was fixed at great expense suddenly reappears.

▸ A developed and tested feature is mysteriously missing.

▸ A fully tested program suddenly does not work.

▸ The wrong version of the code was tested.

▸ There is no traceability between the software requirements, documentation and code.

▸ Programmers are working on the wrong version of the code.

▸ The wrong version of the configuration items is being baselined.

▸ No one knows which modules comprised the software system delivered to the customer.

Configuration Management functions include:

▸ Configuration identification;

▸ Baselining;

▸ Change control;

▸ Configuration Management system (software library);

▸ Configuration Management status accounting;

▸ Configuration auditing;

▸ Interface control;

▸ Control of supplier CM functions.

Let us examine these functions as they are viewed in the CM process area and in related process areas of CMMI®.

Configuration identification
Configuration identification includes the selection, creation, and specification of:

- The products that are delivered to the customer;
- Designated internal work products;
- Acquired products;
- Tools;
- Other items that are used in creating and describing these work products.

Configuration items to be controlled come out of the product life cycle that is chosen for the project and the product architecture, as illustrated in the in Figures 9.1 and 9.2, respectively.

Configuration items that should always be considered for control include:

- Requirements specification;
- Interface specification;
- Architectural specification;
- Design specification;
- Code modules;
- Test plans;
- Test procedures;
- Project plan;
- Quality plan;
- Configuration Management plan;
- Risk management plan;
- Data dictionaries.

Baselining

Change is a fact of life in product development: Customers want to modify requirements; developers want to modify the technical approach; management wants to modify the project approach; and new technological developments introduce new and better materials. Modification is necessary, because, as time passes, all parties know more about what they need, which approach would be best, and how to get it done and still make money. The additional knowledge becomes the driving force behind most changes.

The fundamental success of any development effort is dependent on well-defined reference points against which to specify requirements, formulate a design, and specify changes to these requirements and the resultant designs. The term *baseline* is normally used to denote such a reference point. A baseline is an approved snapshot of the system at appropriate points in the development life cycle. A baseline establishes a formal base for defining subsequent change. Without this line or reference point, the notion of change is meaningless. A baseline could be:

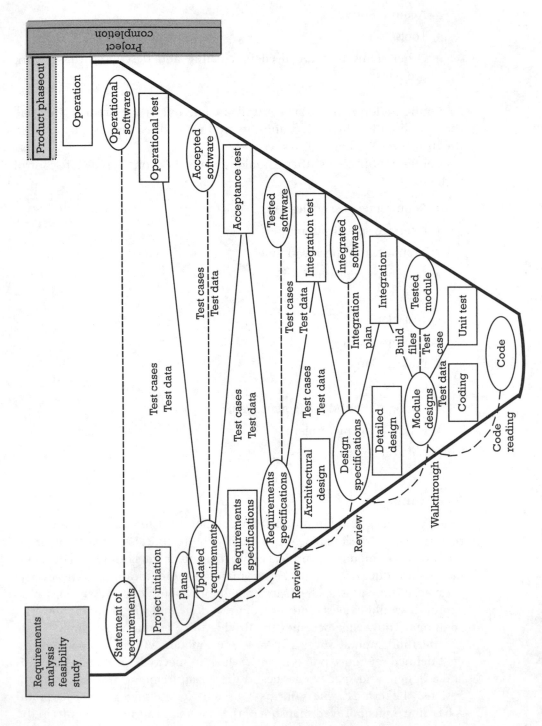

Figure 9.1 V-Model software development life cycle.

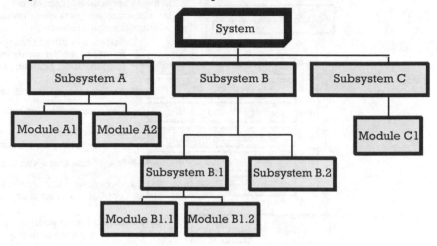

A software product system is composed of subsystems which are in turn composed of systems, which are composed of modules, which are composed of lines of code.

Figure 9.2 Product structure.

> A specification (e.g., requirements specification, design specification);

> A product that has been formally reviewed and agreed upon;

> A partial system.

A baseline is a "record of a contract" and serves as the basis for further development. It should be changed only through an agreed-upon change procedure. A baseline helps a project to control change without seriously impeding justifiable change. It will help a project to control the identified configuration items but not constrain early development excessively from the aspects of time, money, or resources. Before a baseline is established, change may be made quickly and informally. Once a baseline is established, change can be made, but a specific, formal procedure must be applied to evaluate and verify each change. The items in the baseline are the basis for the work in the next phase of the software development cycle. The items of the next baseline are measured and verified against previous baselines before they become baselines themselves.

An example of a baseline is an approved description of a product that includes:

> Internally consistent versions of requirements;

> Requirements traceability matrices;

> Discipline-specific items;

> End-user documentation.

Multiple baselines may be used to define an evolving product during its development cycle. In Figure 9.3 we see a common set of baselines that

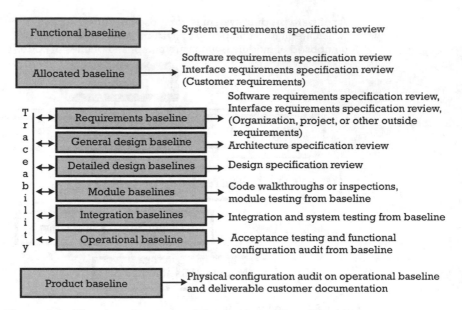

Figure 9.3 Mapping of system and developmental baselines.

includes the system-level requirements, system-element-level design requirements, and the product definition at the end of the development/beginning of production. These are commonly referred to as functional baseline, allocated baseline, and product baseline.

A baseline that is delivered to a customer is typically called a *release*, whereas a baseline for an internal use is typically called a *build*.

Baselines of configuration items should be created or released from the Configuration Management system only with authorization from the configuration control board (CCB) at the organizational level.

Change control

Change requests apply not only to new or changed requirements, but also to system failures and defects in life-cycle work products. Changes at the organizational or system level or even the developmental or project level should follow a change request process. The change request process typically contains the following steps:

▸ The change request is recorded.

▸ The impact the change will have on the work product, related work products, and schedule and cost is determined.

▸ The change request is reviewed and agreement is reached with those affected by the change request.

▸ The change request is tracked to closure.

Change control involves tracking each configuration item, approving a new configuration, and updating the baseline of configuration items.

Check-in and check-out procedures should be used to maintain the correct-ness and integrity of the configuration. It must be mentioned that many organizations use a CM tool to control the check-in and checkout proce-dures. Check-in procedures normally require the change description to be input along with the changed configuration item such as a detailed design document. However, these self-provided change descriptions should be peer reviewed and checked to ensure correct and usable information is being entered into the system for later reporting. Assessment experience has shown that too frequently, the change history does not match the current baselined configuration items. In some cases, change descriptions were "I like peanut butter." All changes and the reasons for the changes must be recorded in sufficient detail to provide change history and support Configu-ration Management status accounting.

Peer reviews, unit testing, and regression testing should be applied to changed configuration items to ensure that the changes have not caused unintended effects on the baseline. Regression testing has been often called *Configuration Management's best friend*, as it shows that the changes have indeed fixed the identified problem and that the functions that worked before still work. Authorization from the configuration control board must be obtained before the changed configuration items are reentered into the Configuration Management system.

Changes are not official until they are released and all relevant stake-holders notified.

A sample change procedure is illustrated in Figure 9.4.

Change control boards

The configuration control board at the organizational level may contain rep-resentatives from different departments and disciplines as suggested here:

- Program management;
- Systems engineering;
- Software engineering;
- Hardware engineering;
- Software quality assurance;
- Hardware quality assurance;
- Configuration Management;
- Integration and systems test;
- Documentation;
- Customer representative.

Change control boards may be established at different levels in addition to the organizational level. Product line CCBs may be established for organi-zations with distinct product lines. Project-level CCBs may be established and may include the project leader, the quality assurance responsible, and

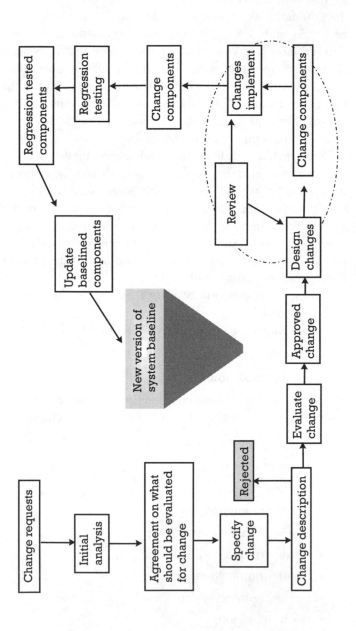

Figure 9.4 Incorporating a change into the current configuration baseline.

an integration and test responsible. The project-level CCB is typically given authority to approved change requests if they do not have any affect on the baselined requirements specifications.

Configuration Management system

The Configuration Management system stores the configuration items created during the product life cycle or references them and prevents unauthorized changes to the baselined items. The Configuration Management system can be viewed as a repository where changes to the baselines and releases of products and product components take place in a controlled fashion. A well-functioning Configuration Management system includes the following functions:

> Managing multiple levels of Configuration Management;

> Storage and retrieval of configuration items;

> Sharing and transferring of configuration items between the different control levels;

> Storage and recovery of archived versions of configuration items;

> Storage, update, and retrieval of Configuration Management records;

> Creation and dissemination of Configuration Management status reports;

> Helping to ensure correct creation of products from the release baseline with authorization from the configuration control board;

> Preserving the contents of the Configuration Management system;

> Backup and restoring of Configuration Management files;

> Recovery from Configuration Management errors;

> Archiving of Configuration Management files;

> Disaster recovery.

The three typical types of Configuration Management systems are:

1. Dynamic (for developers) systems—controlled by the developer;

2. Master (or controlled) systems—used for managing the current baselines and for controlling changes made to them;

3. Static systems—used to archive various baselines released for general use.

Configuration Management status accounting

Configuration Management status accounting is used to maintain a continuous record of the status and history of all baselined items and proposed changes to them. It should be able to answer the questions: What changes have been made to the system? What changes remain to be implemented? The information required for a comprehensive status accounting includes:

> The time at which each baseline was established;
> When each configuration item and change was included in the baseline;
> A description of each configuration item;
> All change requests;
> The description of each product or product component change.

Configuration Management status accounting for systems and software engineering items follows the concepts of financial accounting. Imagine that you went to an automated teller machine and used your bank card to find out your balance. Suppose you felt your balance was around $2,000. When you query the automated teller system, you find out your balance is $1,000. Normally in this situation, you would want to find out what transactions had taken place to result in that unexpected low balance. Most automated teller systems would be able to print out your buying activity for the past 15 or 30 days.

You may find out that your spouse had purchased a new set of golf clubs for $1,000 and that was the reason your balance was not what you expected. Configuration Management status accounting operates in the same way. Status reports on additions and changes to the evolving configuration should be readily available. To support this critical function:

> Configuration Management actions must be recorded in sufficient detail so that the content and status of each configuration item is known.
> All relevant stakeholders, especially project leaders, should have access to and knowledge of the configuration status of the baselined configuration items.
> Previous versions should be able to be recovered.
> The difference between successive baselines must be able to be clearly described.
> The current status and history of each configuration item must be maintained and updated as necessary.
> All relevant stakeholders must have access to and knowledge of the Configuration Management system through defined and understood request procedures that may involve a human being and may be provided by a Configuration Management tool.
> The reports must be detailed enough to support each project's project management needs.
> Standard Configuration Management status reports should be sent out to affected groups and individuals on a periodic basis.

Configuration auditing

Configuration auditing verifies that the product is built according to the requirements, standards, or contractual agreement. It verifies that all product components have been produced, correctly identified, and described, and that all change requests have been resolved.

Baseline audits should be conducted at phase end or other designated point in the product life cycle to continuously ensure that the completeness and correctness of the baselined Configuration Management system contents are verified based on the requirements as stated in the project plan and approved change requests.

The product's functionality and performance should be compared to the requirements. In addition, the documentation that is baselined for maintenance activities (architectural specification and design specification) as well as for operational use (user manuals, operations manuals, installation manuals) should be compared to the requirements.

When the product is ready to be packaged and delivered, this final auditing is often referred to as function configuration auditing (FCA) and physical configuration auditing (PCA). Functional configuration audits verify that the delivered product or product component satisfies the requirements and all approved requirements change requests and nothing more. Physical configuration audits provide an independent evaluation of the system configuration items to confirm that each configuration item that makes up the as-built system maps to its specifications. The audit is held to verify that the product and its documentation are internally consistent and ready for delivery to the customer or end user. Appropriate customer deliverable documentation includes installation manuals, operating manuals, maintenance manuals, and release notes or version description documents.

If the FCA and PCA are based on ongoing baseline configuration audits, shown in Figure 9.5, these audit activities are often not more than a confirmation and a spot check of those baseline configuration auditing reports.

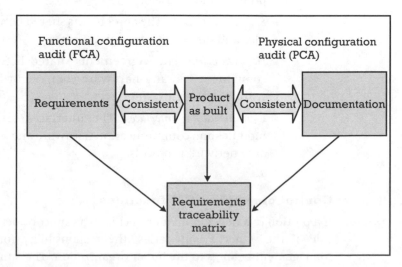

Figure 9.5   FCA and PCA audits.

Interface control

Control of interfaces is becoming one of the most critical tasks in build systems today. This is especially true as many projects are being built at multiple sites, in multiple countries, and within multiple cultures. In addition, suppliers are being used more now than in any other point in history. This simply means that the identification of interface requirements, the establishment of interface descriptions, and the Configuration Management control of those interface descriptions is critical to the success of many of today's projects. CMMI® describes the identification of interface requirements in the Requirements Development process area, the establishment of interface descriptions in the Technical Solution process area, and the control and use of those interface descriptions in the Product Integration process area.

Interfaces are often classified into two major categories:

1. *Organizational interfaces* where the transfer of configuration items is controlled between individuals, the project and support groups, and the customer. Organizational interfaces include interfaces between various organizations or groups involved with the product:

   ▸ Vendor to customer;

   ▸ Project to project;

   ▸ Codeveloper to codeveloper.

2. *Technical interfaces*, which include:

   ▸ *System interfaces:* The explicit interfaces between the system and the software configuration items whose functionality must accomplish the system requirements;

   ▸ *Life-cycle phase:* Transition interfaces between those life-cycle phases of the product;

   ▸ *User interfaces:* Logical characteristics of each interface between the product and its users;

   ▸ *Software interfaces:* The agreements shared between software modules and other software components;

   ▸ *Hardware interfaces:* Agreements shared between other product component and any hardware component in the environment with which it must interface;

   ▸ *Communication interfaces:* The interfaces between the software modules and communication hardware and software such as local area network protocols.

Control of supplier CM functions

If a portion of a development project is to be subcontracted to a supplier outside of the project's boundaries, the responsibility for the Configuration Management belongs to the buyer organization. The supplier is only responsible for the portion of work that has been tasked according to the supplier agreement. Therefore, it is important that the buyer organization thoroughly understand the Configuration Management capabilities of its suppliers. Questions such as the following should be asked and answered:

- What supplier life-cycle work products must be placed under configuration control to ensure consistency with the main development effort?
- What CM concerns need to be added to or removed from the contract with the supplier?
- What audits and procedures need to be established for the supplier?
- What are the supplier's obligations?
- What are the contracting organization's obligations?
- Are the supplier's configuration identification schemes compatible with the buyer?
- Does the supplier have an effective means for managing the interface descriptions?
- Have the frequency and format of the supplier's Configuration Management status reports been agreed upon?
- Does the supplier understand the importance of configuration audits and understand what the buyer expects of it regarding them?

Summary

The quality management functions that are expected to be implemented on any project interested in developing products that satisfy the requirements of product and service quality include but are not limited to:

- Setting quality goals for the project that support the organization's business objectives;
- Conducting peer reviews throughout the product life cycle;
- Performing multiple levels of testing such as unit testing, integration testing, systems testing, and acceptance testing;
- Designing in quality factors such as maintainability, expandability, and reliability;
- Conducting objective evaluations with respect to process quality;
- Controlling the integrity of the evolving product or product component through Configuration Management.

CM is one of the most important process improvement tools that project leaders can use to evolve and deliver their product in a controlled manner. Knowing the state of the product that a project is developing and knowing that it satisfies the customer's requirements are of utmost importance for any project leader. Since many of the most frustrating product or product component problems are often caused by poor Configuration Management, proper Configuration Management is critical.

Enabling the Project Leader to Better Manage and Control Through Supplier Management

Continuing with the project management theme established in Chapter 7, we now turn our attention to supplier management. CMMI® has two process areas that are dedicated to this arena: (1) Supplier Agreement Management, and (2) Integrated Supplier Management.

Supplier Agreement Management

Subcontracting or working with suppliers is becoming a common, but maybe uncomfortable, fact of life. Companies that insisted they would not use subcontractors 1 year ago are suddenly finding themselves in a position of trying to decide how to select a qualified subcontractor or supplier. Too often, these same companies do not have their own requirements engineering, requirements management, project management, or quality management under control and are now faced with managing suppliers in addition to their own project activities. To set the stage, let us define *buyers* and *suppliers*:

- *Buyer:* The project or organization that is setting up an agreement with an entity outside of the project or organization's boundaries to develop a product or product component for delivery. Being outside of the project's boundaries indicates the buyer normally has no control over the supplier's resources.

- *Supplier:* A project inside or outside of the buyer's business unit or organization that agrees to do the necessary product or product component development according to the requirements of the buyer and deliver within

127

specified constraints such as cost, schedule, quality, and performance.

A typical scenario that keeps repeating itself throughout the IT world is one where the buyer organization does not have a sufficiently competent staff to develop or manage the projects that they are being asked to deliver. The senior management team decides to outsource major portions of developing the system to a supplier, but due to their own lack of knowledge about requirements gathering, project management, or quality management, the buyer organization asks the supplier organization to develop not only the requirements but also the acceptance criteria and the acceptance tests. From my point of view, this is a very risky way use suppliers.

While teaching a public supplier management workshop, I explained why the buyer organization should develop the WBS, the requirements, and the project plan to a low enough level to be able to put out a Request for Proposal (RFP) that included a Statement of Work (SOW). Participants asked in an obviously agitated voice, "Are you saying we, the buyer organization, need to do some work before we choose a supplier? Why should we decide to select a supplier if we have to do any of the work? That is why we want a supplier, so we do not have to use any of our resources and do any of the work."

Sound unbelievable? This class was taught in 2001, but the scenario and the questions have been repeatedly presented to me. There are many good reasons to use suppliers and they will be covered in this section. One truth must be kept in mind when a decision is made to use a supplier: *Either you control your suppliers or they control you.*

When and why do we use suppliers?

Let us examine some of the reasons that organizations choose to use suppliers:

- When we don't know how to develop the product or product components;
- When we know how to develop the product or product components but don't have the technology to do so:
  - When someone else knows how to develop the product or product components better;
  - When someone else knows how to develop the product or product components cheaper and with higher quality.
- When we have insufficient in-house resources;
- When it is desirable to create a strategic alliance because the supplier adds to the buyer's competitive position;
- When an organization wishes to pursue new business opportunities;
- When someone else already has a prototype, or a similar product;

> • When using a supplier will result in a more cost-effective solution;

> • When the supplier is willing to share some of the contract risk or entrepreneurial risk.

Different forms of suppliers

Suppliers may take many forms, as indicated next and illustrated in Figure 10.1, including:

> • In-house vendors;

> • Other projects;

> • Fabrication capabilities and laboratories;

> • Commercial vendors;

> • Sister divisions;

> • Commercial-off-the-shelf (COTS) products;

> • Contractors (body shopping).

While there may be arguments against the ideas of reuse components or outsourcing, if we keep in mind the concept that suppliers can be regarded as being "outside of the project's boundaries," these may fit the description as well.

Supplier Agreement Management addresses the need of the project to effectively select and manage those portions of the work that are conducted by suppliers. The term *supplier* is used to identify an *internal or external* organization that develops, manufactures, tests, or supports products being developed or maintained that will be integrated into the buyer's product or will stand alone and be delivered to the buyer's customer.

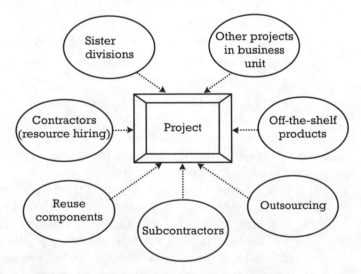

Figure 10.1 Supplier agreement management overview.

Supplier management activities

Supplier Agreement Management involves the following activities:

- Identifying the products and services to be acquired;
- Developing the WBS and requirements that the organization wants the supplier to fulfill;
- Establishing supplier selection criteria;
- Sending out a request for proposal;
- Selecting suppliers;
- Establishing and maintaining requirements and agreements with suppliers;
- Overseeing supplier performance;
- Accepting delivery of the supplied products;
- Arranging for maintenance and support of the supplier products.

What are some of the sources of problems when using suppliers?
Buyers tend to:

- Set unreasonable completion dates;
- Enforce a budget limit without understanding the full scope of the problem;
- Expect an initial project cost and plan that will never be changed without providing a clear definition of the requirements to the supplier;
- Exhibit an us-against-them attitude: conflicts.

Suppliers tend to:
- Fail to identify and specify assumptions and contract performance constraints in the plans/proposal;
- Agree to the buyer-imposed limits too readily—fail to effectively negotiate a win-win solution for both parties;
- Back into a imposed schedule, and therefore skimp on quality over the life of the project;
- Fail to fully identify and manage risks.

As a result, typical problems include: products are not delivered on time, there is no insight to the progress, the quality of products is far below expectations, and costs keep increasing.

When deciding to use a supplier, the buyer organization must decide what acquisition type will provide the best solution that optimizes cost, schedule, performance, and quality. Acquisition types include purchasing off-the-shelf products or services, obtaining products or services through a contractual agreement, obtaining the products or services from another part of the business enterprise (sister division), or combining options such as contracting for a COTS product while have another part of the system developed by a sister division.

Supplier evaluation criteria

Regardless of the acquisition type, it is necessary to develop supplier evaluation criteria in advance. Suppliers should be selected based on their ability to perform the work according to predefined evaluation criteria such as:

- Prior documented performance on similar applications;
- Supplier's performance records on similar work;
- Geographic location;
- Management capabilities;
- Systems engineering capabilities;
- Software engineering capabilities;
- Knowledge, skills, and numbers of staff available to perform the work;
- Available resources such as facilities, hardware, software, and training possibilities;
- The results of an assessment or capability evaluation;
- The project's ability to work with the proposed supplier.

Other requirements for suppliers

Along with the selection criteria, it is important for the buyer to establish the requirements that it wishes the supplier to fulfill. Don't forget to let the supplier know about other requirements beyond the function ones such as:

- Standards and procedures;
- Processes;
- Configuration Management system requirements, including the CM tool that is preferred;
- Quality assurance expectations such as noncompliance audits;
- Design criteria if appropriate;
- Requirements for risk management;
- Deliverables;
- Expected project status reports and frequency;
- Requirements for personal face-to-face visits.

Supplier agreement

Once the supplier is selected, it is necessary to establish the legal and functional way the buyer expects to work with the supplier. This is normally documented in the supplier agreement, which should provide the supplier with the project needs, expectations, and measures of effectiveness. Risk should not be overlooked in the selection of the type of supplier agreement. Fixed price agreements are practical for low-risk projects. Cost or cost plus incentive agreements are generally used when there is a higher degree of risk involved. The supplier agreement typically includes:

- Statement of work;
- Terms and conditions;
- List of deliverables, schedule, and budget;
- Defined acceptance process, including acceptance criteria;
- Identification of buyer and supplier representatives responsible and authorized to agree to changes to the supplier agreement;
- Identification of the process for handling requirements change requests from both sides;
- Identification processes, procedures, guidelines, methods, templates, and so forth that will be followed;
- Identification of critical dependencies between the buyer and the supplier;
- Identification of the form, frequency, and depth of project oversight that the supplier can expect from the buyer (also be dependent upon the amount of foreseeable risk; greater risk will require greater oversight);
- Identification of the supplier's responsibilities for ongoing maintenance and support of the acquired products;
- Identification of the warranty, ownership, and usage rights for the acquired products.

Commercial off the shelf (COTS)

During the middle years of companies using CMM® for Software, most companies did not consider COTS a form of subcontractor and therefore ignored using procedures as they would with subcontractors. At the very least, an organization making the decision to purchase a COTS product needs to define the requirements to a sufficient level of detail in order to objectively evaluate candidate COTS products and determine which ones come the closest to satisfying those requirements. Evaluating candidate COTS products should take into consideration:

- Functionality;
- Performance;
- Quality;
- Reliability;
- Terms and conditions of warranties for the products;

  ▶ COTS supplier's past performance and ability to deliver;

  ▶ Risks associated with the selected off-the-shelf product;

  ▶ Benefits and impacts that may result from future upgrades;

  ▶ Ongoing maintenance plans;

  ▶ Ease of modification;

  ▶ Existence of documentation to support changes.

Supplier: One of the project team's members

It is my opinion that a supplier should be thought of just as if it were one of the project team members. True, the supplier may be another company of 1,000 developers about 4,000 miles away, but, like the project member, the supplier is given an assignment with expected milestones and deliverables. Also like the project member, the supplier needs to write status reports describing accomplishments, issues, risks, considerations for the next reporting period, direction from the project manager, and what did not get accomplished as well as what is planned to be accomplished during the next reporting period.

The supplier's management and technical activities and work products should be evaluated on a periodic and event-driven basis against the supplier agreement. The buyer project manager should be prepared to make recommendations for performance improvement as necessary and provide awards and penalties to the supplier as appropriate in accordance with the contractual agreement. Project management reviews should also be set up to discuss any changes to the supplier's statement of work, terms and conditions, and any other commitments. When contracts are involved, changes to the requirements will involve more money if they are out of scope.

It was mentioned that the requirements should include the buyer's demand regarding Configuration Management and quality assurance. These project management support areas should not be excluded in the periodic progress meetings and status reports. It is up to the buyer to ensure that the supplier is caring for the integrity of the work products and product or product components that it is building. It is also up to the buyer to ensure that the supplier, through its processes, peer reviews, and tests, is able to product the necessary product quality that is expected by the project.

While the supplier's progress reports may be very encouraging, remember that it is the buyer that must integrate the product component(s) produced by the supplier, put their brand on the entire integrated product, and advertise it as quality. Acceptance testing should be done by the buyer. It can be done with support from the supplier, but it is the buyer who is responsible for developing the acceptance criteria and who should be responsible for independent acceptance testing.

The product that is delivered by the supplier must run in the buyer's operational environment and work as the buyer intended it to work. It is perfectly acceptable for the buyer to ask for the systems test results from the supplier along with the results of the functional configuration audit and the physical configuration audit before the buyer even agrees to enter the transition phase and move the product or product component from the supplier to the buyer.

Supplier Agreement Management is about deciding:

‣ What is needed to manage your project's activities?

‣ What part of your project's requirements you would like to be satisfied outside of your project boundaries?

‣ What the effort and cost of acquiring a COTS solution?

‣ What are the effort and cost to manage a supplier?

‣ Where outside of your project's boundaries will you find the most balanced solution for your need?

Integrated Supplier Management

Integrated Supplier Management (ISM) was added to CMMI® in the SE/SW/IPPD/SS model in both the staged and continuous representations to focus projects and organizations beyond the normal activities associated with supplier management. ISM involves monitoring the new products available on the market, evaluating sources of products that might help satisfy project requirements, and using this additional viewpoint to select suppliers. ISM is especially designed for situations in which projects use suppliers to perform functions that are critical to the success of the project.

Achieving project success increasingly demands closely aligned, if not integrated, processes across organizational boundaries. When tight alignment between some of the processes implemented by the supplier and those of the buyer is critical, it is necessary to monitor and analyze those processes closely to help prevent interface problems.

The processes selected for monitoring should include engineering, project management, contracting, and support processes (quality assurance and Configuration Management) critical to successful project performance. The work products selected for evaluation should include critical products, product components, and other work products that provide better insight into the supplier's capabilities. Work products should be evaluated to ensure that:

‣ Derived requirements are traceable to higher-level requirements.

‣ The architecture is feasible and will satisfy future product growth and reuse needs.

‣ Documentation is adequate to operate and support the product.

‣ Work products are consistent with one another.

‣ Products and product components can be integrated.

Summary

The use of suppliers is becoming a common way of life for system developers. To be able to guarantee a fully integrated, working, and effective product or product component on which the business unit is willing to put their logo, project managers must be able to control the project's suppliers as if they were just another member of the project. Applying the basic principles of project management, quality management, and engineering addresses the need of the project to effectively select and manage those portions of the work that are conducted by suppliers.

CHAPTER

11

Contents

Enabling the Project Leader to Better Manage and Control Through Integrated Project Management

Integrated Project Management

Integrated Project Management can be thought of as project management based on the organization's set of standard processes. Integrated Project Management involves:

- Tailoring the project's defined process from the organization's set of standard processes;
- Managing the project using the project's defined process;
- Using and contributing to the organization's process assets;
- Enabling each stakeholder's unique experience and concerns to be identified, considered, and implemented during the development of the product.

A project's defined process

A project's defined process should be based on a minimal set of items, including: the organization's set of standard processes, the customer requirements, the product and product component requirements, commitments made both internally and externally, organizational process needs and objectives, the organizational support environment, the operational environment, and the business environment.

Managing the project's effort, cost, schedule, staffing, risks, and other factors is tied to the tasks of the project's defined process. Integrated Project Management also means that all of the activities associated and supporting the project are

137

coordinated, including the technical activities of requirements development, design, development, and verification and validation. Integrated Project Management also includes the project management support activities of quality assurance, Configuration Management, marketing, and training.

The suggested steps for establishing the project's defined process include:

- Select a life-cycle model from the organization's process assets.

- Select the standard process elements from the organization's set of standard processes that best fit the needs of the project and the life cycle chosen.

- Apply established and maintained tailoring guidelines to the chosen process elements.

- Document the project's defined process.

- Conduct peer reviews of the project's defined process.

- Revise the project's defined process as necessary.

- Incorporate lessons learned from other current and completed projects in the organization.

When performing the estimation that was described in project planning and project monitoring and control in Chapter 7, integrated project management guides the project manager and team members to use the organization's measurement repository. Appropriate data from similar projects can be used to support estimates that the project has conducted on its own. Each project is strongly encouraged to independently validate the historical data and record the assumptions and rationale used to select the historical data.

Plans that affect the project

Integrated project management also has a strong implication that is not present in either the Project Planning process area or Project Monitoring and Control process area. In Project Planning and Project Monitoring and Control, representatives of different groups, departments or disciplines developed or helped the project to develop supporting plans that affect the project, but they were developed as if by independent suppliers.

In applying the principles of Integrated Project Management, these "plans that affect the project" are developed by a more focused and integrated set of individuals who focus not only on the content of a supporting plan but also on how well it is integrated with the other supporting plans.

Integrated project plan

The integrated project plan should incorporate the definitions of measures that will be used to manage the project, identify and analyze overall project risks, and schedules all tasks in a sequence that takes into consideration the critical development factors. It should also identify how conflicts will be resolved that arise between stakeholders involved in the project.

Managing the project using the integrated plans implies tracking risks, commitments, and the adequacy of the support environment on a periodic basis. It also implies that critical dependencies from all relevant stakeholders, including external suppliers, are identified, tracked, and negotiated, and corrective action is again taken as necessary.

To keep the cycle of continuous process improvement going, it is necessary to capture lessons learned and contribute work products, measures, and documented experiences to the organizational process assets. These experiences are placed back into the organizational measurement repository.

Summary of Integrated Project Management

Integrated project management represents the evolution of the basic project management functions. Based on the organization's set of standard processes, Integrated Project Management develops the project's defined process, incorporates other plans that support and contribute to the project's success, and guides the development of the integrated project plan that will be used to manage and control the project to successful completion.

Summary

Project managers today, perhaps more than ever, are under great stress to understand the requirements of the customer and sponsor, develop or lead the development of a work breakdown structure, provide estimates by which to guide the project development, and manage the project to successful completion within the quadruple constraints of cost, schedule, performance, and quality. They must be able to identify risks, analyze them, develop risk mitigation plans with a risk strategy, and monitor the risks in an attempt to prevent them from becoming problems that could hurt the success of the project.

Project managers must be able to coordinate the efforts of different support groups like quality assurance and Configuration Management, different disciplines such as software engineering or hardware engineering, or other departments such as marketing or finance. They must be able to manage their own project members and remotely control the project member of suppliers. They must be able to direct the technical efforts of their project team members, but do so with proper interpersonal skills that must be learned in addition to all the other tasks they are being asked to do.

Today, more than ever, project managers need the processes, procedures, and guidance of the project management and project management support functions that have been described in Chapters 7 through 11 and are emphasized in CMM® Integration.

The Recursive Nature of Requirements Engineering

The requirements phase for many software-oriented projects has been largely restricted to requirements gathering. In probably far too many cases, design and even coding were started before requirements were known or stabilized to a sufficient point. This chapter presents the "recursive" nature of the total requirements gathering and analysis process. It includes concepts from the initial identification of stakeholders, to deriving requirements, to validating requirements at all stages. It will also include the more formal decision making concepts of decision analysis and resolution.

Requirements development

Requirements are the basis for design. Requirements, gathered according to CMMI®, will address the needs of all relevant stakeholders including testing, quality assurance, and database, as well as software, hardware, systems, and so forth. Requirements may be focused on specific life-cycle phases. They may be focused on quality attributes such as maintainability, expandability, or reliability. Requirements may also address constraints caused by the selection of certain design solutions such as using an off-the-shelf database.

What are requirements?

The following list may provide some insight into the question: What are requirements?

- Customer's needs, expectations, and measures of effectiveness;
- Items that are necessary, needed, or demanded;

141

- Implicit or explicit criteria that must, should, or might be met;
- Contain system and software information;
- Will not contain details regarding the internal implementation of a solution;
- May be derived from other requirements during analysis, operational concept and operational scenarios development;
- Describe the services the system is to provide;
- Describe how the system should behave;
- Describe the circumstances under which the system is to operate;
- Provide application domain information;
- Provide constraints on the systems operations;
- Specify the systems properties or attributes;
- Provide constraints on the development process of the system.

Requirements might describe:

- *A user-level facility:* The word processor must include a spell checker and correction command.
- *A very general system property:* The system must ensure that personal information is never made available without authorization.
- *A specific constraint on the system:* The sensor must be polled 10 times per second.
- *How to carry out some computation:* The overall mark is computed by adding the student's examination, project and coursework marks based on the following formula:

  Student Marks

  Total Mark = Exam Mark + 2 · Project Mark + 2/3 · Coursework Mark

- *A constraint on the development of the system:* The system must be developed using the C++ programming language.

Requirements invariably contain a mixture of problem information, statements of system behavior, system's properties, design constraints, and manufacturing constraints. This can and normally does result in conflicts that must be negotiated and resolved. This will be discussed later in more detail.

Requirements come from many sources and stakeholders that must be identified and evaluated as to the true impact that they may have on the project or the impact the project could have on them. Stakeholders, as defined in Chapters 4 and 7, provide the wants, needs, constraints, and interface requirements. It is important for any project to know what the sources of requirements are and to control those sources through requirements gathering and management of requirement's change requests.

These requirements sources include:

- End user;
- Marketing;
- Surveys;
- Systems engineering;
- Software engineering;
- Existing systems and specifications;
- Standards;
- Industry studies;
- Academic research;
- Prototyping;
- Simulation;
- Modeling;
- Quality assurance;
- Configuration Management;
- Testing;
- Regulatory agencies;
- Competitors' products and services;
- Operational environment;
- Application domain.

Requirements are commonly placed into categories. Three examples are: *product* requirements that define the technical criteria that must, should, or might be met by the delivered product; *project* requirements that stipulate resources that will be made available, and how different aspects of the project will be carried out; and *process* requirements that indicate standards, procedures, methods, languages, and engineering and management processes that must be followed.

The needs of stakeholders are the basis for determining customer requirements. Frequently stakeholders' needs, expectations, and constraints are poorly identified or conflicting. In part, this is because developing organizations expect the stakeholders to know exactly what they want the product or product component to look like and act like, how it is supposed to interact with its intended environment, and how long it is expected to exist as a product. In today's fast-paced, technology-driven world, it is very unlikely that the stakeholders will have such insight.

The responsibility to help these stakeholders understand and discover what their requirements really are is the first challenge that must be confronted head-on if the product development is to be successful and the delivered product declared useful in its intended environment. Environmental, legal, and other constraints that may be external to the customer must also be applied when creating and resolving the stakeholders' needs, wants, constraints, and interface requirements into a set of customer requirements.

Elicitation of requirements

In order to go beyond the basic activity of collecting stakeholders' needs, expectations, constraints and interfaces for all phases of the product lifecycle, the Requirements Development process area suggests that they should be elicited. Eliciting goes beyond collecting requirements. Eliciting implies proactively identifying additional requirements not explicitly provided by customers. Examples of techniques to identify and elicit stakeholders' needs include:

> Dialogue;

> Scenario reviews;

> Technology demonstrations;

> Models;

> Simulations;

> Prototypes;

> Brainstorming;

> Observations of existing systems;

> Extractions from sources such as documents, standards, and specifications.

Figure 12.1 illustrates a more detailed process of eliciting requirements.

> *Objective setting:* The overall organizational objectives should be established at this stage. These include general goals of the business, an outline description of the problems to be solved and why the system

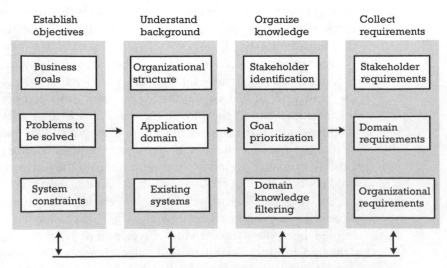

Figure 12.1   Generic requirements elicitation process. (*After:* [1].)

may be necessary, and the constraints on the system such as budget, schedule, and interoperability constraints.

▸ *Background knowledge acquisition*: This is a very important stage where the requirements engineers gather and understand background information about the system. This includes information about the organization where the system is to be installed, information about the application domain of the system, and information about any existing systems which are in use and which may be replaced by the systems being specified.

▸ *Knowledge organization:* The large amount of knowledge that has been collected in the previous stage must be organized and collated. This involves identifying system stakeholders and their roles in the organization, prioritizing the goals of the organization, and discarding domain knowledge that does not contribute directly to the system requirements.

▸ *Stakeholder requirements collection:* This stage is what many people think of as elicitation. It involves consulting system stakeholders to discover their requirements and deriving requirements that come from the application domain and the organization that is acquiring the system.

Customer requirements

The definition of *customer requirements* was first provided in Chapter 4. The set of stakeholders on the left side within the oval is not meant to be exhaustive but to indicate that stakeholders are found inside and outside of the organization and must be seriously considered based on their potential influence on the project. The customer requirements, as defined in Chapter 4 and reillustrated in Figure 12.2, represent the common understanding of

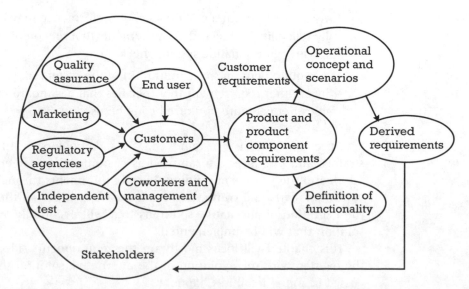

Figure 12.2 Customer, product, and product component requirements.

what will satisfy the stakeholders. This input must be consolidated and have conflicts removed before being captured as customer requirements. Notice that it was stated that conflicts will be removed. There will be conflicts and it is important to thoroughly understand stakeholder relationships before attempting to get them resolved. Stakeholders, by their very nature, want what they want in a product or product component and really do not care what another stakeholder wants. Often these conflicts show up as nonfunctional requirements.

Nonfunctional requirements

Nonfunctional requirements are requirements that are not specifically concerned with the functionality of a system. They place restrictions on the product being developed, the development process, and the external constraints that the product must meet. Nonfunctional requirements define the overall qualities or attributes of the resulting system and place restrictions on how the user requirements are to be met. These nonfunctional requirements are often of critical importance and functional requirements may need to be sacrificed to meet these nonfunctional constraints. Nonfunctional requirements are defined because of the need of the user to achieve certain goals such as:

- Budget;
- Organizational policies;
- Need for intcroperability with other software or hardware;
- Need for certain development processes to be followed;
- Need to care for external factors such as safety and security regulations.

A few examples may help to illustrate the possible conflicts.

- A requirement for a certain level of performance may be contradicted by reliability and security requirements that rely on processor capacity to carry out dynamic system checking.
- A requirement on space utilization of the system may be contradicted by another requirement that specifies that a standard compiler which does not generate optimized code be used.

Once the conflicts are removed, the stakeholders' wants, needs, constraints, and interfaces are captured as customer requirements (see Figure 12.2), and the process of refining those requirements through analysis and validation starts and continues in a recursive manner all the way through the definition of alternative solutions that will eventually lead to the best solution that will be implemented.

This chapter will focus mostly on the requirements side but will show the overlap with the evolution of the alternative solution that will be discussed in more detail in Chapter 13.

Product or product component requirements

The next step in the evolution of the requirements into a product or product component is the translation of the customer requirements into the product or product component requirements. Product and product component requirements define what the system is required to do and the circumstances under which it is required to operate. They define the services that the product or product component should provide and establish constraints on how they will operate. Product and product component requirements should include technical requirements and the criteria that will be used to verify that the products satisfy the requirements. The process of determining what the systems are intended to do is also referred to as the definition of functionality, or more commonly referred to as functional analysis. The definition of functionality should include actions, sequences, input, output, and other information that clearly describes how the product will be used. When we define functions, place them into logical groupings, and associate them with the requirements, we refer to this as the *functional architecture*.

Operational concept and operational scenarios

The requirements evolution focuses on deriving a more detailed and precise set of technical requirements that, if implemented, will satisfy the customer requirements. To accomplish that, the requirements team should analyze the customer requirements concurrently with the development or refinement of the operational concept. Analysis of one level of requirements makes sure that they are necessary and sufficient to meet the objectives of higher levels of the product hierarchy. The analysis of requirements may produce derived requirements that result from design decisions and should also address the cost and performance of other life-cycle phases to the extent possible with the organization's business objectives.

The *operational concept* is a general description of how the system operates, where in the operating environment the system will be distributed, how long the system must operate, and how effective the system's performance must be. An initial understanding of the operational concept may appear during the elicitation of the requirements but is expected to continue as the development team strives to refine their understanding of the requirements to eventually choose between alternative solutions to implement them.

Operational scenarios classify as a requirements elicitation technique but are most often used together with the operational concept to refine and discover new requirements, needs, and constraints. An operational scenario is a sequence of events that might occur; it includes the interaction of the product with its environment and users, as well as the interaction among its product components. The operational scenario should be consistent with the level of detail in the stakeholders' needs, expectations, and constraints in which the proposed product is expected to operate.

Operational concepts and scenarios should focus not only on the system's functionality but also on its performance, maintenance requirements, support requirements, and methods of disposal when its productive use is over. The operational concept should also describe the environment in which the product is to operate, including boundaries and constraints. Operational concept and scenario development is an interactive process that continues into technical solution development.

Product and product requirements that come out of the refinement of the customer requirements should address the satisfaction of customer, business, and project objectives and any associated attributes such as effectiveness and affordability. The relationships between requirements should be established and maintained for consideration during change management and requirements allocation.

Architectural and interface requirements

The gathering and analysis of customer requirements and their translation to product and product component requirements not only include functional requirements but also focus on architectural and interface requirements.

Architectural requirements that are commonly included are critical product quality factors like maintainability and expandability. Maintainability refers to the characteristic of the system that makes it easy to repair if a problem is discovered in one of its product components or subsystems. Expandability refers to how easy it is to expand or add another function or product component to the existing integrated system. We have much to learn about architecture from building houses. Deciding to knock out a wall to expand the house when it is nearly 95% complete may not be possible if it was not built to allow that expansion to happen. Similarly, if a system is built that is not highly cohesive and loosely coupled, trying to find and fix an error may result in many other parts of the system being negatively affected. Companies that have chosen not to consider these quality factors relating to architecture often find themselves in a position that they can no longer fix a problem or enhance the existing system without serious negative side effects. These same companies frequently elect to outsource their system to another company that has less ability than they do and soon they are totally out of business.

Interface requirements between product and product components should be identified in the product architecture and should be defined. The interfaces between functions must be defined and controlled as part of the product and product component integration. As the interface designs are defined, the design becomes a requirement for products and product components that are affected by the interface. As the design progresses, the product architecture may be altered by the technical solution processes creating new interfaces between product components and those components external to the product.

Allocation of requirements

As indicated in Figure 12.3, the process of evolving the requirements from stakeholders wants, needs, constraints, and interface requirements to

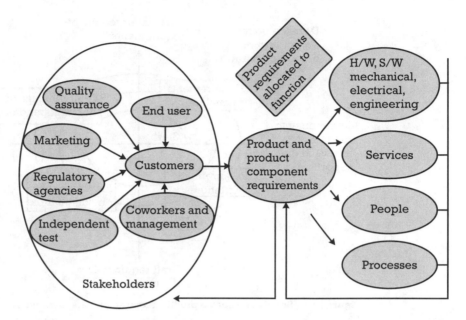

Figure 12.3   Product requirements allocated to functions.

product and product component requirements and to alternative solutions is also affected by how we allocate those requirements to the various engineering functions, services, processes, and people. When we say allocate requirements to hardware, we are really saying that we intend to satisfy those requirements through a hardware implementation solution. Likewise, allocating requirements to software implies that we intend to implement those requirements through software. We shall see in Chapter 13 that the decision to allocate requirements to hardware, software, or other engineering or manufacturing functions may be altered as we strive to find the optimal alternative solution.

Validation of requirements

There is one more important concept that is brought out in the Requirements Development process area and that is the concept of *validation of requirements*. Perhaps when you hear the phrase "validation of requirements," you think of conducting testing near the end of the project life cycle. CMMI® clearly shows us that validation needs to start almost immediately after we have gone through the first round of gathering customer requirements and needs to continue until the best alternative solution has been chosen and implementation has begun. This is illustrated in Figure 12.4 as a spiral model adapted from [1].

In the early rounds of requirements gathering and analysis, validation of requirements may mean meeting with the customer and relaying the understanding of how the operational needs may be met. As the requirements are refined and lower-level requirements derived, techniques such as

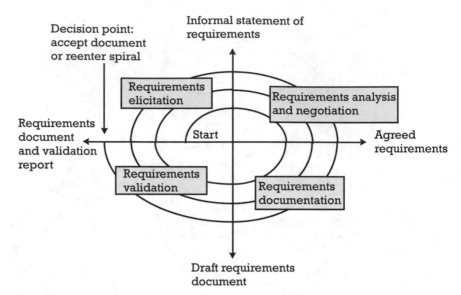

Figure 12.4 Spiral model of the product requirements engineering process. (*After:* [1].)

those used during the elicitation of the requirements may be used to gain the customers' confidence that the project is capable of using the customers' requirements to develop the product that indeed will meet their operational needs.

Requirements Management

While the requirements elicitation, analysis, documentation, and validation are evolving, it is important that the organization have strong management control of those requirements. Requirements control must continue throughout the remainder of the project life-cycle phases including when:

- The optimal alternative solution is chosen.
- The product is being implemented.
- Change requests to the requirements are received.

The relationship among RD, TS, and RM

Figure 12.5 illustrates Requirements Management's (RM) ongoing and continuous relationship with Requirements Development (RD) and Technical Solution (TS). As RD and TS are "running" around the track eliciting, analyzing, refining, and deriving more requirements, RM is running around in parallel to ensure that their efforts are managed and controlled. As RD captures its initial customer requirements, RM reaches in periodically and captures those requirements, identifies them, and places them in a baseline for control purposes. When RD validates the requirements with the customer,

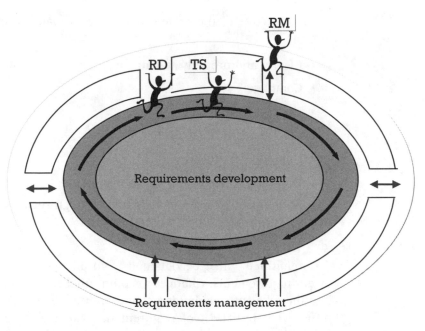

Figure 12.5 Requirements Management and Requirements Development Partnership.

RM is again there to capture the improved understanding of the requirements and control them until the next improvement version is offered. This process continues even through the definition and selection of alternative solutions.

For example, if a design decision is made to use an off-the-shelf product, the interfaces to that COTS product become the requirements for the other product components that will interface with it. For this example, RM would be there again to support the capture and control of the new requirements into the evolving baseline.

Configuration Management of requirements change requests

Requirements Management is essentially Configuration Management of requirements change requests. This was how it was originally stated in CMM® for Software. However, due to my assessment experience during the years I was at the SEI, it became a process area on its own to indicate the great importance of not only gathering and analyzing requirements but also ensuring that all relevant stakeholders inside and outside of the project's organization were kept aware of the current state of those requirements. One way that can be accomplished is to make sure that the requirements are reviewed by a multidisciplined team to ensure that each discipline and support function that is necessary for the project success has a shared understanding of the requirements. The review would take into consideration the viewpoint of software, hardware, systems, quality assurance, independent test, and marketing, for example.

The objective of the review would be to make sure the requirements were:

- Clearly and properly stated;
- Complete;
- Unambiguous;
- Consistent with each other;
- Uniquely identifiable;
- Feasible and appropriate to implement;
- Able to be verified and validated through reviews and testing;
- Traceable.

Commitment must be obtained from all relevant stakeholders on the current requirements. Changes to commitments must be renegotiated with all of the relevant stakeholders that were involved in the review and baselining of the initial set of requirements. Changes to commitments made external to the organization should be reviewed by senior management, as one of the relevant stakeholders, to ensure that commitment can be accomplished along with the other previously approved commitments. In the past many people thought that this meant the senior management team was supposed to be conducting a technical review of the requirements. This is not the case. This is a business case review to ensure that the organization can indeed make this commitment or change in commitment along with all other commitments that have been made or are in the process of being made. As the requirements evolve according to the practices described in Requirements Development and Technical Solution, Requirements Management ensures that all project participants commit to the current, approved requirements and commit to the resulting changes in project plans, activities, and work products. Requirements Management also emphasizes that all changes to existing commitments should be negotiated before project participants commit to the requirement or requirement change.

Changes to the requirements must be controlled as they evolve over the product life cycle due to changing needs and derived requirements. All relevant stakeholders must review and agree on the change requests to the requirements before they are applied. Approved changes to the requirements are tracked and a change history is maintained for each requirement along with the rationale for the change.

Impact analysis

To effectively analyze the impact of the changes, it is necessary that the source of each requirement is known and the rationale for any change documented. To make sense of this, it is helpful to remember the different elicitation techniques that were used to obtain the requirements from the customer in the first place. An impact analysis procedure should take many things into consideration before the requirements change request is approved. The following is a list of items that should be examined at a minimum for the impact on them:

- Development schedule;
- Release schedule;
- Changes required to this system;
- Staffing;
- Components;
- Development and target equipment;
- Risks;
- Scope;
- Costs;
- Changes required to other systems or interfaces within the project;
- Other existing products or product lines.

Bidirectional traceability

The practices found in Requirements Management also point out another critical function that must be put in place and exercised for successful control of requirements. That function is bidirectional traceability. Bidirectional traceability was only mentioned at Maturity Level 3 in CMM® for Software but is more properly stated as a Maturity Level 2 activity in CMMI®. It should be clear that without requirements traceability, it would be very difficult if not impossible to conduct an effective impact analysis when a requirements change request was received, much less prove that the delivered system actually matched the requirements and approved requirements change requests. A requirement is traceable if you know:

- The source of each requirement;
- Why the requirement exists;
- What requirements are related to it;
- How the requirement relates to other information such as systems designs, implementations, and user documentation.

Traceability information is needed to find other requirements that might be affected by proposed changes. Bidirectional traceability helps determine that all source requirements have been completely addressed and that all lower-level requirements can be traced to a valid source.

Frequently I am asked: "Is it OK to have the life-cycle work products on a PC-based system and the source code (for software) on a mainframe computer?" My answer is always, "Yes, as long as the traceability is in place to trace from the requirements through the associated life-cycle work products of architecture specifications, detailed design specifications, code, unit test plans, integration test plans, system test plans, and so forth and back." This is often referred to as *vertical traceability*. *Horizontal traceability* refers to the traceability from the requirements to the associated plans such as the project plan, quality assurance plan, Configuration Management plan, risk management plan, and so forth.

Keeping life-cycle work products consistent

The important benefit of having bidirectional traceability is to ensure that all of the life-cycle work products, plans, and related activities are updated as necessary to keep them consistent with the approved changes made to the requirements. This guarantees that the integrity of the system is kept.

Summary

During the iterative process of requirements analysis, the following guidelines should be continuously applied:

- Analyze stakeholder needs, expectations, constraints, and external interfaces to remove conflicts and to organize into related subjects.
- Determine what impact the intended operational environment will have on the ability to satisfy the stakeholders' needs, expectations, constraints, and interfaces.
- Analyze requirements to ensure that they are complete, feasible, realizable, and verifiable.
- Analyze derived requirements to determine whether they satisfy the objectives of higher-level requirements.
- Identify key requirements that have a strong influence on cost, schedule, functionality, risk, or performance.
- Identify technical performance measures that will be tracked during the development effort.
- Analyze operational concepts and scenarios to refine the customer needs, constraints, and interfaces and discover new requirements.

Requirements management processes manage all requirements received or generated by the project, including both technical and nontechnical requirements and those that are imposed on the project by the organization. When the Requirements Management, Requirements Development, and Technical Solutions processes are all implemented, their associated processes are normally tied closely together and performed concurrently.

Reference

[1]   Kotonya, G., and I. Sommerville, "Requirements Engineering with Viewpoints," *BCS/ISS Software Engineering Journal,* Vol. 11, No. 1, 1996, pp. 5–18.

Alternative Solutions

This chapter presents the concepts and guidelines that CMMI® has to offer on establishing criteria and selecting product or product component solutions from alternative solutions. It includes the concepts of decision analysis and resolution for more formal decision making. Critical insight is provided that shows that alternative solutions not only are different ways of addressing the same requirements but also reflect a different allocation of requirements among the product components comprising the solution set. This chapter will also focus on the design and implementation of the product or product component.

Selecting the best alternative solution

Alternative solutions need to be identified and analyzed to enable the selection of a balanced solution across the life of the product in terms of cost, schedule, performance, and quality. This concept first appeared in Chapter 7 as the quadruple constraint that needed to be optimized.

To illustrate why identifying and selecting the best alternative solution is such an important consideration, let us build a possible scenario.

The Problem: Provide a product or product component solution across the life of the product that optimizes the quadruple constraints of:

- Cost;
- Schedule;
- Performance;
- Quality.

The Solution: This may be accomplished through the allocation of the requirements to:

- Software;
- Hardware;
- Electronics;
- Mechanics;
- Hydraulics;
- Manufacturing processes;
- Services;
- People.

It may be accomplished through:

- In-house development;
- Purchase of commercial-off-the-shelf products;
- Use of suppliers;
- Use of reuse components.

It will be influenced by the proposed product architecture that addresses the critical quality factors of the product such as maintainability and expandability.

Satisfying the quadruple constraints

Given this scenario, it is obvious that for reasonably large and/or complex systems, the combinations and permutations possible will require us to identify alternative solutions and, based on selected criteria, select the best solution to solve our originally stated problem. *Best* must be understood before the concept of alternative solutions is clearly understood. The alternative solutions must fit within the range of given values for cost, schedule, performance, and quality. It is possible that a project will find that it cannot fit within those given ranges for one of more of the quadruple constraints. This may necessitate a change to the product architecture. It may cause a reallocation of the requirements to the engineering functions or processes or services. It may cause a renegotiation with the stakeholders to determine if any of the constraints can be eased. In any event, "best" is not meant to be "the guaranteed best solution," but the alternative solution that best optimizes the given constraints.

Allocation of requirements as a solution set

In the general case, solutions are defined as a set. Alternative solutions are not only different ways of addressing the same requirements, but they also reflect a different allocation of requirements among the product components as a solution set—not as single product components. The objective is to optimize the set as a whole. Detailed alternative solutions and selection criteria, consistent with business objectives, typically include:

- Cost (development, procurement, support);
- Technical performance;
- Complexity of the product component;
- Robustness to product operating and use conditions, operating modes, environments;
- Product expansion and growth;
- Technology limitations;
- Sensitivity to construction methods and materials;
- Risk;
- Evolution of requirements and technology;
- Disposal;
- Capabilities and limitations of end users and operators.

Choosing an alternative solution under the conditions described above may well require a formal evaluation process that focuses on identified alternatives against established criteria. The CMMI® process area Decision Analysis and Resolution may be called upon to assist in the selection of the best alternative solution that will satisfy the technical solution needs of the project. Decision and Analysis and Resolution involves making good business decisions by:

- Selecting a decision-making technique and level of structure.
- Identifying criteria that will be the basis of the decision:
  - This criteria should address design issues for the life of the product, such as provisions for easy insertion of new technologies or the ability to better utilize available commercial products.
  - The criteria needed for decision-making techniques range from consensus-based decisions to the use of probabilistic models and decision theory.
- Identifying alternatives.
- Evaluating the alternatives against the criteria.

The final selection of an alternative should be accompanied by:

- The selected technique, criteria, and alternatives;
- The rationale for the selection of the final solution;
- The rationale for not selecting one of the other alternative solutions.

While the use of formal decision analysis techniques should always be considered, some guidelines for requiring formal decision making include:

- When a decision is directly related to topics assessed as being of medium or high risk;
- When a decision is related to changing work products under Configuration Management;
- When a decision would cause schedule delays over a certain percent or specific amount of time;
- When a decision has an impact on the ability to achieve project objectives;
- When a decision's costs are reasonable compared to the decision's impact.

Selection of the best solution set establishes the requirements provisionally allocated to that solution as the set of allocated requirements that will be designed and implemented.

Commercial off-the-shelf products

If the decision is to purchase an off-the-shelf product, the requirements should be used to establish the supplier agreement. Factors that can affect the make-or-buy decision include:

- Functions that the products or services will provide;
- Available project resources and skills;
- Costs of acquiring versus developing internally;
- Critical delivery and integration dates;
- Strategic business alliances;
- Market research of available products;
- Functionality and quality of available products;
- Skills and capabilities of potential suppliers;
- Stability of potential suppliers (i.e., length of time in business, reliability of existing products ongoing technical support services);
- Impact on core competencies;
- Licenses, warrantees, responsibilities, and limitations associated with products being acquired;
- Product availability;
- Proprietary issues;
- Risk reduction.

Designing and implementing the product or product component

Product or product component designs must provide the appropriate life-cycle content for implementation, modification, maintenance, sustenance, and installation. Product design consists of two broad phases that may overlap during actual execution: preliminary design and detailed design. Preliminary design establishes product capabilities and the product or systems architecture. Detailed design fully defines the structure and capabilities of the product components.

Preliminary design

Defining the architecture requires that:

» Processes exist that need to take place in order that the system accomplish its intended functions.

» The individual processes transform either data or materials that flow between them.

» The processes or activities or operations follow rules that establish the conditions under which they occur.

» The components that will implement the design (hardware, software, personnel, and facilities) must be described.

Systems or product architecting has been defined as the process of creating complex, unprecedented systems. Building systems in today's fast-moving world is difficult at best. Requirements of the marketplace are ill-defined. The rapidly evolving technology provides new services at a global level instantly. Uncertainty is increasing about the way the system will be used, the components that will be incorporated, and the interconnections that will be made.

Traditional approach to systems architecting

Many methodologies have been developed to support a traditional systems development model. The steps normally consist of defining the requirements, considering several options, and emerging with a well-defined design through a process of elimination. This is illustrated in Figure 13.1.

The traditional approach to architecting is effective when the requirements are well defined and remain essentially constant during the system development period. If the implementation of the system is long, on the order of years, the requirements may change due to changing needs and new technology that offers different alternatives and opportunities that the traditional approach to systems architecture cannot handle.

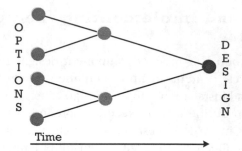

Figure 13.1   The traditional approach.

Evolutionary approach to systems architecting

There is a new systems architecture approach that is emerging with its roots in software systems. It is called the evolutionary approach and is oriented to deal with the uncertainty in requirements and technology, especially for systems with a long development time and an expected long life cycle. This is illustrated in Figure 13.2. Requirements are allowed to be more abstract and, therefore, subject to interpretation. Alternative solutions are explored and pursued further as new technology options become available. Intermediate designs are saved and some of them are implemented as prototypes but not operationally implemented. Others are implemented in traditional ways. At any time in the development process, when there is a need to build a system, the available solution that best meets the current requirements is selected and implemented using any systems engineering approach.

Architectures may include standards and design rules governing the development of product components and their interfaces, as well as guidance to assist product developers. In the context of the architectural requirements, multiple architectures supporting alternative solutions may be developed and analyzed to determine the advantages and disadvantages. Operational concepts and scenarios are used to generate the use cases and quality scenarios that become the guidelines to refine the architecture as well as evaluate the suitability of the architecture.

Detailed design

During detailed design, the product architecture details are finalized, product components are completely defined, and interfaces are fully characterized. Design criteria are often established to ensure that the product or product component exhibits one or more of the following quality attributes:

- Modularity;
- Clarity;
- Maintainability;
- Expandability;
- Portability;

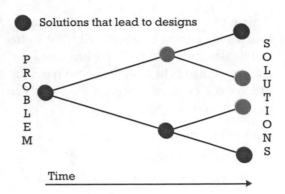

Figure 13.2 Evolutionary approach.

- Efficiency;
- Reliability;
- Security;
- Usability;
- Scalability.

These quality factors can be defined following the Goal–Question–Metric–Paradigm approach as shown in Figure 13.3. The criteria that define the quality factors and the metrics that help measure the extent the product or product component exhibits that characteristic or quality factor must be used for design purposes. It can be used to verify that the quality factors are being built into the product or product component. It can be further used to validate that the product operates in the operational environment and will indeed exhibit the required quality characteristic.

There is much talk about effective design methods. Whether or not a design method is effective depends on how much assistance it provides the

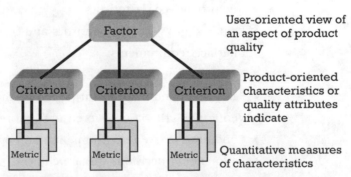

- Product quality is described through a number of factors (reliability, maintainability).
- Each factor has several attributes that describe it called criteria.
- Each criterion has associated with it several metrics, which, taken together, quantify the criterion.

Figure 13.3 Product quality metrics.

designer and the cost-effectiveness of that assistance. Criteria must be established and maintained against which the effectiveness of the design methods can be determined. Highly sophisticated methods are not necessarily effective in the hands of designers who have not been trained in the use of the methods. Examples of techniques and methods that facilitate effective design include:

- Prototypes;
- Structural models;
- Object-oriented design;
- Entity relationship models;
- Design reuse;
- Design patterns.

Technical data package

The design should be recorded in a *technical data package* that is created during the development of the preliminary design to document the architecture definition and should be maintained throughout the life of the product to record essential details of the product design. The technical data package is similar to the unit record folder or the software development file descriptions from the 1970s and 1980s. A technical data package provides the developer with a comprehensive description of the product or product component as it is developed.

The technical data package should include:

- Product architecture description;
- Allocated requirements;
- Product-component descriptions;
- Product-related life-cycle process descriptions;
- Key product characteristics;
- Required physical characteristics and constraints;
- Interface requirements;
- Materials requirements;
- Fabrication and manufacturing requirements;
- Verification criteria used to ensure that requirements are achieved;
- Conditions of use (environments) and operating/usage scenarios;
- Rationale for decisions (design choice).

Interface descriptions

As mentioned in Chapter 12, interfaces are one of the most important configuration items to be identified and controlled throughout a project life cycle. Projects must develop detailed interface descriptions during the refinement of the product and product requirements and during the selection of alternative solutions. Interfaces must be defined with other product components and external items. When that external item is a COTS product, the interface description to the COTS product becomes a requirement to which all of the other product components that will interface with that COTS product must adhere.

The criteria for interfaces frequently reflect a comprehensive list of critical parameters that must be defined or at least investigated to determine their applicability. Interface designs include the following:

- Origination;

- Destination;

- Stimulus and data characteristics for software;

- Electrical, mechanical, and functional characteristics for hardware.

Implementation

The product design to be implemented is described in the Technical Solution process area as:

- Software is coded.

- Data is documented.

- Services are documented.

- Electrical and mechanical parts are fabricated.

- Facilities are constructed.

- Materials are produced.

- Unique manufacturing processes are put into operation.

Peer reviews and unit testing

The requirement to conduct *peer reviews* and *unit testing* is also in the description of the Technical Solution process area. Peer reviews will be further discussed in Chapter 14, which covers Product Integration, Verification, and Validation.

Examples of peer reviews include structured walkthroughs and inspections. Examples of unit testing methods include:

- Statement coverage testing;

- Branch coverage testing;

- Path coverage testing;

- Boundary value testing;

- Special value testing.

Product support documentation

While the focus within the description of Technical Solution is on architecture, design, and implementation, it is important to note that this is not complete until the documentation that will be used to install, operate, and maintain the product is also developed, reviewed, and revised as necessary. It is recommended that the project develop preliminary versions of the installation and that operator and user's manuals should be developed in the early phases of the project life cycle and reviewed by all relevant stakeholders inside and outside of the organization. This documentation will be part of the delivery package that will be described in Chapter 14.

Summary

Choosing a technical solution that will implement the product or product requirements in the operational environment requires alternative solutions to be identified and analyzed. The selection of the best technical solution will enable the selection of a life cycle that is a balanced solution in terms of cost, schedule, technical performance, and quality. Identifying and selecting the criteria to guide the selection of the best alternative solution may require a formal decision analysis and resolution procedure. The rationale for the chosen alternative solution and the rationale for alternative solutions that were not chosen must be documented for future reference.

From Components to Products: Gluing the Pieces Together

This chapter presents CMMI® process areas of Product Integration, Verification, and Validation as a "triple." Here we show how their use guides projects from the building blocks developed during technical solution to an integrated, verified, and validated set of product components that are ready for packaging and delivery.

The Product Integration process area addresses the integration of product components either into more complex components or subsystems or into complete products. While it is not wrong to think of product integration as a one-time assembly of the product components, today this is normally an iterative process of assembling product components, evaluating them, and then assembling more product components until the complete product is assembled and the system is fully tested.

Product Integration can be a very deceptive process area to those who read its goals and practices as if all of the events were to be executed in sequential order. Its real value appears when one regards Product Integration as a main program of events that must take place to assemble the product components, and Verification and Validation as subroutines that are called upon for the performance of peer reviews, testing, simulation, and other verification and validation activities.

The integration strategy

The performance of effective product integration involves the establishment and the maintenance of an integration sequence, the environment for performing the integration, and the development and usage of integration procedures.

An *integration strategy* should be developed early in the project, concurrently with product development plans and

167

specifications. Some life cycles require that the integration and test strategy be one of the very first documents developed for the project following the successful baseline of the allocated requirements.

During the establishment of the product integration strategy, the following 11 questions should be answered:

1. When will the product components be available?
2. Which ones are on the critical path?
3. What alternative integration sequences have been considered?
4. What work needs to be done to prepare and conduct the integration activities?
5. Who is responsible for each integration activity?
6. What resources will be required?
7. What schedule is to be met and what are the expectations?
8. Are the necessary procedures to be followed documented and in place?
9. Are there any special tools required during the integration?
10. What must be included in the product integration environment?
11. What personnel skills are required for the individuals conducting and supporting the integration?

Other considerations include:

- What modules should be integrated first?
- How many modules should be integrated before integration testing starts?
- What order should be used to integrate the modules?
- Should there be more than one skeleton?
    - How is each skeleton defined?
    - Are there distinct build levels?
- How much testing should be done on each skeleton?

Alternatives for the order of product component integration include top-down product component integration, bottom-up product component integration, critical product components first, related functional product components first, as-available product components, and complete product component integration.

Integration environment

The establishment of the integration environment needed to support the integration of the product components is of great importance. The requirements of an integration environment can widely vary the product components that are integrated into the deliverable product. For contrast, imagine the integration environment needs for a software accounting system. Now compare these to the integration environment required for the development of a Boeing 747 aircraft. The space, safety concerns, assembly equipment, required personnel, tools, recording equipment, and so forth take a long time to plan and set up to support the integration for a Boeing 747. This integration environment is considerably different both internally to the systems themselves and externally to the users.

The environment may include test equipment, simulators, pieces of real equipment, and recording devices. It may be purchased or developed. The product integration environment may also include the reuse of existing organizational resources as long as that reuse is planned for early enough in the project life cycle.

It is also quite possible that the integration, verification, and validation activities share the same environment. One IT company in Asia and one in Central Europe set up "mirror" environments for their development, integration and systems test, and production functions. This company believed that it is cheaper in the long run to duplicate these environments with the same software and hardware rather than to worry about what effects partial or different environments may cause to the development, implementation, and test results.

Product Integration procedures

In order to carry out the integration sequence, product integration procedures must be developed, or reviewed for usefulness if they already exist. These procedures may include guidance on the number of iterations that are planned to be performed and expected test results for each iteration. Criteria should also be established indicating the readiness of the product component for integration. Criteria may include the degree of simulation permitted for a product component to pass a test.

Readiness for integration

One of the most important *readiness criteria* needed for product integration is the assurance that all of the product components are confirmed to be compliant with their *interface requirements*. Interface requirements drive the development of the interfaces necessary to integrate the product components.

The interface requirements may have been collected during requirements elicitation, expanded during product architecture development, and managed throughout the product life cycle.

The interface descriptions defined during requirements evolution and the definition of alternative solutions must be placed under Configuration Management as one of the project's most important configuration items.

Change requests to these interface descriptions must strictly follow the change control process. Many product integration problems arise from unknown or uncontrolled aspects of both internal and external interfaces. Effective management of product-component interfaces helps ensure that implemented interfaces will be complete and compatible.

To ensure product component readiness for integration:

> Ensure that the product components are delivered to the product integration environment in accordance with the planned product integration strategy.

> Verify the receipt of each product component.

> Ensure that each product component meets its description.

> Check the configuration status of the product component against the expected configuration.

> Confirm that each product component is compliant with its interface requirements.

Assembly of product components

Once the readiness criteria of the product components have been established, the actual process of integrating these product components can commence. This is normally carried out in an iterative fashion from the initial product components, through the interim assemblies of product components, to the product as a whole. The readiness of the product integration environment should be ensured and the product components assembled according to the product integration sequence and integration procedures.

Evaluation of assembled product components

Throughout the evolution of the product from the iterations of assembly or product components, each interim state or final product state must be evaluated to show satisfaction of functional, performance, and quality requirements. Actual product evaluation results should be compared against the expected results and spot-checked by an independent party, such as quality assurance. The assembled product components must therefore be verified and validated according to the integration sequence and the verification and validation strategies.

Verification techniques and methods

Verification techniques ensure that the integrated product meets the specified requirements. In other words, it assures that the project "built the product right." Methods of verification include, but are not limited to:

> Inspections;

- Peer reviews;
- Audits;
- Walkthroughs;
- Path coverage testing;
- Simulations;
- Functional testing;
- Load, stress, and performance testing;
- Operational scenario testing;
- Observations and demonstrations.

Verification methods commonly applied prior to packaging and delivery include:

- Load, stress, and performance testing;
- Functional decomposition–based testing;
- Operational scenario testing.

Validation procedures and criteria ensure that the product or product component will fulfill its intended use when placed in its intended environment. To validate a product means to demonstrate that you have "built the right product." Validation methods should be selected based on their ability to demonstrate that user needs are indeed satisfied.

Packaging and delivery

Prior to packaging and delivering the product, the requirements, design, product, test results, and documentation are reviewed again to ensure that all issues affecting the packaging and delivery of the product are identified and resolved. Configuration audits are conducted prior to packaging and delivery to ensure that:

- The product or product component that is included satisfies the customer, product requirements, and all approved change requests and nothing more.
- The documentation that is to be delivered to the customer/end user matches the delivered product or product component.

Verification and validation results that have been conducted throughout the development life cycle are used as input to this final configuration audit.

Final delivery includes satisfying the applicable packaging requirements, preparing the operational site for the installation of the product, delivering the product and related documentation, and ensuring that it can be installed at the operational site.

Acceptance testing may satisfy the final verification and validation criteria. The purpose of acceptance testing is to confirm that a product or product component is ready for operational use. The acceptance test is performed for or in conjunction with someone else to demonstrate that the confidence is justified. The primary quality factors addressed are usability and reliability in order to answer the question: Will the product or product component support operational use? Acceptance testing should also include the review of user documentation to verify its technical correctness compared to the system functionality, its completeness, and its ease of use.

Verification and Validation

Verification not only focuses on the final assembled product but also includes verification of the intermediate work products against all selected requirements, including customer, product, and product component requirements. Verification methods address the technical approach to work product verification and the specific actions, resources, and environments that will be used to verify specific work products. Verification typically begins with involvement in the definition of product and product component requirements to ensure that these requirements are verifiable. The verification environment must be appropriate to support the verification method and may be shared with product integration and validation.

When verification activities are performed, the results must be documented. This includes the "as-run" verification method and the deviations from the strategies and procedures that were necessary during its execution that may be used later for process improvement purposes.

The development of Validation procedures should include the test and evaluation of maintenance, training, and support services. As pointed out in Chapter 12, validation activities are performed as early in the product life cycle as possible, starting with the customer and product requirements. As the validation activities are performed, the "as-run" validation procedures should be documented and the deviations that occurred noted.

During validation it is important to remember to:

▶ Demonstrate that the maintenance tools are operating in the actual product;

▶ Verify in the field that support of the product is effective as specified by the customer (e.g., mean time to repair);

▶ Demonstrate adequate training of the products and services.

The final task during validation is to answer the question: Did the product perform as expected in its intended environment?

Summary

The steps leading up to product delivery include integrating the product components according to the integration sequence and utilizing verification and validation techniques throughout the project life cycle as appropriate. Sequences of triples may be required to be carried out before the final product is assembled, verified, and validated:

- (PI_1, VER_1, VAL_1)
- (PI_2, VER_2, VAL_2)
- (PI_3, VER_3, VAL_3)
- ....
- ....
- (PI_N, VER_N, VAL_N)

A delivered product is not considered to possess quality unless it can be shown that it satisfies all of the specified requirements and performs as anticipated in the operational environment.

Improving Processes at the Organizational Level

Ever since Mr. Watts Humphrey[1] started the Process Program at the Software Engineering Institute (SEI) in 1986, he has emphasized having an organizational focus on developing processes. He also stressed the need to have process improvement champions at all levels while making the statement, "Process improvement is not going to happen by itself." As early as 1988, when a handful of people at the SEI and I were learning about assessments from Mr. Humphrey, he would recommend to any organization that they establish a process group who would facilitate the process improvement program for that organization. Looking at CMM® for Software or CMMI® shows us that the Organizational Process Focus process area is at Maturity Level 3. Yet Mr. Humphrey recommended that an organization establish their Software/Systems Engineering Process Group (SEPG) as one of the first actions that they took even if the organization was assessed at Maturity Level 1. His thinking was that the SEPG would not only facilitate the development of the necessary processes but also serve as an example by acting or behaving at a maturity level at least one above where their organization was assessed. Thus, an organization would not only have champions who kept a constant vigil on the process improvement activities but also have champions who would serve as an example for other projects on how it should be done.

This chapter describes the organizational components necessary to establish and keep the organization on a path of continuous process improvement. It includes CMMI® process areas of Organizational Process Focus and Organizational

---

1. Watts S. Humphrey founded the Software Process Program of the Software Engineering Institute (SEI), where he is a Fellow and staff research scientist, at Carnegie Mellon University. From 1959 to 1986, he worked for IBM Corporation as the director of programming quality and process.

Process Development. It will provide a sample process improvement infrastructure and description of the roles and responsibilities that are necessary to make a process improvement initiative successful.

The description of the Organizational Process Development process area will emphasize the various components that must be in place before an organization can claim compliance to the requirements and guidance provided by this process area. It will distinguish between a product life cycle and a process description. It will clearly show the importance of establishing and enforcing tailoring guidelines for project use of organizational processes and it will show the importance of collecting, advertising, and using good examples for project uniformity and success.

Focusing your organization's process improvement efforts

One of the most important activities that the process group has is to determine the strengths, weaknesses, and improvement opportunities for the organization's processes. This is normally carried out relative to a process standard such as CMMI®. It is important to remember that the organization's vision and business objectives must be supported by the process improvement effort. In all of my experience, it is rare that a process improvement initiative will be kept going and be successful if it is not directly linked to the vision and business objectives set by the senior management team. It is wise to consider the issues related to finance, quality, human resources, and marketing for process improvement and not just technology.

It is also important to identify the process performance objectives such as time to market and product and service quality when putting together a process improvement initiative for your organization. Other commonly used process performance objectives include cycle time, defect escape rates, and productivity.

What processes currently exist?

In order to focus the organization's process improvement efforts, it is necessary to look at what currently exists and within what constraints the organization must work and to examine other input that can provide valuable process improvement hints and suggestions. To start the process, process group members may choose to identify the policies and standards applicable to the organization's process. They may also examine relevant process standards and models for good and best practices.

To further understand and define or refine the characteristics of the organization's processes, the process group can evaluate processes that are currently being used in the organization, process and product standards imposed by the organization, and process standards and product standards imposed by customers/end users.

Assessment or appraisal

A classic approach to determining the organization's process capabilities is to conduct an assessment or appraisal. Process appraisals normally result in:

▸ Strengths and weaknesses of the organization's processes;

▸ Improvement recommendations for the organization's processes;

▸ Understanding of the business consequences from following or not following organizational processes.

Other process improvement sources

While the assessment is a very effective mechanism to determine the organization's process capabilities and make process improvements as necessary, there are other candidate process improvement sources that can offer insight into the organization and project's processes. Some of these sources include:

▸ Measurement and analysis of the processes;

▸ Effectiveness and suitability of deployed processes;

▸ Lessons learned from tailoring the organization's set of standard processes;

▸ Lessons learned from process implementation;

▸ Process improvement proposals;

▸ Senior management inputs;

▸ Peer review results and defect trends;

▸ Testing results;

▸ Trouble reports;

▸ Results of other organizational initiatives.

Realizing a successful process improvement program requires the cooperation and coordination of all levels of management and practitioners. Process improvement for any organization can never be the sole responsibility of the process group. Figure 15.1 illustrates a sample process improvement infrastructure. A description of the components of that infrastructure follows.

Sample improvement infrastructure

The sample improvement infrastructure shown in Figure 15.1 is based on the original Software Engineering Process Organization developed in 1988 by Westinghouse Electronic Systems Group (ESG) in Baltimore, Maryland. Westinghouse ESG established the steering committee, the working groups, and the SEPG. This model was subsequently adopted by the Software Engineering Institute and published in [1].

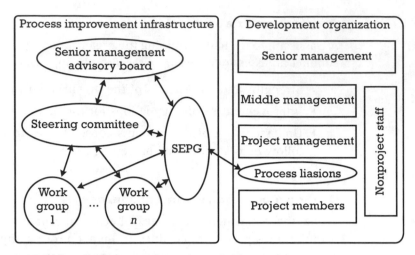

Figure 15.1   Sample process improvement infrastructure.

The sample improvement infrastructure is shown in Figure 15.1 on the left side of the diagram. The right side of the diagram is composed of members from the organization represented.

This, in no way, indicates that an organization needs to reorganize itself in order to engage in process improvement. It merely illustrates, as stated earlier, that process improvement requires the support of all levels of management and the practitioners. Senior managers, middle managers, project leaders, and practitioners must be committed and visibly participating to make process improvement work.

Senior management advisory board

A senior management advisory board is necessary to initially and then continuously share the organization or business unit's vision and business objectives. This ensures that the process improvement effort supports that vision and provides measurable improvements to support the business objectives. It is vital for the success of the process improvement effort for each person in the organization to be able to relate the changes they see in their immediate environment and daily work to the broader goals of the organization. People at all levels like to know that what they are doing is supporting the overall health of the organization. They want to be a part of success. They are not happy with starting projects then stopping them with no apparent reason.

Understanding the vision and business objectives helps all individuals to realize the value of their individual efforts and the value of the process improvement effort. Only visible senior management support can provide that guidance. Senior management must demonstrate regular and consistent visible support for specific change actions and for continuous process improvement in general. Senior management needs to proactively let the organization know why the process improvement initiative is indeed one of the organization's most important projects and communicate to the organization why the proposed changes are needed.

Last but not least, senior management needs to ensure that the necessary resources for the process improvement initiative are available in a timely manner. This does not mean that the senior management team must approve and support everything required for improvement at one time.

Improvement efforts like any other project have to be prioritized and have to support the organization to stay in business so that they can improve and become more competitive in the future. Process improvement efforts, however, do require:

> Dedicated people for the steering committee, working groups, and the SEPG;

> Training courses at many levels;

> Computers;

> Databases;

> Internal and external consultants;

> Hand-holding support for the projects as they strive to accomplish their project objectives while incorporating new processes and procedures to accomplish those tasks.

Virtually all of the process improvement success stories have a strong senior management involvement. Dr. Edwards Deming stated that the process belonged to the senior management. It is the senior management that must be willing to support the process improvement initiative or it will flounder and possibly die altogether. That was true 50 years ago and it remains true today.

The proposed membership of the senior management advisory board is:

> Organization senior manager and/or product line manager;

> Key line managers;

> Key product managers;

> Quality director;

> Chief financial officer;

> Marketing director;

> Software process manager (also on steering committee).

Steering committee

Without senior management involvement, the process improvement initiative may flounder and not be oriented toward supporting the organization's business objectives. Without middle management involvement, the critical process improvement resources and other individuals that are needed to work on specific focus area improvements will probably not be made available. Middle management must be on board to ensure that the right people are provided where they are needed for as long as they are needed.

Westinghouse Electronics Group recognized the critical role that middle managers play in process improvement in 1988 and created the concept of a steering committee. The steering committee became the management implementation mechanism representing senior management on a daily basis.

Middle managers constantly receive pressure from above to guide projects under their authority to completion on time, within budget, and with the promised functionality or better. Middle managers also receive constant pressure from below as the software developers are continually asking for new state-of-the-art software tools including computers, databases, languages, file servers, workstations, and Web-enabled applications. Each request comes with a high price tag but with the promise that the productivity may be increased by 10%, 15%, or even 25%.

Many middle managers have climbed the corporate ladder by being good hardware engineers. Yet suddenly they find themselves managing projects where 80% of the project is software. They are being asked to make decisions for which most of them have little or no training or experience. The process improvement initiative can be invaluable because it can give control back to middle managers so that they are in a position to make informed risk management decisions based on data and not emotion.

Too many organizations allocate expendable resources to SEPGs and Working Groups. Individuals with software/systems experience and product line knowledge are required for a truly successful process improvement initiative.

If individuals are to devote 20% of their time to a process improvement working group, that 20% must be made as important to them as the 80% they are being asked to devote to project work. They must be evaluated for their contributions to the process improvement effort in the same manner they are evaluated for their development efforts. In addition, if an individual is asked to devote 20% of his or her time to process improvement, this must not be 20% above the 120% that he or she are already working. It is middle management who owns these resources and who must balance their work to accomplish business goals set by the senior management team. It is *middle management* who must protect the time allocated and spent on the working groups, or the entire process improvement effort will be in danger from day one.

The steering committee is normally involved in the following activities:

▶ Ensuring that the software process improvement activities are in line with the vision and business objectives that have been established by the senior management advisory board:

  ▸ Reviewing the proposed budget for the improvement effort;

  ▸ Making recommendations to the senior management advisory board regarding program direction, budget, and program risks.

> ‣ Ensuring that the necessary resources for the working groups and SEPG are available in a timely fashion:
>
>   › Establishing the working groups to concentrate on prioritized focus areas (e.g., commitment process, estimation procedures, testing methods);
>
>   › Supporting, where needed, negotiations for people's dedicated time to the process improvement effort.
>
> ‣ Conducting process improvement program oversight reviews on a periodic basis (recommended once per month):
>
>   › Ensuring that software process improvement activities progress are in line with documented budgets and plans;
>
>   › Performing reviews and approval of working group deliverables.
>
> ‣ Providing visible support for the SEPG and working groups.

The proposed membership of the steering committee is:

‣ Functional managers;

‣ Project managers;

‣ Chief systems engineers;

‣ SQA manager;

‣ HQA manager;

‣ Software process manager;

It is appropriate to make the case at this time for the middle manager to be considered the *process owner*. Process owners are often associated with those individuals who have the most technical expertise and interest to lead a working group or process action team. However, as argued earlier, it is the middle managers who truly own the resources that must make the project successful and the process improvement efforts to happen. By making the middle managers the process owners, the senior manager is ensured that his or her vision and business objectives are being considered for each piece of the process improvement effort. Furthermore, it becomes the middle managers' responsibility to ensure that the working groups have the proper resources, tools, and guidance to develop new processes or revise existing ones and get them deployed on the projects. The middle managers do not have to have responsibility to actually do the process development work, but to work with the working group that is taking care of improving the process areas they are responsible for as a sponsor. This means that the middle managers must communicate with the SEPG and the working group and understand the issues being faced along with the progress and future activities. They can then offer guidance to the working groups from their interaction with the senior manager and can report accurate process improvement progress to the senior manager. In every instance from my experience, when the middle managers have been made the process owners, the organizational process improvement initiative has had measurable success.

Software/systems engineering process group (SEPG)

Software/systems engineering process group, process action group, process group, process improvement group, or whatever name it is referred to throughout the world, is a focal group for action planning, process improvement, technology insertion, training, and awareness and expectation setting. SEPGs are frequently viewed as a channel for institutionalizing the organization's knowledge of process methods, practices, and technology. SEPGs are the organization's *champion of change* and its members are *change agents*. An SEPG must facilitate the process improvement efforts at the organization, project, and individual levels.

What does the SEPG have to know? Collectively the members of the SEPG need to be able to demonstrate their ability to manage, develop, coach, and guide process improvement initiatives and their accompanying cultural changes. First and foremost, they need to understand senior management's vision and the organization's business objectives to be able to efficiently and effectively guide the process improvement effort. Without this explicit knowledge the organization's process improvement effort may demonstrate compliance to a model such as CMMI® but may not be supportive of the organization's business needs at all.

SEPG members must have a solid engineering background. They must have a general knowledge of the organization's application domains and knowledge of modern software/systems engineering techniques and methods. They must be up-to-date on the accepted software/systems engineering standards (DoD, MoD, IEEE, ISO, ESA, NASA, and so forth). They must also have a good understanding of the quality management functions such as quality assurance and Configuration Management. They must be respected by the managers and product engineers alike. They must have a strong knowledge and good experience in project management and a working knowledge of metrics to help the project managers better manage and control their projects.

SEPG members must be people-oriented with superior communication skills and willing to perform most of their work in the labs of the product developers who need their support to understand just how the process improvement ideas fit into their daily lives. They should always be ready to provide hand-holding support for the managers and practitioners on the various projects where the process ideas are being introduced.

While SEPG members must have the technical background to maintain credibility with the product developers, they must also be knowledgeable in the organizational development skills as well (i.e., managing technological change, team building, collaborative consulting) to effect successful technology transition.

The SEPG should strive to show by example how process improvement should be accomplished: walk the talk.

While the many tasks attributed to the SEPG are important ones for its members, it must be stressed that the job of the SEPG is to be the champion of the process improvement effort. The SEPG is expected to facilitate the process of change, *not be responsible* for the process change. SEPG responsibilities include but are not limited to:

- Coordinating the process improvement initiative up, down, and across the organization:
  - Participating in the senior management advisory board reviews;
  - Participating in the steering committee reviews;
  - Facilitating the activities of the working groups, which means staying on top of what is going on, what difficulties are being encountered, and what successes are being realized;
  - Promoting technical awareness and education about process improvement—this is a continuous job for the SEPG—the process liaisons help the success of this function.
- Managing/facilitating the process improvement initiative:
  - Facilitating the definition/improvement of the technical and managerial processes, methods, techniques, and tools for developing and maintaining products and product components;
  - Assisting in the evaluation of new tools and techniques based on their understanding of the existing processes;
  - Facilitating the definition and maintenance of organization policies and standards for processes and products;
  - Discovering good practices, getting them adapted for general use on the projects throughout the organization, and baselining them as best practices;
  - Overseeing and facilitating pilot projects and implementation of improvements into the projects and across the organization.
  - Directing the definition of process metrics, initiating the collection of data, and assisting the working groups and projects in the analysis and use of the resulting information.
- Ensuring that the processes are living:
  - Maintaining a dialogue with project personnel regarding the application and performance of developing processes:
    - Sharing good ideas from other parts of the organization;
    - Listening to issues/ideas from the practitioners.
  - Initiating periodic process improvement progress checks and reassessments;
  - Initiating a practitioner-driven review of specific processes.
- Maintaining a process asset library of product and product component process assets:

> • Overseeing the process asset library for product and process assets used across the organization;
> • Facilitating the development and retention of tailoring guidelines for specific use of the assets in the process asset library.

An SEPG must have some full-time members. Watts Humphrey suggested that 1–3% of the product development and maintenance budget should be devoted to the SEPG. It is certain that one SEPG member is not enough. The SEPG may have part-time members as well, but it should be recognized that less than 50% of a person's time will not be very effective.

The proposed membership of the SEPG is:

- Process improvement manager (SEPG leader);
- Process champions:
  - Motivated and respected;
  - Knowledgeable;
  - Team players.
- Associate members who may be drawn from pilot projects and/or product segments;
- Associate members who may represent function, product line, or other affected organizational entities.

Process improvement manager

Each process improvement infrastructure should have an identified process improvement manager. This individual is a senior person with most of the attributes listed in the section on what SEPG members should know. The process improvement manager is responsible for coordinating all of the process improvement activities throughout the organization. He or she serves as the link among the senior management advisory board, the steering committee, and the SEPG. The process improvement manager serves as the link between the process improvement initiative and the organization's line, function, and project management.

Working groups

Working groups or process action teams or cluster teams are the most common mechanism used for the development and/or revision of processes that will be piloted on selected projects and eventually implemented throughout the organization. Working group members may be involved in the development of the action plan for a particular focus area, may be involved in supporting the implementation of a process or procedure on a project or projects, or both. Some working group members are required to be committed long term to ensure continuity. Working group members may be involved with the action planning up to 100% of the time but are normally involved with the subsequent process development, process revision, problem fixing, and so forth, and the associated implementation and support is involved 20% of the time. SEPG members often facilitate multiple working groups and coordinate the activities of the working groups to avoid duplication of effort.

Working group members are interested in contributing to the improvement of a particular focus area and usually have some background/experience in that focus area. Working group members are involved with supporting process improvement in a focus area for at least 9 months but normally rotate out after 1.5 years. Examples of activities that working groups take on are:

- Developing the action plan for a specific focus area;
- Developing new or improved processes, procedures, guidelines, templates, and so forth based on a formally documented and approved plan;
- Identifying, screening, and evaluating technologies based on the organization and project's processes;
- Suggesting and/or developing training plans;
- Supporting the piloting of those processes;
- Evaluating the pilot performance and revising the processes as necessary;
- Reporting process improvement progress to the steering committee;
- Sharing lessons learned on the working group with other working groups and project members;
- Supporting the institutionalizing of the tested and approved processes.

The proposed membership of the working groups is:

- Working group leader (high percentage effort: ≥ 50%);
- Core members (high effort: 40–50%);
- SEPG representative (moderate to high effort: ≥ 30%);
- QA representative (low to moderate effort: 20%);
- Members (low to moderate effort: 20%);
- Internal consultants (low effort: 10%);
- Reviewers (low effort: 5%).

Process liaisons

Process liaisons were also added along with the senior management advisory board in 1993 to the sample improvement infrastructure that was presented to organizations as a guide. The concept of process liaisons is very simple. Usually on a project, there is at least one person who is quality minded or process improvement minded. While this person may not be ready to change his or her career and join the SEPG full-time, he or she is probably interested in process improvement and willing to spend about 5% of the time keeping up with the process improvement progress and sharing process improvement news with the other project members. Process liaisons can help transition the process improvement ideas into their projects.

General activities for process liaisons should include the following:

- Acting as the point of contact between the process improvement organization and the project practitioners:
  - Keeping project members informed of software process improvement activities;
  - Providing input to the SEPG/working groups regarding good practices being performed on the project and possible candidates for working group involvement;
  - Serving as the process improvement advocate for the project.
- Providing information and feedback to the SEPG and working groups regarding:
  - Issues impacting development performance;
  - Use of new processes in the project.

Establishing, maintaining, and implementing action plans

Process action plans are detailed implementation plans. These plans differ from the overall organizational process improvement plan. They are normally focused on improving processes that belong to one or more related process areas. These process action plans normally address weaknesses revealed by appraisals or one of the other sources of process improvement considerations.

Figure 15.2, taken from the Kasse Initiatives Action Focused Assessment method, is a generic working group model (GWGM) that can be used to establish, maintain, and implement action plans. The following steps provide the details behind the flowchart in the figure.

Provide management direction   Understand the vision, business objectives, quality goals, and priorities from the senior management team. Ensure that the process improvement effort is in line with the vision and business objectives of the organization. Management direction and authority are necessary to ensure that allocated resources are protected and unforeseen obstacles are addressed appropriately. Identify the members of the steering committee and from which organizational departments they should come. Create the steering committee to:

- Review/approve process improvement priorities;
- Conduct monthly process improvement progress checks with the SEPG and the working group chairpersons;

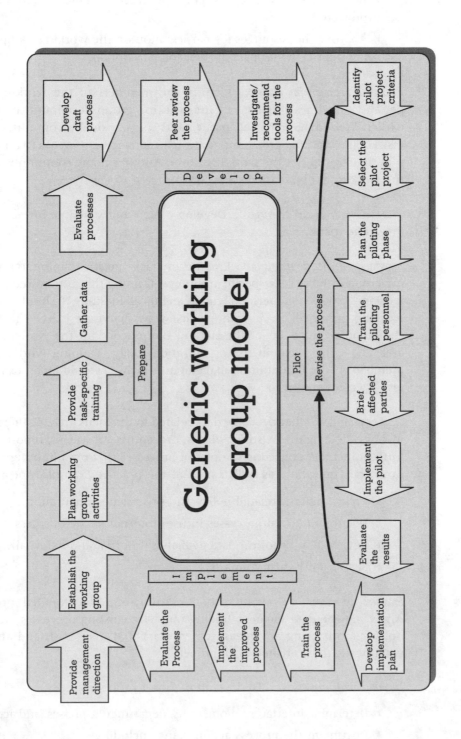

Figure 15.2 The GWGM.

  ‣ Report progress to the senior management advisory board;

  ‣ Ensure that resources assigned to process improvement tasks are protected;

  ‣ Approve the resources for participation on the working groups, making their activities part of their job description.

Establish the working group   Identify the members of the working group per the guidelines provided in the working group description mentioned earlier. This implies that all participants are personally committed to the tasks of the working group and that their management agrees to and schedules time to support the working group. Another name commonly used for the working group is the process action team (PAT).

Plan working group activities   Develop a plan and schedule for each working group focus area.

Provide task-specific training   Provide any task-specific training to the working group or PAT. Task-specific training is training that is required to put all working group members on equal technical footing. It should help the working group fill in any knowledge gaps that may exist. The training should be an overview of the state of the practice for the particular focus area and what exists in the organization today. Training working group members in Configuration Management functions would be an example of task-specific training.

Gather data   Gather available data related to the focus area. Gathering data means collecting the existing policies, procedures, processes, reports, and so forth. It includes collecting samples of processes that exist in other business units or organizations as well as state-of-the-practice examples and articles:

  ‣ Collect all task-related policy and process documentation.

  ‣ Document actual processes in use (internal to the business unit).

  ‣ Review any historical data available (internal and external).

  ‣ Search for industry data.

Evaluate processes   Evaluate actual existing and documented processes. Analyzing the data includes finding out why existing processes are or are not used, analyzing any measurement data that may exist, and analyzing what needs to be created or improved.

Develop draft processes   To develop the draft processes:

  ‣ Determine interfaces among units, departments, phases, and activities.

  ‣ Document the process action plans, including:

    ‣ Process improvement infrastructure;

    ‣ Process improvement objectives;

- Improvements that will be covered;
- Procedures for planning and tracking progress for each process action;
- Strategies for implementing the process actions including the identification and selection of pilot projects;
- Training, mentoring, and coaching needed for the pilot project members;
- Responsibility and authority for implementing the process actions;
- Resources, schedules, and assignments for implementing the process actions;
- Evaluation criteria for successful implementation of the process actions;
- Methods for determining the effectiveness of the process actions;
- Risks associated with the process action plans.
- Develop guidelines for tailoring to project-specific needs.
- Identify the means for measuring the effectiveness.

Peer review the processes   To peer review the processes:

- Submit the process for peer review (all affected parties).
- Revise the process if necessary.
- Submit the revised process to the steering committee for approval.

Investigate/recommend tools for the process   To investigate/recommend tools for the process:

- Investigate tools in use or available within the unit/organization/world.
- Match tool functionality to the process.

Implementing process actions   This is project management for the process action plans including:

- Negotiating commitments among the process action team members;
- Coordinating with other process action teams;
- Tracking progress on action plan implementation;
- Monitoring progress and results of the process actions;
- Communicating status, activities, plans, and results of the process action plan implementation;
- Comparing the results against the organization's process improvement objectives;
- Using pilot projects to test selected improvements.

Identify pilot project criteria   Establish and maintain pilot project selection criteria. The criteria should include:

- Criticality to the organization (it is OK for the project to be important to the organization's business success);
- Life-cycle phase;
- Willingness of the project manager to support the new and/or revised processes;
- Attitude of the project team towards process improvement;
- Stress on the project;
- Ability of the SEPG and quality management group to support the pilot project.

Select the pilot project   The use of pilots should be institutionalized within the organization. The use of pilots minimizes the widespread impact to people and projects throughout the organization while the process is exercised and real-world problems are identified and handled. Pilot projects were chosen because they were not in the main stream of the organization and were thought to be safe. I recommend that a project be identified as a pilot if it is critical to the success of the organization and intervention along with new or revised processes might make a measurable difference for that project.

Plan the piloting phase   Create implementation plans for each pilot project that the process actions are tested on. An implementation plan is necessary to gain the commitment of the pilot project leader and practitioners to the process, to establish the contract for SEPG/WG support to the pilot project, and to provide a basis for measuring and verifying the performance of the process.

- Determine how to introduce the new methods/procedures.
- Determine success criteria.
- Establish the contract within the pilot implementation plan.

Train the piloting personnel   Train the pilot project members and others who interface with that project in the new process. This step prepares pilot practitioners to perform the activity. Training also involves teaching practitioners how to use any tools built or purchased to support the process.

Brief affected parties   While many other groups internal and external to the organization may have requested or even demanded change, these same groups may not react well to pilot projects actually exhibiting different behavior. It is often necessary to brief other relevant stakeholders or affected parties to set their expectations during the time they interact with the pilot project.

Implement the pilot   Implement the process actions on the designated projects and record measurement data.

Evaluate the results   Evaluate the results and process performance data based on implementing the new or revised processes on the pilot project(s):

- Collect process performance data.

- Compare the performance data to the established evaluation criteria.

- Get feedback from the pilot project participants.

- Brief all participants on pilot results.

Revise processes   Revise processes based on pilot results:

- Modify the process action plan if necessary.

- Repilot, reevaluate, revise, and repilot until readiness for full implementation is determined.

Develop implementation plan   Develop the implementation plan for expanding the process improvement throughout the entire organization. Even when the pilot project(s) have been successful, a plan still needs to be developed for implementing the improved processes throughout the entire organization. The broadening approach may have to be project by project.

Train the processes   Provide training, mentoring, and appropriate coaching to all of the other projects in the organization in support of full-scale use of the piloted processes.

Implement the improved process   To implement into full-scale use:

- Draft and publish a policy for the application of the process actions.

- Provide general training in each approved process action.

- Ensure that all support mechanisms including tools are in place and functioning.

- Conduct quality assurance audits on process compliance.

Evaluate the processes   Monitor, evaluate, and improve processes. Process improvement is not a monotonically increasing function. Even if a pilot project achieved success and the organization appeared as if it were accepting of the new processes, progress could be slowed down, start to regress, or even stopped entirely.

It is important to remember that continuous process improvement means looking at existing processes to see if they need further support to keep them living as well as working on getting new ones implemented and institutionalized:

- Processes deteriorate without continuing emphasis/support.

- Environments change and processes must evolve with them.

Incorporating lessons learned

Of course, process improvement is continuous and the intent is not just to get things implemented into full scale use but to conduct periodic reviews of the effectiveness and suitability of the organization's set of standard processes and related process assets, obtain feedback, and derive lessons learned from defining, piloting, implementing, and deploying the process assets. An important step in the maturity of any organization is to set up a visible and easy-to-use mechanism for handling process improvement proposals similar to the setup for handling trouble reports. This signals that the process improvement effort is really one of the most important projects in the organization, and ineffective processes are going to be analyzed and improved as if they were a problem report against a fielded product.

Communicate status and results of process improvement activities

It is important to not only achieve process improvement success but also to communicate that success on a regular basis through all multiple media mechanisms available. Publish achievements of culture change and business objectives. Let everyone know the successes that have been achieved, no matter how small!

Continue to improve

Process improvement is not a monotonically increasing function. Even if a pilot project achieved success and the organization appeared as if it were accepting of the new processes, progress could be slowed down, start to regress, or even stopped entirely. It is important to remember that continuous process improvement means looking at existing processes to see if they need further support to keep them living as well as working on getting new ones implemented and institutionalized. Processes deteriorate without continuing emphasis and support. Environments change and processes must evolve with them.

Process assets

According to CMMI®, the purpose of the Organizational Process Definition process area is to establish and maintain a usable set of organizational process assets. An asset is defined to be "an item of value," according to *Merriam-Webster's Collegiate Dictionary*. A process asset, then, is anything of value that helps to implement the practices of a given process area and achieve its goals. Organizational process assets are artifacts that help describe, implement, and improve processes such as:

> ‣ Policies;
> ‣ Process descriptions;

> ▸ Templates;
> ▸ Measurements;
> ▸ Process implementation support tools.

The term *process assets* also indicates that these artifacts are developed or acquired to meet the business objectives of the organization and are not just developed to satisfy an audit and then become shelfware. They should represent an investment by the organization that is expected to provide current and future business value.

CMM® for Software referred to the organization's standard software process (OSSP). For many organizations, this was interpreted to mean that an organization had to have only one standard process that was applicable to all of the projects that were ongoing or were to be implemented throughout the organization. This was never the intent of the authors of CMM® for Software and certainly would not work in organizations with multiple product lines or multiple systems needs. CMMI® indicates that an organization needs to establish and maintain the organization's set of standard processes. The operative word in CMMI® definition is *set*. The set of standard processes should be able to be tailored for each of the organization's business areas or product lines. The organization's set of standard processes refers to the standard processes established at the organizational level and typically includes technical, management, administrative, support, and organizational processes. Multiple standard processes may be needed to address the needs of different application domains, life-cycle models, methodologies, and tools.

It is my opinion that the name itself, Organizational Process Definition, is one of the most misleading process area names and has been since the original CMM® for Software was released. For many individuals, *process definition* seems to connote software or hardware methodology or a Systems Development Lifecycle (SDLC) document. While there is that aspect that is described in the Process Definition process area, there is much more to understand, implement, and take advantage of when the Process Definition process area is implemented completely and correctly. Figure 15.3 provides a graphical view of the components that make up the description of the Process Definition process area. We will examine the components in more detail.

Process asset library

The organization's process asset library is a collection of items maintained at the organizational level for use by the people and projects within the organization. This collection of items includes descriptions of processes and process elements, descriptions of life-cycle models, process tailoring guidelines, and process-related documentation and data.

Examples of these process asset library items include:

> ▸ Organizational policies;

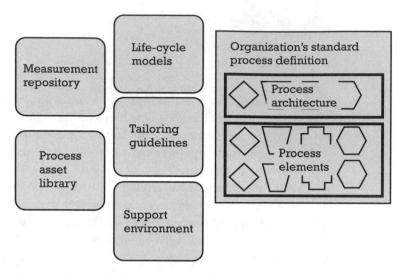

Figure 15.3 Organization's process assets.

- Projects' defined standards and procedures;
- Projects' development plans;
- Quality assurance and Configuration Management plans;
- Projects' measurement plans;
- Projects' process training materials;
- Checklists and templates;
- Lessons learned reports.

Process elements

A process element is the fundamental (primitive or atomic) unit of process definition. Process elements may be templates, fragments to be completed, and abstractions to be refined, or complete descriptions to be tailored or used as is. The elements must be described in sufficient detail such that the process can be consistently performed by appropriately trained and skilled people.

Process elements can be described by critical attributes which include:

- Process roles;
- Applicable process and product standards;
- Applicable procedures, methods, tools, and resources;
- Process performance objectives;
- Entry criteria;
- Inputs;
- Tasks;
- Product and process measures to be collected and used;

> ▸ Verification points (e.g., work product inspections);

> ▸ Outputs;

> ▸ Interfaces;

> ▸ Exit criteria.

Process architecture

The relationships among the process elements can be described in a process architecture. Much like the product architecture or software architecture, the process architecture refers to the rules for describing those relationships, including:

> ▸ Ordering of the process elements;

> ▸ Interfaces among the process elements;

> ▸ Interfaces with external processes;

> ▸ Interdependencies among the process elements.

One of the original process architectures was built and described by Ron Radice in [2]. Its elegance was in its simplicity that allowed multiple IBM divisions make use of the common architecture and still utilize specialized process elements. See Figure 15.4.

Product life-cycle models

Life-cycle models may be used for a variety of customers and applications, as one life cycle many not be appropriate for all projects. Life cycles that are included in the process asset library must be approved for use; approved for

Family	Stage	
Requirements and planning	1.	Requirements and planning
Design	2.	Product level design
	3.	Component level design
	4.	Module level design
Implementation	5.	Code
	6.	Unit test
Testing	7.	Functional verification test
	8.	Product verification test
	9.	System verification test
Packaging and validation	10.	Package and release
	11.	Early support program
General availability	12.	General availability

Figure 15.4   Process architecture stages.

use means that the descriptions of these life-cycle models are documented, trained, supported, and maintained. This does not mean that a project cannot choose another life-cycle model if it would be more appropriate to satisfy the project's demands. What it does mean is that each project that chooses to use a nonapproved life-cycle model must be assessed for the risk involved due to the lack of organizational support and must be approved by the process improvement steering committee.

Examples of life-cycle models include:

- Waterfall;
- Overlapping waterfall;
- Evolutionary;
- Incremental;
- V-Model;
- Spiral.

The spiral model is shown in Figure 15.5.

Support environment

Parallel to the earlier discussion on life-cycle models, the organization's process assets may include state-of-the-practice tools and methods that have been chosen to be applied across the organization's projects. Examples of methods include:

- Object-oriented design;
- Web-enabled development;
- Joint application development (JAD).

Examples of tools that may be included in the support environment include:

- QSM (project management estimation tool);
- PVCS (Configuration Management tool);
- DOORS (requirements management tool).

Methods should be documented, trained, supported during real project use, and objectively evaluated. Support environment tools should be trained, coached, and supported. Use of new methods and tools on a project should be accompanied by an understanding that productivity will go down before it goes up. It is the training, coaching, and support of the methods and tools on pilot projects that reduces the risk of them being inadequately applied and producing poor results.

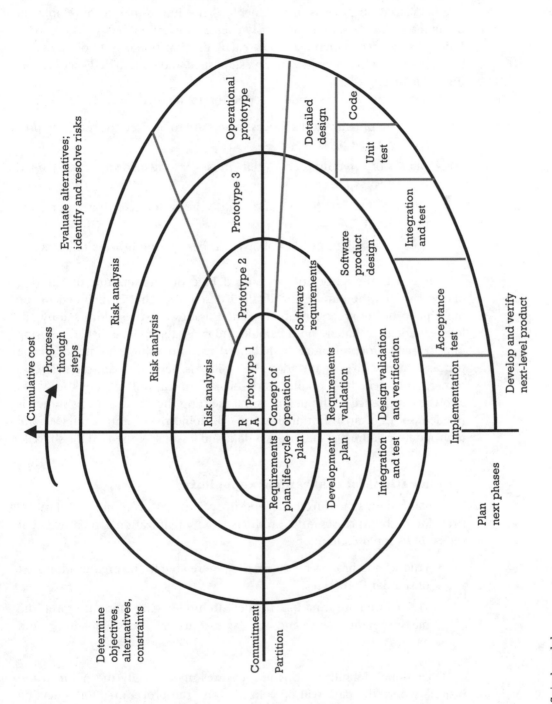

Figure 15.5 Spiral model.

Tailoring guidelines

With the variety of projects, application domains, product lines, and constraints placed on projects, it is difficult, if not impossible, to develop a set of standard processes that will satisfy each and every project with no adaptation. It is recommended that each organizational set of standard processes be complemented with an established and maintained set of tailoring guidelines.

Tailoring guidelines should describe the following:

- How the organization's process assets are to be used to create the project's defined processes;
- Mandatory requirements that must be satisfied by the defined processes;
- Options that can be exercised and criteria for selecting among the options;
- Procedures that must be followed in performing process tailoring.

There will always be the ongoing debate on the amount of tailoring allowed versus the amount of detailed description that is included in the description of the process elements. These issues must be addressed by tailoring guidelines that are both flexible and consistent. Flexibility in tailoring and defining processes must be balanced with ensuring consistency in the processes across the organization. Flexibility is needed to address the customer, costs, schedule, quality trade-offs, technical difficulty of the work, and the experience of the people implementing the process. Consistency is needed so that organizational standards, objectives, and strategies are appropriately addressed and process data and lessons learned can be shared.

Organizational measurement repository

The organization's measurement repository contains a common set of measures for both processes and products. The organization's measurement repository should contain:

- Product and process measures that are related to the organization's set of standard processes;
- The related information needed to understand and interpret the measurement data and to assess it for reasonableness and applicability.

Operational definitions for the measures must specify the point in the process where the data will be collected and the procedures for collecting valid data.

Examples of classes of commonly used measures include:

- Size of work products (lines of code, function or feature points, complexity);

 ‣ Effort and cost;

 ‣ Actual measures of size, effort, and cost;

 ‣ Quality measures;

 ‣ Work product inspection coverage;

 ‣ Test or verification (peer review) coverage;

 ‣ Reliability measures.

Summary

Process improvement requires the support of all levels of management and the practitioners. Senior managers, middle managers, project leaders, and practitioners must be committed and visibly participating to make process improvement work. The SEPG is a focal group for action planning, process improvement, technology insertion, training, and awareness and expectation setting. SEPGs are the organization's champion of change and its members are change agents. An SEPG must facilitate the process improvement efforts at the organization, project, and individual levels. Each organization must establish and maintain a usable set of organizational process assets to help implement the practices of a given process area and achieve its goals. These organizational process assets, or artifacts, are developed or acquired to meet the business objectives of the organization.

References

[1]   Software Engineering Institute, *Software Engineering Process Group Guide*, Technical Report CMU/SEI-90-TR-24, Pittsburgh, PA, September 1990.

[2]   Radice, R., "A Programming Process Architecutre," *IBM Systems Journal*, Vol. 24, No. 2, November 1985, pp. 79–90.

The Knowledge and Skills Base

As stated in CMMI®'s process area Organizational Training, the real need that every organization must address is the need to develop the knowledge and skills of all of its people so that they can perform their roles effectively and efficiently.

Organizational training focus

Organizational training programs must support the organization's strategic business objectives and the tactical training needs that are common across projects and support groups. The basic focus of the Organizational Training process area is the identification of process training needs that are primarily based on the skills that are required to perform the organization's set of standard processes that are, in turn, based on business objectives and core competencies. The knowledge and skills may be categorized as technical, organizational, or contextual. Technical knowledge and skills refers to the ability of the workforce to use the equipment, tools, materials, data, and any processes required by a project or process. Organizational knowledge and skills refers to behavior within and according to the employee's organizational structure, roles, and responsibilities and general operating principles and methods. Contextual knowledge and skills refers to self-management, communication, and interpersonal skills.

Core competencies

The focus on an organizational training program and its link to building core competencies should not be taken lightly. With increasingly complex software and hardware systems being built today, finding and keeping good people are also becoming increasingly difficult. Two managers have been quoted as saying: "The most important ingredient on this successful project

201

was having very smart people," and "The only rule I have in management is to ensure that I have good people—real good people—and that I grow good people, and that I provide an environment where good people can produce."

As previously stated, however, finding and/or growing these good people can and will be a difficult task.

Therefore, organization's need to take on a more aggressive and people-oriented approach to providing training for its workforce. First and foremost, it is imperative that the senior management team not only be able to state current business objectives, but be able to clearly state what business the organization is in. This may not be as trivial as it sounds. One definition of what business the organization is in may only result in the workforce becoming frustrated with the management team and understanding what is expected of them. Another definition of what business the organization is in may make it clear for all employees such that some will leave the organization immediately and others will increase their efforts to gain the necessary core competencies and become more valuable assets to their organization.

Once it is clearly defined what business the organization is in, the organization must identify and define the core competencies required to perform the organization's business and remain competitive. The management team and the practitioners must understand just what these core competencies are and why they are so critical. All efforts to increase the core competency of the workforce must be totally supported by management and practitioners alike. Departments that are responsible for training and career development, such as human resources, must work closely with project managers, lead engineers, quality managers, and process improvement specialists to find ways to develop and/or acquire the core competencies that support the business.

Following the definition of the core competencies, it is now appropriate and necessary for the organizational training focus to determine just what the organizational knowledge and skills base are. Personnel records and training records are input for this activity. Strategic and near-term plans must be developed to build up the necessary knowledge and skills and thus the core competencies. Career development must be planned to support the core competency development for each individual and thus for the organization. Workforce practices must be adapted to reward the knowledge and skills growth that leads to higher core competency.

Recruiters must also change their focus, looking first for candidates that either have the necessary knowledge and skills that fulfill the core competency need or a base of knowledge and skills combined with a proven ability to learn that can be used to grow the critical core competencies for the organization.

Organizational and project level training

The organization's strategic business objectives and improvement plans should be analyzed to plan for current, intermediate, and future training needs in order for the organization to remain competitive. Examples of sources of strategic training needs include:

- Organization's set of standard processes;
- Organization's strategic business plan;
- Organization's process improvement plan;
- Enterprise-level initiatives;
- Skill appraisals;
- Risk analyses.

Once the strategic training needs are captured, it must be determined what the training needs of the organization are versus the project training needs. Steps to accomplish this include:

- Identify the training needs required at the organizational level.
- Analyze the project and support groups' needs that can be most efficiently addressed organization-wide.
- Negotiate specific training needs with the various projects and support groups.
- Consider "economy of scale" at every opportunity when planning for organizational versus project-level training. Economy of scale refers to training the most people for the least amount of money by taking advantage of organizational training if it is needed by multiple projects.

Training capability

To establish the required organizational training capability, three areas must be defined:

1. Instructor or trainer's proficiency;
2. Training approach;
3. Training descriptions.

All instructors must be required to demonstrate current proficiency in the topics with which they have been identified and intend to teach. There are many approaches used to learn. It is therefore appropriate that different training approaches are developed and used, some in combination with others, to teach or train as well. Some training approaches that can be effectively used by an organization include:

- Classroom teaching;
- Computer-aided instruction;
- Guided self-study;

- Formal apprenticeship and mentoring program;
- Facilitated videos;
- Structured on-the-job training.

It is equally important that detailed outlines are provided of the training opportunities so that the organization's workforce members will know what is available. This will enable them to be able to pick and choose courses as well as other training opportunities with assurance that it will help them gain the desired knowledge and skills. Such a detailed outline may contain:

- Course abstract;
- Objectives;
- Intended audience;
- Length of the training;
- Prerequisites and preparation for participation in the training;
- Format of the training;
- Training topics;
- Criteria for determining the participant's satisfactory completion.

Training delivery

Increasing the knowledge and skills of a target group of participants is much more than assigning an instructor and telling him or her to deliver the training material. Indeed, my experience in providing quality management and process improvement training over the past 15 years points to ensuring that guidelines and expectations are clearly set and then reset again. Participants should be more carefully selected through documented procedures and checklists rather than just determining who needs training hours logged and who is available.

A starter-kit list of participant selection guidelines is shown here:

- Do they have the prerequisite background?
- Do they have the skills and abilities to perform their roles?
- Is there a need for cross-discipline technical and management training?
- Do the managers need training for their level as well?
- Is there a need for training in basic engineering principles?
- Is there a need for training in the project support functions like quality assurance or Configuration Management?
- Is there a core competency that needs to be built?

In addition to properly screening the participants, it is important to plan for each training session, including the time each participant must have to take advantage of the learning opportunity. Nonstop interruptions, daily crises to be resolved, and electronic leashes (mobile phones) are not conducive to learning. It is also critical to choose experienced instructors who not only can present the material but can also speak from their experiences in order to enhance the value of the material.

Effectiveness of the training

Most organizations hand out a participant evaluation form. They ask that it be filled it out at the end of the course in order to determine its effectiveness and that of the instructor. Personal experience has shown that this offers little insight into the "true" effectiveness of the training or, more importantly, the knowledge and skills gain that is the objective of the training anyway. Following the lead and examples of Tom Gilb [1], a quantitatively measurable effectiveness-of-training definition is offered here:

▸ Experience and knowledge of the participants prior to the training;

▸ Preparation by the participants prior to the training;

▸ Expectations of the participants (overview course or in-depth study of a subject compared to the course objectives);

▸ Training materials;

▸ Experience and knowledge of the instructor;

▸ Ability of the instructor to train adults;

▸ Ability of the instructor to add value to the materials from his or her experience;

▸ Time after the training that the participant has an opportunity to put the training concepts to use;

▸ Mentoring and coaching that the participant has available following the training;

▸ Management support that the participant has following the training to attempt to use the new concepts he or she was taught;

▸ Whether or not training on a subject was part of the participant's job.

Training, mentoring, and coaching

The gaining of knowledge and skills leading to increased core competencies requires an approach that is focused on successful technology transfer. This may be accomplished by:

▸ Providing *training* in order to convey technical and organizational change concepts to individuals and groups who need to have an in-depth knowledge of the topics. Training should not be regarded or used to transfer years of experience to the participants.

- Providing *mentoring* in order to share with a select group of individuals the psychology and philosophy behind the concepts of training, processes, procedures, guidelines, templates, and so forth. Mentoring sessions are with an expert and up to four mentorees. Experiences and war stories are shared in order to bring about a sense of reality and understanding for those who are being mentored.

- For many companies, training is really reduced to *on-the-job training*. This usually translates into trial by fire. The next step is providing *coaching* of individuals and small groups while they are working on the project so that they can see the practicality of the ideas. Organizational experts may provide such coaching in one of three consulting modes:

  - *Expert:* The consultant leads the development of a plan or leads the peer review or other artifact with minimal input from the project manager or members.

  - *Collaborative:* The consultant and the client own 50% each of the problem to be solved. This assumes a certain level of knowledge on the part of the client's personnel.

  - *Observer:* The consultant basically reviews work that has been done and provides direction and/or guidance on implementation.

If organizations are to succeed in the face of increasingly complex tasks that demand large amounts of good people, they must view their people as critical corporate assets. The following set of questions should be used in an organizational survey to determine if the workforce believes they are viewed as critical corporate assets or not.

Am I considered a critical corporate asset?

To help you determine if you are considered a corporate asset in your own organization, try answering the following questions:

1. What is your educational background?

2. What job experience do you have that helps you do your current job?

3. Do you know what the organization's business is and what core competencies are required to support that business?

4. Do you have the skills you need to do your job?

5. What training have you received in the past year related to your current job?

6. What mentoring have you received in the past year related to your current job?

7. What coaching have you received in the past year related to your current job?

8. Are you able to conduct self-study?

9. How do you respond to classroom training?

10. How well do you absorb training on the job?

11. What training related to the management of people has your manager or supervisor had in the past year?

12. How would you rate your manager's people skills? (Circle one.)

    a. Does not care about people;

    b. Shows some care, but not much and not often;

    c. Tries to incorporate concern for people in everyday management;

    d. Balances focus on people and technical tasks;

    e. Is a real people person.

13. Do you feel you have an equal chance to get promotions in your application areas?

14. Are there opportunities for you to test your skills in other areas?

15. Do you feel you are adequately compensated at present?

16. Do you think your organization's overall compensation plan is acceptable? Why or why not?

17. Do you think your actions are aligned with the direction in which your organization is going?

18. Do you believe the others in the organization are aligned with the direction in which your organization is going?

19. Do you feel like you have grown technically and emotionally since you have joined the organization?

20. Is your career development path defined and in line with the organization's competency needs?

21. How long have you been with this organization?

22. How long were you with the organization in your previous job?

23. What motivated you to stay or leave?

24. Are you planning on a long-term relationship with this organization?

25. Do most people and most projects in the organization have the capability to deliver high quality software?

26. What motivates you to enjoy working for a organization and stay with that organization?

27. Is the organization prepared to hire talented people as well as help them grow internally?

28. Is your organization prepared or preparing for future competition?

29. Are people in your organization considered human capital and treated as corporate assets?

Summary

To really treat people like critical corporate assets, organizations must minimally do the following:

- Clearly understand, define, and communicate what business the organization is in.

- Identify and define what core competencies are needed to support the organization's business.

- Identify the knowledge and skills necessary to be considered competent in the core competencies.

- Determine the knowledge and skill levels of the people for each department throughout the organization.

- Set up training, mentoring, and coaching programs for the employees in the organization's core competencies.

- Assist employees in their career development planning in order to enhance their capability to perform their assigned tasks and responsibilities along the identified core competencies.

- Hire new employees based on how well their background matches the core competencies and how well their knowledge and skills complement the knowledge and skills base that already exists in the organization or project.

- Provide incentives in the form of promotions, money, time off, and so forth based on an employee's ability to grow in the organization's core competencies while producing high quality processes and products.

- Coordinate all of the workforce activities with the current and future business needs.

- Align the motivation and growth of the people with that of the organization.

The bottom line is that people count. Too often people are viewed as commodities. They are, in fact, the most important assets of a corporation. Their knowledge, ability to grow, and belief in the honesty and integrity of the organization are invaluable. Getting the maximum output from employees means investing the maximum in their potential and affording them opportunities for growth.

Reference

[1] Gilb, T., *Principles of Software Engineering Management*, Reading, MA: Addison-Wesley, 1988.

Integrated Teams

An integrated team, also known as an integrated product team, is composed of members who are collectively responsible for delivering the work product. Team members include empowered representatives from both the technical disciplines and business functional organizations involved with the product and have a stake in the success of the work products produced. Within defined boundaries, these representatives have decision-making authority and the responsibility to act for their representative organizations. These integrated teams may be viewed as a microversion of the company or business unit itself.

This chapter describes the conditions under which integrated teams are considered, built, and managed. It includes CMMI® process areas of Integrated Project Management, Integrated Teams, and Organizational Environment for Integration.

The concept of the integrated team

Establishing self-managed and empowered teams, whose members are collectively responsible for delivering the work product in order to support clear business objectives, could be equivalent to achieving CMMI® "Maturity Level 3.5." Integrated product teams are only established to satisfy specific business objectives that the project manager or higher-level managers of the organization believe cannot be reached without the skills and abilities of a special group of people. These special people are to be provided with the necessary tools, equipment, and training that may not normally be provided for standard project members. They should be highly skilled in their own disciplines or functions and have demonstrated the ability to learn. They have demonstrated the ability to get along with and work cooperatively with others. These integrated team members do not have to be solicited to share their skills. They will do whenever the integrated team needs them.

The concept of integrated team is not the same as a project team as it is normally defined at CMMI® Maturity Level 2 or even Integrated Project Management at CMMI® Maturity Level 3. It is not a concentration on team-building skills, although those skills may certainly be taught. It is not related to the team software process, although again those skills may be taught as part of the integrated team scope. An integrated team may consist of the entire project but more often is a subset of the project. Integrated teams are more like Special Forces units that are brought together at considerable expense, are highly trained, and are asked to perform specific tasks with significantly higher expected results. To decide to put such an integrated team together requires understanding the business objectives and determining if the effort will be cost-effective.

We will now examine some of the requirements brought out in CMMI® with respect to integrated teams.

Shared vision

The most important characteristic of having successful integrated product teams is to establish and maintain the organization's shared vision. A "shared vision" is a common understanding of guiding principles including mission, objectives, expected behavior, values, and final outcomes that are developed and used by the organization, project, or integrated team.

The purpose of creating a shared vision at any level in the organization is to achieve a unity of purpose. The value of a shared vision is that people understand and can adopt its principles to guide their actions and decisions. Shared visions help team members to focus on the end state while still allowing room for personal and team innovation, creativity, and enthusiasm.

The shared vision of a project's integrated team should be consistent with the shared vision of the project, which in turn must be consistent with the shared vision of the organization as illustrated in Figure 17.1. It is important that the individual's vision be aligned as well.

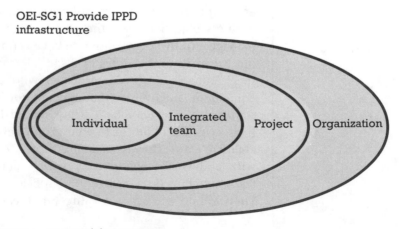

Figure 17.1   Shared vision context.

Organizational environment for integration

Along with the shared vision, successful integrated teams will have organizational environments established for them to promote the highest possible productivity, quality products, and services. The organization's set of standard processes and organizational process assets need to be augmented to support the integrated teaming concepts.

Integrated work environment

In addition, an integrated work environment must be established and maintained according to the needs of the integrated team. The integrated work environment includes the physical infrastructure such as facilities, tools, and equipment to allow the integrated team to perform their jobs effectively.

Integrated work environments are and should be viewed as capital assets that:

- Are often expensive;
- Have unique implementations;
- Are irreversible—their implementation can destroy or make unusable the assets being replaced;
- When modified can disrupt ongoing activities.

Integrated work environments must be evaluated to determine if the performance improvements are worth the costs and risks; hence, the reference to the business objectives stressed earlier.

Examples of integrated work environment technologies, tools, and resources include:

- Computing resources;
- Software productivity tools;
- Communication systems, tools, and resources;
- Engineering or simulation tools;
- Proprietary engineering tools;
- Prototyping or production equipment.

Examples of communication tools include meeting rooms, e-mail, Web sites, and video teleconferencing capabilities.

Integrative leadership and interpersonal skills

Managing integrated teams demands a different view of product development and requires integrative leadership and interpersonal skills beyond those typically found in traditional environments where people tend to work alone. Some of those skills were mentioned earlier. Others include:

- The skills to integrate all appropriate business and technical functions;
- The interpersonal skills to coordinate and collaborate with others;
- The leadership skills to act, influence others, and achieve the shared vision.

Higher leadership skills for those who will lead an integrated team are also required. These include:

- Ensuring that all team members mutually understand their roles and responsibilities;
- Actually using the people in their intended roles;
- Effectively accessing the expertise that exists in the organization and integrating it to strengthen the team effort.

Implementing integrated teams requires cultural changes as people and integrated teams are empowered and decisions are driven to the lowest level as appropriate. However, empowerment does not necessarily mean that every decision must occur at the lowest level; decision making is influenced by the decision type that the team agrees will be used to resolve issues and that the project manger and higher-level managers have agreed to support. Examples of decision types include:

- *Command:* The leader examines the issue and makes the decision alone.
- *Consultative:* The leader receives and examines input on the issue from relevant stakeholders and then makes the decision.
- *Collaborative:* Issues are raised, discussed, and voted upon. Rules are established to determine when this vote is binding for the leader.
- *Consensus:* Issues are discussed among all members of the integrated team until the entire team agrees they can accept and support the decision.

While integrated teaming normally corresponds to team-related incentives, individual excellence must also be valued. To purposefully support the use of integrated teams, the recognition and reward systems need to shift from a focus on the success or failure of an individual (program manager) to integrated team success or failure. Care should still be taken to continue to recognize individual excellence as long as it was not achieved at the expense of the established integrated team behaviors.

Integrated Project Management (IPPD)

As indicated in Figure 17.1, a project does not operate in isolation. If a project understands organizational expectations and constraints, it can align its direction, activities, and shared vision with the same in the organization, and it can help create a common purpose within which its activities can be coordinated. A project's shared vision context has both external and internal aspects:

▶ External aspects deal with the interfaces outside of the project.

▶ Internal aspects deal with aligning project members' personal aspirations and objectives with the project's vision and purpose.

To support integrated teams, the project manager must determine the integrated team structure within the guidelines of the organization's set of standard processes that will best meet the project objectives and constraints. The basis for defining integrated teams, their responsibilities, authorities, and interrelationships should come from the evaluation of factors such as:

▶ Product requirements;

▶ Cost;

▶ Schedule;

▶ Risk;

▶ Resource projections;

▶ Business processes;

▶ Project's defined process;

▶ Organizational guidelines.

The team structure should be tied into the work breakdown structure used by the project, allowing each integrated team to be responsible for its own specific tasks and work products. The integrated team structure should facilitate the partitioning of responsibilities, requirements, and resources so that the right expertise and abilities are available to produce the assigned products. As the project evolves, the integrated team structure must be reevaluated for applicability. This reevaluation may result in the integrated team being reorganized, including the appointing of a new integrated team leader.

Preliminary distribution of requirements

The requirements should be *preliminarily distributed* to integrated teams even before the teams are officially formed as a sanity check to verify that the selected team structure is workable and covers all the necessary requirements, responsibilities, authorities, tasks, and interfaces. Potential representatives from the required disciplines should be identified even though the integrated team is not yet formed to ensure an objective evaluation of the ability to satisfy the requirements that were preliminary assigned to the integrated team.

Responsibilities and authorities

The team leader should be chosen along with the assignment of planned responsibilities and requirements for each team. Integrated teams require a great deal of autonomy, which necessitates at the organizational and project levels a high degree of confidence in the team leader. Organizational and project influences on selecting the team leader should be used judiciously. When a new team leader and/or new team members join the team, the match between the new composition and the current responsibilities should be reviewed and appropriate changes should made as necessary. When defining the integrated team responsibilities and authorities, consider the following factors:

- Authority of the integrated team to pick its own leader;
- Authority of the team to implement subteams;
- Reporting chains;
- Reporting requirements such as cost, schedule, and performance status;
- Progress reporting measures and methods.

The integrated team

An integrated team focuses on the product life cycle to the extent required by the project. The sponsor, usually the project manger/leader typically provides the integrated team with the product requirements they will be responsible for implementing, initial technical and business interfaces, and high-level tasks from the *work breakdown structure* (WBS) and work packages. The project manager also needs to clearly define the relationship between the integrated team and the project and organization.

Selection criteria for integrated team members

Team members must be selected and positioned according to established criteria, including:

- Knowledge, skills, and functional expertise related to tasks and responsibilities associated with the team's assigned work products;
- Interpersonal skills and ability to work in a team environment;
- Ability to complement the mix and knowledge and skills in the team;
- Potential to fulfill a significant responsibility in the team;
- Ability to acquire additional knowledge and skills or expertise related to the team's tasks;
- Educational and cultural background;
- Personal self-motivation.

The functional knowledge and related job skills within the integrated team are directly related to specific team tasks and responsibilities. Organizational business objectives must be identified, the core competencies required to support those business objectives must be defined and the knowledge and skills profiles required for each core competency must be established.

Integrated team charter

Once the team has been selected, it is important to establish the team charter. The team charter is the contract among the team members and between the team and its sponsor for the expected work effort and level of performance. It is meant to solidify the rights, guarantees, privileges and permissions for organizing and performing the team's objectives and tasks. It should establish the team's level of empowerment and independence. It should also identify how the team and individual performance and accomplishments will be measured.

Operating procedures and ground rules must also be developed to define and control how the team will interact and work together. They define the expectations and rules that will guide how the team works collectively, the degree of collective decision making, the level of consensus that is needed for team decisions, and how conflicts will be addressed and resolved.

It is important that while the integrated team members have been chosen for their ability to get along with other team members, they are also chosen due to their highly crafted technical skills and possibly their individual contributions on other projects. Establishing the team charter, operating procedures, and ground rules simply serves to remind each individual that he or she has been chosen for an integrated team and must abide by that team's decisions. To complete the rules of the game, it is necessary to clearly establish the roles and responsibilities of each member of the integrated team, including each team member's anticipated contributions, level of involvement and realm of influence each member is expected to have on the success and functioning of the team. Setting of the roles and responsibilities also includes determining:

▸ How assignments are accepted;

▸ How resources and input are accessed;

▸ How works gets done;

▸ Who checks and reviews work;

▸ How work is approved;

▸ How work is delivered and communicated.

Summary

Deciding to put such an integrated team together requires an understanding of the business objectives and the ability to determine if the results will be cost-effective. It can be expensive and politically charged unless an organization's culture has been evolved to support and nurture integrated teams. Not everyone is a candidate to be a member of an integrated team. Those who are chosen will become a part of the *vision chain*. They will align their personal aspirations with the vision of the integrated team that is aligned with the vision of the project and, in turn, is aligned with the vision of the organization.

Reducing Variation

Understanding variation

When the topic of variation is discussed, the context is normally control charts and statistical process control. One of the specialists in understanding variation that has influenced members of the SEI as well as many other diverse fields such as transportation, manufacturing, utilities, and aerospace is Dr. Donald Wheeler. Dr. Wheeler is an internationally recognized speaker and trainer in the understanding and use of data in business and industry. Dr. Wheeler holds a Ph.D. in statistics from Southern Methodist University and was a student and associate of Dr. W. Edwards Deming for 19 years. Dr. Wheeler has written numerous technical books on statistical process control and related topics, but the one book that continues to have a visible impact on those who strive to fully understand and use CMMI® at higher maturity levels is [1].

In Chapter 2 of [1], Dr. Wheeler discusses Dr. Walter Shewhart's approach to interpreting data:

> We analyze numbers in order to know when a change has occurred in our process of system…. Some variation is routine, run-of-the-mill, and is to be expected even when the process has not changed. Other variation is exceptional, outside the bounds of routine, and therefore to be interpreted as a signal of process change…. The key to effectiveness of the process behavior chart is contained in the way in which the limits are computed from the data…. If over a reasonably long period of time, all of the points fall within the limits of a process behavior chart, and if the points are well-behaved, then the process can be said to display nothing but routine variation…. However, when points fall outside the limits of a process behavior chart they are interpreted as signs of exceptional failure. Exceptional variation is attributed to assignable causes which, by definition, dominate the many

common causes of routine variation.... Eliminating the effects of
assignable causes of variation from your process can ensure that the
process you are following will operate more consistently, predictably
and more reliably.

Statistical process control and a more detailed explanation of common
and assignable causes of variation will be presented in Chapter 19. These
ideas of variation are presented here to provide the backdrop for the main
theme of this chapter; using the CMMI® model as the basis for an organization's process improvement initiative can be viewed as a continuous journey in reducing variation.

This chapter presents an evolutionary path within the CMMI® model that
illustrates how process improvement steps taken to move from an individual
focus to a project focus, to a measurement-oriented organizational focus, and
to a quantitative management focus can be regarded as successive steps in
reducing variation in an organization's processes and business results. The
process areas of Project Planning, Project Monitoring and Control, Measurement and Analysis, Organizational Process Definition, Integrated Project
Management, Organizational Process Performance, and Quantitative Project
Management will be used to support this chapter's concepts.

Variation among individuals

Figure 18.1 shows a "Staged" view or representation of the CMMI® model.
At the initial maturity level, the process is described as being unpredictable,
poorly controlled, and reactive. In CMM® for Software, we often described
this state as "chaotic." One of the traits of CMMI® Maturity Level 1 is that
the process "belongs" to the people. If others follow a process, it is normally
due to the strong personality of someone on the project who has experienced using processes in another environment. From a variation point of
view, a Level 1 organization has a great variation based on its individual
employees following their own process paths. This is why Maturity Level 1
companies depend so heavily on the heroics of their people.

Projects' processes to reduce variation

At CMMI® Maturity Level 2, processes normally belong to the project and
are enforced by the project manager. The processes, standards, guidelines,
checklists, and templates are enforced for all of the project members to
achieve more uniformity in development and product quality. Assuming
that all projects follow some form of process, the amount of variation that
was seen in organizations of Maturity Level 1 is reduced even if all of the
projects followed a different process.

In addition, the new process area of Measurement and Analysis helps
the organization to develop and sustain a measurement capability that can

Level	Process characteristics	Process areas	
5 Optimizing	Focus is on quantitative continuous process improvement.	Causal Analysis and Resolution Organizational Innovation and Deployment	
4 Quantitatively managed	Process is measured and controlled.	Quantitative Project Management Organizational Process Performance	
3 Defined	Process is characterized for the organization and is proactive.	Requirements Development Technical Solution Product Integration Verification Validation Organizational Process Focus Organizational Process Definition Organizational Training	Integrated Project Management Integrated Teaming Organizational Environment for Integration Integrated Supplier Management Risk Management Decision Analysis and Resolution
2 Managed	Process is characterized for projects and is often reactive.	Requirement Management Project Planning Project Monitoring and Control Supplier Agreement Management Product and Process Quality Assurance	Configuration Management Measurement and Analysis
1 Initial	Process is unpredictable, poorly controlled, and reactive.		

Figure 18.1 CMMI® overview.

be used to support management information needs. It will further provide a measurement foundation that can be built upon as the organization evolves towards CMMI® Maturity Level 3 and a set of standard processes. The process area of Measurement and Analysis guides an organization to define measures to be used along with the data collection process, the storage mechanisms, the analysis processes, the reporting processes, and the feedback processes. This is a critical step for an organization to move to CMMI® Maturity Level 3 and to have the proper foundation to move to CMMI® Maturity Level 4.

Organizational processes to reduce variation

As described in Chapter 15, an organization that wishes to achieve CMMI® Maturity Level 3 needs to have its processes owned by the organization for economy of scale to be realized and process measurement to make practical sense. Referring to Chapter 3, the organization's set of standard processes contains the definitions of the processes that guide all of the activities in an organization. A standard process enables consistent development and maintenance across the organization and is essential for long-term stability and improvement.

These process definitions are tailored and incorporated into the project's defined processes throughout the organization and thus variation in project development and product and service quality is again reduced. In addition to the standard processes, an organization at CMMI® Maturity Level 3 also establishes its organizational measurement repository. This measurement repository contains both product and process measures that are related to the organization's set of standard processes. It also contains the information needed to understand and interpret the measures and assess them for reasonableness and applicability. With this measurement repository, trends can be seen and predictability can be achieved. In addition, process performance baselines can now be developed to support quantitative management later.

Quantitative Project Management

Finally, at CMMI® Maturity Level 4, the ownership of the processes reverts back to the projects. This is because individual projects must determine if the requirements and constraints placed upon them demand the use of Quantitative Project Management techniques, even though the tailored processes still come from the organization's set of standard processes. The data collected in the organization's measurement repository is used to develop a process performance database or set of databases.

Quantitative Management is tied to the organization's strategic goals for product quality, service quality, and process performance. When higher degrees of quality and performance are demanded, the organization and projects must determine if they have the ability to improve the necessary processes to satisfy the increased demands. Achieving the necessary quality and process performance objectives requires stabilizing the processes that contribute most to the achievement of the objectives and reducing process variation to support the quantitative management objectives.

Summary

Figure 18.2 provides a process capability prediction view of CMMI®. It illustrates the theme of reduction of variation that we have discussed so far. At the *Initial* level target dates of cost, schedule, performance and quality are often missed by wide variation. At the *Managed* level, the variability of the actual results around the target decreases. At the *Defined* level, variability again decreases. Target hits increase and the target begins to move in toward the *y*-axis due to reduced rework. At the   *Quantitatively Managed* level,

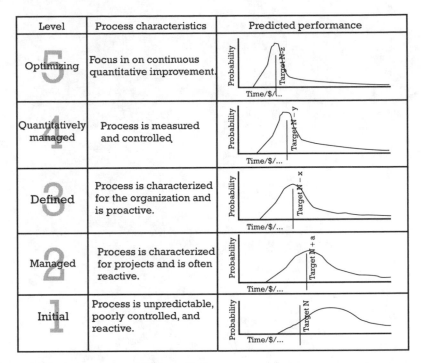

Figure 18.2 Process capability prediction.

variability continues to decrease. Target results improve, and development time becomes shorter while productivity and quality increase. Continuing to the *Optimizing* level, defect prevention helps to reduce rework further and variation continues to be reduced.

There are many different views of CMMI®. There are also many different ways that CMMI® can help an organization that are not always obvious on the surface. Helping an organization to reduce variation as it improves in its process capability is a benefit of using CMMI® that all organizations should strive to utilize.

Reference

[1]   Wheeler, D. J., *Understanding Variation: The Key to Managing Chaos*, Knoxville, TN: SPC Press (Statistical Process Control), 1999.

Techniques for Establishing a Measurement Program

This chapter illustrates the strong measurement focus that is found within CMMI®. Basic project management measures are defined in the Project Planning and Monitoring and Control process areas. An understanding of getting a measurement program started is provided through the implementation of the concepts found in the Measurement and Analysis process area (PA). Continuing on the evolutionary path, CMMI® guides the reader to the establishment of an organizational measurement repository, the collection of peer review and test data, and the evolution of the organizational process measures that provide the building blocks for statistical process control and quantitative project management. The Measurement and Analysis, Organizational Process Performance, and Quantitative Project Management process areas will be examined in detail. The special cause of variation will also be discussed. Chapter 20 addresses the common cause of variation.

Measurement: Is it really necessary?

The following are questions that a project manager must consider and be able to answer to management while a project is starting.

- Can it be done?
- How long will it take?
- How much will it cost?
- How many people will it take?
- What are the risks?
- What are the trade-offs?
- How many potential errors?

- How much does your current development process cost?

- How much value does each piece of the process add?

- What would the impact be of deleting, modifying, or adding a procedure to the process?

- What activities contribute the most to the final product cost?

- Have you tried to improve the current development process?

- What changes in cost/value resulted from that improvement effort?

- What processes represent the greatest potential for return on improvement investment?

- How would you quantify the value of the process improvement investment?

- Do you really want to know where the money is going in your software development projects?

- What value do you think you are delivering to your customers? Do they agree?

Measurement and Analysis

The Measurement and Analysis common feature found in CMM® for Software was, in my opinion, one of the weakest parts of CMM® that was written. Striving to not present specific metrics, but yet giving guidance on measuring status and effectiveness of processes, my view of CMM® is that the measurement requirements were not very clear and did not give much guidance for organizations as they tried to improve their process capability.

In the past, many individuals, projects, and organizations have mistakenly believed, when embarking upon their journey to achieve CMM® Levels 2 and 3, that measurement was not necessary until the organization had actually accomplished CMM® Maturity Level 3. They believed that measurement only played a significant role once they began a Maturity Level 4 initiative and embarked on an implementation of the Quantitative Process Management and Software Quality Management key process areas (KPA). Obviously, it was not possible to achieve a legitimate Maturity Level 2 or 3 rating without having also satisfied the Measurement and Analysis common feature.

These same organizations focused upon the usage of status information to achieve their CMM® Maturity Level 2 objectives. They added a few measures once they developed their organization's standard software process but found out they did not have the right data to actually consider putting their process or subprocesses under statistical process control. CMMI® authors have created a new process area called Measurement and Analysis that helps organizations to establish their measurement program and create a measurement foundation that can be added to as the organization moves from CMMI® Maturity Level 1 to Level 2 to Level 3 and beyond.

Let us examine some of the key concepts found in the Measurement and Analysis process area.

The Measurement and Analysis purpose statement states that an organization should develop and sustain a measurement capability that is used to support management information needs. This means that the measurement objectives that are specified at the project level are aligned with the established information needs and business objectives of the organization. The essential message of the Measurement and Analysis process area is contained in the following two points:

1. Define the measures to be used, the data collection process, the storage mechanisms, the analysis process, the reporting processes, and the feedback processes.

2. Provide objective results that can be used in making business judgments and take appropriate corrective actions.

Let us explore the details of these two guiding statements.

Establish measurement objectives

Consider the Goal–Question–Metric Paradigm developed by Dr. Vic Bacilli and Dr. Dieter Rombach and document the purpose for which any measurement and analysis is done. Ensure that the kinds of actions that may be taken based on the results of the data analysis are specified up front. Much like the concept of criticality and verification techniques discussed in Chapter 14, actions should be based on expected results and project risks. Debating what should be done once the data indicates something should be done is often a waste of resources and is not effective. It is simply best to specify what will happen given situation X, and then do it.

One of my strong recommendations is to continually ask the question: What value will this measurement be to the people who will be asked to supply the raw measurement data and to those who will receive the analyzed results? Some years ago, I was working for a business unit of a large company in Europe. The CIO of the company had wanted to establish a peer review culture in his organization. He turned over the implementation of this program to his deputy CIO. The deputy CIO instructed the quality assurance manager to go to each project and demand to know what increased percent peer reviews did the project conducted this past month have compared to previous months. Project managers and members alike saw no value in this exercise but realized they had to find a way to "show" compliance each month. Many of the projects would hold at least one more peer review at the local tavern with a round or two of beers a day or two before the quality assurance manager was to come around to be able to say the percentage had increased. Over a period of 6 months each project was reporting around a 70% increase in the use of peer reviews. During an assessment, the practitioners told me (I was serving as the lead assessor) that they really did not conduct peer reviews. I reported this during the senior management presentation. The CIO was very upset and the deputy CIO was angry at being put in a compromising situation. When the CIO demanded that I substantiate this claim, 65 practitioners stood up and said, "That is what we told the assessment team." Measures should always be useful to those who collect the data and use it!

Specify measures

Candidate measures should be based on documented business objectives and refined into precisely defined, quantifiable measures that have unambiguous operational definitions associated with them. There are numerous potential sources for business objectives. This is because in today's world a corporation may include several different business units such as software development, patents and licenses, and so forth. Therefore, the business objectives may not necessarily be those defined at corporate level. They may, more appropriately, be those defined for the business unit itself.

Derived measures are more quantitatively reliable and meaningful than the base measures used to construct them. Derived measures are often expressed as ratios or composite indices and are based on combinations of data that are collected for the defined basic measures.

Examples of commonly used derived measures include:

> *Earned value:* Actual cost of work performed compared to the budgeted cost of work performed;
> *Defect density:* Number of defects found per thousand lines of code;
> Peer review coverage;
> Test coverage;
> *Reliability measures:* Mean time between failure.

Specify data collection and storage procedures

The procedures that will be used to collect and store the data for each measure must be established and maintained. Explicit specifications of how, where, and when the data will be collected must be defined. Procedures for ensuring the data collected is valid must be developed and the data must be stored so that it is easily accessed, retrieved, and restored as needed. The following questions should be considered when an organization sets up its measurement collection and storage procedures:

> Has the frequency of data collection been established?
> Have the points in the process where the measurements will be made been determined?
> Has the time required to move measurement results from the points of collection to databases or end users been estimated?
> Has it been decided who is responsible for collecting the data?

> Has it been decided who is responsible for data storage, retrieval, and security?

> Have the necessary supporting tools for data collection, storage, analysis, and feedback been developed or acquired?

> If a database is used for storage of metrics data, would there be a value for real-time generation of graphics?

It is important to remember that effective data collection is always dependent upon the actions of people. Therefore, consideration must be given to how easy it is for people to record metrics and to generate the required graphics. Initially, usage of a spreadsheet may be sufficient. However, as an organization transitions to the usage of an intranet to facilitate communication, the use of a spreadsheet may not be the most efficient way to generate graphics. The use of a database and active server pages to enable publishing of real-time graphics may be a better approach. If the interface between the person recording the metrics data is easy enough to find and use, then the likelihood that data will be recorded increases. Also, if the graphics display requires little to no effort on the part of the person recording the data, then the likelihood that the metrics displayed will be current and actually used substantially increases. After all, metrics are of no use if all of the data is not recorded and is not translated into an output, suitable for analysis, within a reasonable time frame.

Specify analysis procedures

Analysis procedures must be defined and agreed upon in advance. Consideration must be given to how the results will be reported to the project manager and project members and what the most appropriate method of display of the results should be to ensure maximum understandability and usefulness. It is always important to factor in the audience who will receive these measurement results. The feedback, content, and interpretation will differ if the audience is an intended user, a sponsor, a data analyst, or a data provider.

Collect and analyze the measurement data

The measurement data should be collected as defined at the points in the process that were agreed upon. Derived measures should be generated from the basic data and initial analyses should be conducted. The results from the initial analysis should be interpreted and reported to the stakeholders to determine if the results are understandable and decisions can be taken from them. It is most important for those who collect and analyze the measurement data to follow up and coach those who receive it to ensure their understanding and interpreting of the measurement results. Creation of a common metrics style guide is suggested. This ensures that expected output will be reasonably consistent and professional in appearance.

Store the measurement data and analysis results

A major point that the authors of CMMI® made regarding the storage of the measurement data is repeated in the definition of the Organizational Measurement Repository, and repeated again in the description of the Quantitative Project Management process area. That point states: "Measurement-related information should be stored together with sufficient context so that the measures can be understood and interpreted for reasonableness and applicability." Throughout the years, I have assessed many companies around the world who collected a lot of data but without any context at all. In addition, this data was normally know by the "metrics expert" and was almost never used by the project manager or members for decision purposes. I strongly suggest that one or two sentences should always be provided to explain what the graphics are displaying. For example, the sentences could say "A rising line means this...and a falling line means this..."

The use of sentences like this should also be a mandatory part of the metrics style guide recommended earlier. It should also be part of the organization's metrics policy in order to ensure that no metrics will be published in the organization without some form of explanation of what the graphics mean. Thus, other people who may not be familiar with the graphics can understand what is being communicated. After all, the purpose of metrics is to facilitate communication of data in a visual manner so that it can be more easily understood. Metrics are nice, but if no one can interpret them, they are useless.

Basic measures

A measurement program should always include the basic project management measures. These measures were discussed in Chapter 7 and include:

- Attributes of the work products:
  - Size;
  - Complexity;
  - Weight;
  - Form, fit, or function.
- Cost and expended effort;
- Schedule;
- Technical performance (completion of activities and milestones against the schedule);
- Staffing profiles;
- Resources:
  - Physical facilities;
  - Computers, peripherals;
  - Networks;

> Security environment;

> Processes.

▸ Knowledge and skills acquisition of project personnel;

▸ Training needs;

▸ Commitments;

▸ Quality: defects or quality attributes.

In addition to the basic project management measures, it is important for each project manager to know if the processes that his or her project members are following are working in the way that they were expected to work. In other words, are the processes *effective*?

Effectiveness of processes

When we discuss effectiveness of processes, we want to know how well the process or processes are working for those who are following them. Many measures related to Measurement and Analysis focused on status. Here are a few examples that should illustrate the difference between the status of following a process and its effectiveness.

We will look at the process area of Requirements Management. If a project had 1,000 requirements, how effective would the Requirements Management process be? The status of 1,000 requirements is just that—a status number. It does not give any more information than if we said we had 10,000 requirements. We might expect the project to be more complex if we had 10,000 requirements compared to 1,000 but there is nothing to be said of the effectiveness of the Requirements Management process itself. What if we had the input that the project had 100 requirements change requests? Would that be enough information to give us reason to believe we could discuss the effectiveness of the Requirements Management process? The answer is still no. We do not know what type of requirements change requests are included in that 100, but if we had the data that told us we had 100 requirements change requests and 25 of them were showstoppers, we would be able to state we had an indicator of effectiveness of the Requirements Management process.

We would not consider that process to be very effective and would start the search to determine what was not working right. Perhaps the requirements elicitation process was faulty. Perhaps the requirements analysis process was not adequate. Perhaps the impact analysis was inadequate. If the data stated that of the 100 requirements change requests, 100 of them were "nice to have," then we would believe that our Requirements Management process to be sufficiently effective.

Like all measures, effectiveness of processes measures produce indicators that must be evaluated if they are good or not. Here are a few other examples of effectiveness of Requirements Management measures that could be useful for a given project:

> Time spent on change requests up until a yes-or-no decision is given from the senior contract group;

> Impact of the change requests on project progress: effort spent on the change requests versus the amount of effort to execute the original project;

> Actual cost of processing a change request compared with budgeted or predicted costs:

  › Actually make the change;

  › Filling in the forms;

  › Impact analysis;

  › Authorization;

  › Replanning;

  › Rescheduling;

  › Renegotiating commitments;

  › SQA effort;

  › SCM effort;

  › Review effort;

  › Test effort.

Organization's set of standard processes

Besides being a CMMI® Maturity Level 3 requirement, developing a set of organizational standard processes builds a common vocabulary and allows others to anticipate the behavior of other groups and be more proactive in their interactions. Having a set of organizational standard processes allows the organization to measure a *controlled set* of processes to gain economy of scale. Trends can be seen and predictability can start to be achieved. Process performance baselines can be economically developed to support quantitative management later. One of the major components of the Organizational Process Definition process area is the organization's measurement repository that was defined and discussed in Chapter 15. CMMI® description is based on the foundation laid by the Measurement and Analysis process area.

Organization's measurement repository

The organization's measurement repository contains:

> Product and process measures that are related to the organization's set of standard processes;

> The related information needed to understand and interpret the measurement data and assess it for reasonableness and applicability;

▸ Operational definitions for the measure should specify the point in the process where the data will be collected and the procedures for collecting valid data;

▸ Examples of classes of commonly used measures include:

  ▸ Size of work products (lines of code, function points, complexity);

  ▸ Effort and cost;

  ▸ Actual measures of size, effort, and cost for software;

  ▸ Quality measures;

  ▸ Work product inspection (peer review) coverage;

  ▸ Test or verification coverage;

  ▸ Reliability measures.

Slightly more advanced measure

When discussing defects discovered during peer reviews, it is much more interesting to think about defects in terms of *major* or *minor* defects where the boundary line between the two classifications depends on the influence of the defect on the cost, schedule, performance, and quality of the product that is received by the end user.

Even the classification of defects into major and minor defects is not as informative as one would need to focus limited resources and care for product quality at the same time. Placing major and minor defects into categories allows the peer review team and the measurement team that will analyze the defects to see trends and focus energy on improving processes that will result in a greater benefit to the organization's business on the whole. Categories of peer review defects may include imprecisely stated requirements, ambiguous requirements, performance variables not quantified, requirements that are not testable, missing items, interface errors, and logic errors.

Peer review data can also reveal effectiveness of the peer review calculated by comparing the number of major defects found in a life-cycle stage compared to the total number of defects found so far. After an organization has collected peer review data for life-cycle work products throughout the entire life cycle and can start to see trends, it is possible to mathematically calculate the remaining defects in a given life-cycle work product. A caveat about peer review metrics is to ensure that the metrics are not used in a negative fashion against the person who authors the peer-reviewed document or code. Remember, a hallmark of effective peer review is that the results cannot be attributed to any person.

Defects identified through the performance Process and Product Quality Assurance (PPQA) process area activities and audits after an item has completed peer review are a rich source for potential defect prevention activities. If the peer review process has been effective, then the amount of defects in the product reviewed should be little to none. If there are significant defects identified, then the result of the PPQA audit of the product must then point to a very inefficient peer review process. Remember, that is the purpose of peer review: to catch the defects before the product is approved for release. QA is not a substitute for an ineffective peer review process. So if QA is finding defects after a product has completed peer review, the peer review process must be broken. This requires a corrective action on the part of PPQA personnel.

Testing defects can also be subdivided into categories and testing effectiveness can also be calculated. The defects found in testing can be compared to those found in peer reviews leading to a more focused causal analysis on the origin of the defects and the effectiveness of the engineering processes that are allowing the defects to be injected into the evolving system. Test coverage measures are another measurement that helps project members to more accurately report the extent of the testing that is being carried out and understand the product quality that is being shipped more thoroughly.

Quantitative project management

When higher degrees of quality and performance are demanded, the organization and projects must determine if they have the ability to improve the necessary processes to satisfy the increased demands. Quantitative management is tied to the organization's strategic goals for product quality, service quality, and process performance. Achieving the necessary quality and process performance objectives requires stabilizing the processes or subprocesses that contribute most to the achievement of the objectives. Assuming that the technical requirements can be met, the next decision is to determine if it is cost-effective.

Process performance baselines

In order to determine if a requirement for a higher degree of quality or performance can be achieved, it is necessary to know what the process capability of the existing organizational processes and subprocesses is across the organization's projects. CMMI® has defined a process area called Organizational Process Performance that guides an organization to maintain a quantitative understanding of the performance of the organization's set of standard processes in support of quality and process-performance objectives. Process performance data, baselines, and models are established and maintained to quantitatively manage the organization's projects.

Before going further, it is important to define process performance. The introductory notes for the Organization Process Performance process area provide excellent insight. "Process performance is a measure of the actual results achieved by following a process" [1]. Process performance is characterized by both process measures and product measures. Typical process measures include effort, cycle time, and defect removal effectiveness. Typical product measures include reliability and defect density.

The common measures for the organization are composed of process and product measures that can be used to summarize the actual performance of processes in individual projects in the organization. The organizational data for these measures are analyzed to establish a distribution and range of results which characterize the expected performance of the process when used on any individual project in the organization.... The expected process performance can be used in establishing the project's quality and process-performance objectives and can be used as a baseline against which actual project performance can be compared. Each quantitatively managed project, in turn, provides actual performance results that become a part of the baseline data for the organizational process assets [1].

When the organization has measures, data, and analytic techniques that it knows how to properly apply, it has the ability to:

» Determine whether processes are behaving consistently or are predictable.

» Identify processes that perform within consistent natural bounds.

» Establish criteria for identifying whether a process or process element should be statistically managed.

» Identify processes that show unusual behavior.

» Identify parts of the processes that can be improved.

» Identify implementations of processes that represent good and best practices.

Earlier interpretations of quantitative project management approaches based on CMM® for Software led companies to believe that they needed to get all of their organizational standard processes under statistical process control. Selection of the processes and/or process elements is based on the needs and objectives of both the organization and the projects. It is extremely important to understand that CMMI® provides the guidance that it is typically not possible, useful, or economically justifiable to apply statistical process control (SPC) techniques to all process or process elements of an organization's set of standard processes (OSSP).

Measures that provide appropriate insight into the organization's process performance need to be chosen. The obvious question is: Based upon what criteria? Examples of the criteria suggested by CMMI® include:

» Relationships of the measures to the organization's business objectives;

» Coverage that the measures provide over the entire life of the product;

» Visibility that the measures provide into the process performance;

» Frequency at which the observations of the measures can be collected;

» Extent to which the measures are controllable by changes to the process;

‣ Extent to which the measures represent the user's view of effective process performance.

Organizational process performance baselines must be established to measure the performance for the organization's set of standard processes for each of the major phases of the approved project life cycles. An organization may have to establish several process performance baselines to characterize performance for subgroups of the organization. These subgroups include:

‣ Product line;

‣ Application domain;

‣ Complexity;

‣ Team size;

‣ Work product size.

CMMI® suggests that each organization establish and maintain its organization's process performance baselines from the collected measurements and analyses by:

‣ Establishing a distribution and range of results that characterize the expected performance for selected processes when used on any individual project in the organization;

‣ Using measurements from stable processes (other data may not be reliable).

At the SEI-sponsored SEPG Conference held in Phoenix, Arizona, in 2002, a representative from PRC-Litton presented his company's successful journey into statistical process control. While many attempts were made to have only one process performance baseline, the degree of variation was found to be so great that this gentleman's organization ended up developing five process performance baselines.

Quantitative project management

Statistical management involves statistical thinking and the correct usage of a variety of statistical process control tools such as run charts, control charts, confidence intervals, prediction intervals, and tests of hypotheses.

Quantitative management uses data from statistical management to help the project predict whether it will be able to achieve its quality and process performance objectives and identify when corrective action should be taken.

Process performance is a measure of the actual process results achieved and is characterized by both process measures and product measures as indicated earlier. Organizations are encouraged to use statistical management to have the ability to predict the extent to which its projects can fulfill its quality and process performance objectives.

Any necessary corrective action is based on understanding the nature and extent of the variation experienced in actual process performance and recognizing when the project's actual performance may not be adequate to achieve the project's quality and process performance. Reducing process variation is an important aspect to quantitative management. Some variation is routine and run-of-the-mill and is to be expected even when the process has not changed. Other variation is exceptional, outside the bounds of routine, and therefore to be interpreted as a signal of a process change.

In order to distinguish or separate variation into these two components, Dr. Walter Shewart created the control chart. The control chart illustrated in Figure 19.1 is created by plotting data in a time series. A central line is added as a visual reference for detecting shifts or trends, and limits are computed from the data. These limits are placed on either side of the central line at the distance that will allow them to filter out virtually all of the routine variation. The key to effectiveness of the control chart is contained in the way in which the limits are computed from the data. Dr. Donald Wheeler describes these calculations in a clear manner in [2]. By characterizing the extent of routine variation, the limits on a control chart allow you to differentiate between routine variation and exceptional variation. If over a reasonably long period of time, all of the points fall within the limits of a control or process behavior chart, then the process can be said to display nothing but routine variation. When this happens, the process can be thought of as being predictable within those limits, and it is reasonable to expect that, unless something is changed, it will continue to operate that way in the future.

Thus, the limits of a control chart allow you to characterize the behavior your process as predictable or unpredictable and define how much routine variation you should expect in the future. However, when the points fall outside of the limits of the control chart, they are interpreted as signs of exceptional or assignable causes of variation. Assignable causes of variation dominate the many common causes of routine variation; thus, it is worthwhile to try to identify the assignable cause of variation so its effect upon your process can be eliminated. It is worthwhile, assuming that if project managers or members know about an assignable cause of variation, they would not allow it to dominate the process(es) that the project members were required to follow. Thus, control charts allow a project to learn about dominant cause and effect relationships that may have not been realized in the past and help the project to realize a more predictable and reliable process.

Understanding variation

Understanding variation is a fundamental premise of statistical control. Understanding variation is achieved through the collection and analysis of process and product measures so that special causes of variation can be identified and addressed to achieve predictable performance. Wheeler used the term *routine variation* compared to exceptional variation. Routine or

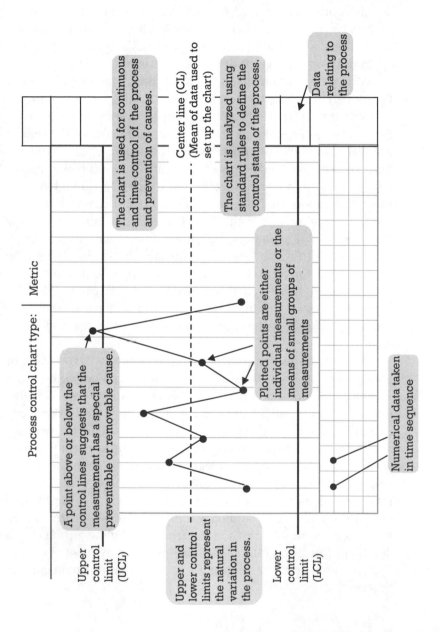

Figure 19.1 Process control chart type: metric. (*After:* [3].)

common causes of variation are variation in process performance due to the normal interaction among the process components (people, machines, material, environment, and methods). Variation due to common cause is random but will vary within *predictable* bounds. Special or assignable causes of variation arise from events that are not part of the normal process. These special causes of variation represent sudden or persistent abnormal changes due to one or more of the process components. The special cause may manifest itself as a faulty input to the process environment or through the way the processes themselves are executed. Examples of assignable causes of variation include inadequately trained people, tool failures, and failures to follow the process.

Assignable cause and exceptional cause

Assignable causes of variation dominate the many common causes of routine variation; thus, it is worthwhile to try to identify the assignable cause of variation so its effect upon your process can be eliminated, assuming that if project managers or members know about an assignable cause of variation, they would not allow it to dominate the process. Thus, control charts allows a project to learn about cause and effect relationships that may have not been realized in the past and to help the project to realize a more predictable and reliable process.

It is important to remember to focus on subprocesses that can be controlled to achieve a predictable performance as well as the overarching processes. Subprocesses should be selected from the process elements in the organization's set of standard processes. It is helpful to know if the subprocesses showed stable performance in previous comparable instances or that the performance data for that subprocess showed satisfaction of the project's quality and process performance objectives. It is also useful to analyze the interaction of the subprocesses to understand the relationships that exist among the subprocesses. This can certainly have an effect on your ability to bring them under statistical control.

During the process of deciding which subprocesses to select, it is helpful to identify the criteria to be used that will result in selected processes that are the main contributors to achieving the identified quality and process performance objectives and for which predictable performance is important. Examples of sources for criteria used in selecting subprocesses include:

- Customer requirements related to quality and process performance;
- Quality and process performance objectives established by the customer;
- Quality and process performance objectives established by the organization;
- Organization's performance of the subprocess on other projects;
- Laws and regulations.

Remember: It may not be possible to statistically manage some processes nor economically justifiable to apply statistical techniques to certain subprocesses.

When the selected subprocesses are brought under statistical control, their capability of achieving quality and process performance objectives can be determined. It is, therefore, also possible to predict whether the project will be able to achieve its objectives. Statistical process control is then based on collecting and analyzing process and product measures so that the special or assignable causes of variation can be identified and addressed in order to achieve predictable performance.

Voice of the process: Voice of the customer

Before you can improve any system or system process, you must listen to the voice of the process defined by the natural bounds and variation within those bounds of process performance. You must be able to change the inputs in order to achieve the desired results. However, comparing numbers to specifications will not lead to the improvement of the process. You must also listen to the voice of the customer. This means being able to achieve the goals established for the product and process performance such as:

- Product specifications:
  - Amount of downtime;
  - Mean time to failure;
  - Response time.
- Management specifications:

  - Meeting the schedule;
  - Meeting the budget.

Capable processes

From a statistical control point of view, a capable process is one that satisfies both the voice of the process and the voice of the customer. See Figure 19.2.

The focus of this description of quantitative management has mainly been on the control chart. There are many continuous improvement and quantitative project management tools and techniques that include:

- Cause and effect (fishbone diagrams);
- Pareto analysis;
- Scatter diagrams;
- Run charts;
- Interrelationship diagraphs;
- Check sheets;
- Histograms;
- Control chart.

QPM-SG2 Statistically manage
subprocess performance

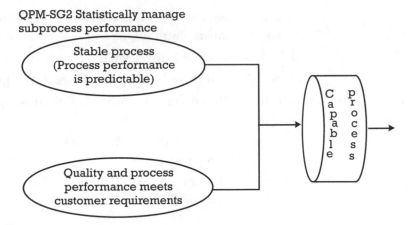

Figure 19.2   Capable process.

Cause and effect or fishbone diagrams, Pareto analysis charts, scatter diagrams, run charts, and interrelationship diagraphs are examples of statistical process control (SPC) tools that are used for the determination of cause and effect relationships. Some of these cause and effect techniques are described in more detail in Chapter 20.

Two quantitative management techniques are most useful for quantifying process behavior (voice of the process) and in answering the question: Is the process capable of meeting my customers' requirements (voice of the customer)? These two techniques are the control chart, discussed previously in this chapter, and the histogram.

Control charts

A control chart:

- Allows a project team to monitor, control, and improve process performance over time by studying variation and its source;
- Distinguishes special or assignable causes of variation from common causes of variation as a guide for management decision making;
- Serves as a tool for ongoing control of a process;
- Helps improve a process to perform consistently and predictably for higher quality, lower cost, and higher effective capacity;
- Is most effective when used within the broader context of established goals and the activities performed to achieve those goals.

Histograms

A histogram:

- Allows a project team to take measurement data and display the distribution of the observed values;

- Shows the frequencies of events that have occurred in ways that make it easy to compare distributions and see central tendencies;
- Illustrates quickly the underlying distribution of the data;
- Helps indicate if there has been a change in the process;
- Provides useful information for predicting future performance of the process;
- Helps answer the question: Is the process capable of meeting my customers' requirements?
- Is created by grouping the results into "cells" and then counting the number in each cell (Figure 19.3).

Summary

The strong measurement focus that can be found and utilized from CMMI® has been presented. Beginning with basic project management measures and an understanding of getting a measurement program started through the implementation of the concepts found in the Measurement and Analysis PA, it guides the reader to the establishment of an organizational measurement repository, the collection of peer review and test data, and the evolution of the organizational process measures that provide the building blocks for statistical process control and quantitative project management.

The measurement implications view of the CMMI®, shown in Figure 19.4, sums up this powerful feature of CMMI®:

- *Initial:* Measurements are hard to make and data is difficult to collect due to the chaotic processes.

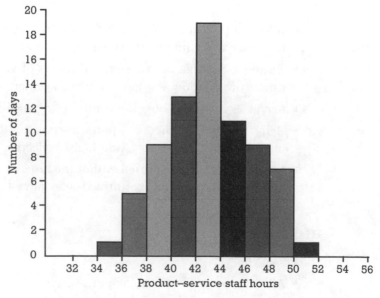

Figure 19.3 Histograms.

Level	Process characteristics	Measurement implications
5 Optimizing	Process improvement is institutionalized.	Continuing improvement is based on business objectives and cost-benefit analysis.
4 Quantitatively managed	Product and process are quantitatively controlled.	Data analysis is based on the principles of statistical process control. Actuals are compared to expected values of mean and variance.
3 Defined	Technical practices are integrated with management practices and institutionalized.	Consistent definitions exist across projects. Management and quality data is collected across the organization.
2 Managed	Projects management practices and institutionalized.	Projects collect management data about cost, effort, size, schedule, and so forth. Different projects may use different definitions.
1 Initial	Process is informal and ad hoc.	Measurement is haphazard, but may yield cost and effort data.

Figure 19.4   Measurement implications of process maturity. (*After:* [4].)

- *Managed:* The project can collect measures based on the actuals to estimates they collect including size, effort, schedule, technical activities, risks, and staffing.

- *Defined:* The organization's standard software process allows the start of quantitative measurement data to be collected and placed into the process database.

- *Quantitatively Managed:* As stated, the data collected allows trend analysis to be carried out. Statistical Process Control methods are used to manage the project quantitatively.

- *Optimizing:* Organization can quantitatively decide how much improvement to try for and its cost benefit. Organizations can look into new businesses and determine the feasibility of doing it from a technical and now financial point of view.

References

[1]   CMMI Product Development Team, *CMMI for Systems Engineering/Software Engineering/Integrated Product and Process Development/Supplier Sourcing, Version 1.1 Continuous Representation* (CMU/SEI-2002-TR-011, ESC-TR-2002-011), Pittsburgh, PA: Software Engineering Institute, Carnegie Mellon University, March 2002, p. 152.

[2]   Wheeler, D. J., *Understanding Variation: The Key to Managing Chaos*, 2nd ed., Knoxville, TN: SPC Press, 1999.

[3] Burr, A., and M. Owen, *Statistical Methods for Software Quality*, Boston, MA: International Thomson Computer Press, 1996.

[4] Kasse Initiatives, "Multiple Views of the CMMI," presentation, Amsterdam, 2001.

Beyond Stability

CMM® for Software and CMMI® indicate a distinction between achieving an organizational process capability at Maturity Level 4 and performing the prescribed activities to achieve an organizational process capability at Maturity Level 5. For many process improvement professionals, the distinction between Maturity Levels 4 and 5 is a very fine shade of gray indeed. As indicated in Chapter 19, reducing the variation of a process or subprocess by eliminating the special causes of variation and stabilizing the process is only the first step in attempting to achieve the process performance and/or quality. The second and most important step is to find an innovative or incremental solution that will actually result in producing a product that meets the expectations or requirements of the customer. This was called the *voice of the customer*. The approach to stabilizing the process within its natural bounds was referred to as *voice of the process*. It was shown that both are needed to have a capable process. The innovations or incremental improvements needed to achieve customer requirements will be explored further in this chapter.

While eliminating the special causes of variation is a necessary step for stabilizing the process and reducing variation, a more interesting next step is to improve the process further by eliminating the common causes of variation. The process area of Causal Analysis and Resolution was developed to support the identification of causes of defects and take action to prevent them from occurring in the future.

This chapter describes the causal analysis and process innovations that can be built upon the quantitative and predictable knowledge of an organization's processes to solve business needs that otherwise could not be solved simply through hard work and management concern.

Causal analysis

Causal Analysis and Resolution is the process of improving quality and productivity by preventing the introduction of defects into a product. Relying on activities such as peer reviews and testing to detect and eliminate the defects after they have been introduced into the system is not cost-effective. Based on an understanding of the defined process in use and how it is implemented, the root causes of the defects and the future implications of the defects can be determined. Causal Analysis and Resolution also provides a mechanism for projects to evaluate their processes and look for improvements that can be made. If the project improvements are shown to be effective, they become candidates for process improvements at the organizational level.

Causal analysis may also be used to solve problems unrelated to defects. For example, causal analysis can be used for analysis of improvement suggestions and new business directions.

In order to have an effective process for finding the root cause of a defect so that it can be removed, it is important to gather relevant defect data from multiple sources, including:

- Project management problem reports requiring corrective action;
- Defects reported by the customer;
- Defects reported by the end user;
- Defects found in peer reviews;
- Defects found in testing;
- Defects found by project and process measures;
- Process capability problems that have been identified.

To select defects to analyze further, other issues might be taken into consideration such as:

- The frequency of occurrence;
- The similarity between defects;
- Cost of analysis;
- Time and resources needed;
- Safety considerations.

Quantitative project management techniques for causal analysis

There are many continuous improvement and quantitative project management tools and techniques, as described in Chapter 19. Examples of methods for determining causes and other relationships that exist among critical issues include:

- Cause and effect (fishbone diagrams);
- Pareto analysis;
- Scatter diagrams;
- Run charts;
- Interrelationship diagraphs;
- Check sheets.

Cause and effect (fishbone) diagrams (Figure 20.1):

- Allow the project team to identify, explore, and graphically display all of the possible causes related to a problem to discover its root cause;
- Help the team to probe, map, and prioritize a set of factors that are thought to affect a particular process, problem, or outcome;
- Help to elicit and organize information from people who work within a process and know what might be causing it to perform the way it does;
- Focus the project team on causes, not symptoms.

Pareto charts [a special form of histogram or bar chart (Figure 20.2)]:

- Help focus investigations and solution finding by ranking problems, causes, or actions in terms of their amounts, frequencies of occurrence, or economic consequences;
- Based on the proven Pareto principle, 20% of the sources cause 80% of any problem;
- Help prevent shifting the problem, where the solution removes some causes but worsens others.

Scatter diagrams (Figure 20.3):

- Display empirically observed relationships between two process characteristics;

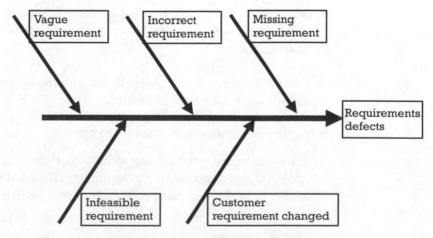

Figure 20.1   Cause and effect diagrams (fishbone).

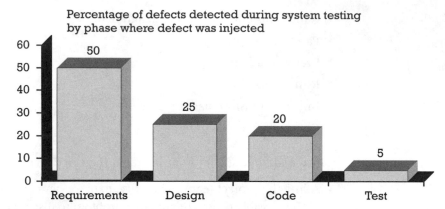

Figure 20.2 Pareto charts.

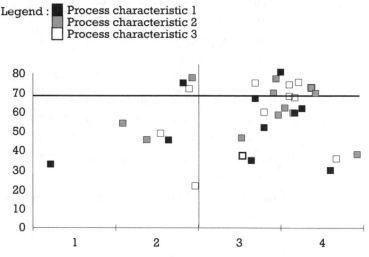

Figure 20.3 Scatter diagrams.

> A pattern in the plotted points on a scatter diagram may suggest that the two factors are associated, perhaps with a cause-and-effect relationship.

Run charts (Figure 20.4) are a specialized, time-sequenced form of scatter diagram that can be used to examine data quickly and informally for trends or other patterns that occur over time.

Interrelationship diagraphs (Figure 20.5):

> Allow a team to systematically identify, analyze, and classify the cause and effect relationships that exist among all critical issues so that key drivers or outcomes can become the heart of an effective solution;

> Encourage team members to think in multiple directions rather than linearly;

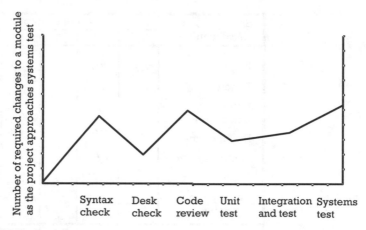

Figure 20.4 Run charts.

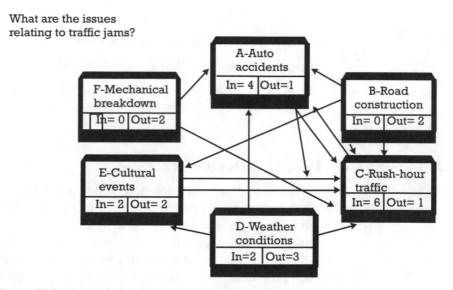

Figure 20.5 Interrelationships diagraph. (*After:* [1].)

▶ Explore cause-and-effect relationships among all the issues;

▶ Allow a team to identify root causes even when credible data does not exist.

Check sheets (Figure 20.6):

▶ Allow a project team to systematically record and compile data from historical sources or observations as they happen;

▶ Clearly detect and show patterns and trends;

▶ Build with each observation a clearer picture of the facts as opposed to opinions of the team members;

Errors classification	Book chapters					
	1	2	3	4	5	Total
Spelling	////	///	//	////	///	16
Punctuation	//	///	//	//	///	12
Missing information	/	//	//	/		6
Redundancy	//	///	/	/	//	9
Technical errors	//	/	//	/	//	8
Format errors			//	/		3
Incomplete concepts						
Total	11	12	11	10	10	54

Figure 20.6 Proof and checking errors. (*After:* [1].)

- Ensure that recordings are made consistently;
- Make patterns in the data become obvious quickly;
- Must collect data over a sufficient period of time to be sure the data represents typical results during a typical cycle for the business.

Addressing defect causes

Following the analysis of the selected defects and other problems to determine the root causes, it is often helpful to group the selected defects based on their root causes. For example, the root causes of defects may include inadequate training, not paying attention to all of the details of the task, or even a process deficiency. The grouping of root causes needs to be accompanied with proposed actions that will be taken to prevent the future occurrence of similar defects. Specific actions include:

- Providing training in common defects and techniques for preventing them;
- Changing a process so that error-prone steps do not occur;
- Automating all or part of a process;
- Reordering process activities;
- Adding process steps to prevent defects.

Before these actions are implemented, it is useful business-wise to analyze the action proposals and determine priorities such as:

- Implications of not addressing the defects;
- Cost to implement process improvements;

- Expected impact on quality;

- What other similar defects may exist in other processes and work products.

Was the change successful?

Before declaring victory, it is necessary to evaluate the impact of the changes by gathering evidence that the process change has corrected the problem. Has the process performance improved? Has the capability of the project's defined process improved? Will the customer's expectations and requirements be satisfied?

Bottom line: Has the process change corrected the problem and improved performance?

Enabling the selection and deployment of improvements

The focus of the Organizational Innovation and Deployment process area is process improvement that is based on a quantitative knowledge of the organization's set of standard processes and technologies and the expected quality and performance of those processes and technologies in predictable situations.

Organizational Innovation and Deployment supports projects and process groups in selecting and deploying improvements that have the possibility to meet the quality and process performance objectives as derived from the organization's business objectives. These product and service quality and process performance objectives include increased productivity and greater customer and end-user satisfaction. Process performance is a measure of the actual process results achieved and is characterized by both process measures and product measures.

Process measures include:

- Effort;

- Cycle time;

- Defect removal efficiency.

Product measures include:

- Reliability;

- Defect density;

- Response time.

Process and quality performance objectives that will be deployed are selected from proposals based on the following criteria:

- A *quantitative* understanding of the organization's current quality and process performance;

- The resources and funding available for that deployment;

- Estimates of the improvement resulting from the deployment;

- The expected benefits *weighed against the cost and impact* to the organization.

Collecting and analyzing improvement proposals

Organizational Innovation and Deployment can be seen as an extension of the activities described in Organizational Process Focus (OPF). OPF provided candidate process improvement sources, including measurement and analysis of the processes, lessons learned from process implementation, and peer review defect trends. In a similar manner Organizational Innovation and Deployment directs project members and project group members to search for process and quality performance objectives proposals that propose *incremental* and *innovative* improvements to specific processes and technologies. Examples of sources for process and technology improvement proposals include:

- Analysis of customer problems;

- Analysis of project performance compared to quality and productivity objectives;

- Analysis of data on defect causes;

- Measured effectiveness of process activities.

It is quite possible that a project or organization could show the technical prowess to reach the product quality or process performance being demanded by the customer, industry, or competitors, but, figuratively speaking, go out of business achieving those results. The Organizational Innovation and Deployment process area clearly stresses that a cost-benefit analysis must be conducted before the decision is made to implement the improvements or innovations suggested. Items that must be considered in that cost-benefit analysis include:

- Estimating the contribution of each candidate process improvement proposal toward the organization's process and technology improvement objectives;

- Estimating the effects of each improvement proposal to mitigate identified project and organizational risks;

- Estimating the effect on related processes and assets;

- Estimating the effects of each candidate process improvement proposal on the ability to respond quickly to changes in project requirements, market situations, and the business environment;

‣ Estimating the expected life span of the proposed innovation.

Deploying improvements

As in any standard process improvement activity, pilot projects should be identified to test the innovative or incremental improvements before they are broadly implemented. Each pilot should be implemented in an environment that is characteristic of the environment in a broadscale deployment. The results of the pilot project must be evaluated to determine if the pilot should be terminated, whether the pilot needs to be replaned and reimplemented, or whether improvements should be deployed throughout more of the organization.

All candidate processes and technology improvements that have been piloted should be prioritized against the organization's business objectives before broadscale deployment begins. The final selection of process and technology improvement proposals for deployment across the organization should always be based on quantifiable criteria derived from the organization's quality and process performance objectives. It is important to always keep in mind that all incremental and innovative improvements that are selected for deployment must measurably improve the organization's processes and technologies.

A deployment plan for each selected process improvement should be developed. The deployment plan must take into consideration:

‣ How each process improvement needs to be adjusted for organization-wide deployment;

‣ What changes are needed to deploy each process and technology improvement, including possible changes to:

  ‣ Process descriptions, standards, and procedures;

  ‣ Development environments;

  ‣ Organizational culture and characteristics;

  ‣ Existing commitments;

  ‣ Knowledge and skills of workforce.

Measures and objectives must be established to determine the value of each improvement with respect to the organization's business objectives. These measures may examine:

‣ Return on investment;

‣ Time to recover the cost of the process or technology improvement;

‣ Measured improvement in the project or organization's process performance;

‣ Ability to respond quickly to changes in project requirements, market situations, and the business environment.

The actual deployment of the process and technology improvements must be carried out in a controlled and disciplined manner. The use of an incremental approach is encouraged. Suggested steps to support the actual deployment process include:

- Providing updated training materials to reflect the improvements to the organization's process and technology assets;
- Providing consultation support;
- Tracking the deployment against the deployment plan;
- Determining if the process and technology improvement deployment actions are complete;
- Documenting and reviewing the results of the deployment:
  - Identifying and documenting lessons learned;
  - Revising process and technology improvement measures, objectives, priorities, and deployment plans as necessary.
- Measuring the effects of the deployed process improvements:
  - Measuring the actual cost, effort, and schedule for deploying each process improvement;
  - Measuring the value of each process improvement;
  - Measuring the progress toward achieving the organization's quantitative objectives for process improvement;
  - Storing the measures in the organizational measurement repository.
- Providing feedback to the organization on the status and results of the process improvement deployment activities.

Summary

The Causal Analysis and Resolution process area guides an organization to manage the removal of the root causes of defects or problems from the project's defined processes. In the Organizational Innovation and Deployment process area, planning is done to manage the deployment of improvements to the organization's processes and technologies that can be quantified against the organization's business objectives. Both process areas are designed to assist an organization to move beyond stabilizing processes to improving them based on the quantitative understanding of those processes and meeting not only the voice of the process but also the voice of the customer.

Reference

[1]   Brassard, M., and D. Ritter, *The Memory Jogger II*, Salem, NH: GOAL/QPC, 1994.

Repeatable, Effective, and Long-Lasting

Defining, implementing, and institutionalizing processes are necessary if any organization expects them to be repeatable, effective, and long-lasting. Questions we may ask ourselves include: Just what does it take for a process to be repeatable, effective, and long-lasting? Why should organizations care? Another question may be: What is institutionalization anyway? Yet another related question may well be: Why does CMMI® place such a great emphasis on this concept?

Are your project members using effective processes?

Before answers to these and other related questions will be provided, the reader ought to take out a blank piece of paper and list as many factors as possible on what an organization might put in place, do, or direct to ensure that its developers and managers are not using ineffective processes. It is probable that you listed training, because training is certainly an activity that helps us to be effective in utilizing the concepts that are offered. Naturally, all processes that an organization asks its people to follow should be documented, reviewed, and implemented. There should also be tailoring guidelines that each individual and project can use to obtain the maximum benefit from them. As lessons are learned, the documented processes ought to be updated to reflect the current understanding of business. You have probably also listed resources because it takes money, time, people, and tools and technology to make processes repeatable and long-lasting. Perhaps your list includes measures, and, just possibly, it includes policies that come from the senior management team to direct the everyday behavior and activities of the organizational work force.

If your list included some of the items listed above and perhaps a few that were not listed, it is an indicator that you understand the technical, managerial, and cultural efforts that it takes to truly develop processes for an organization's projects that can be repeated with measurable results, are effective so no one is thrashing about, and will be long-lasting.

One of the most important reasons that organizations should strive to ensure its processes are repeatable, effective, and long-lasting is that process improvement is not free. Developing processes that are not intended to truly support measurable results is a waste of the organization's money and the time and energy of the people who engage themselves to develop these critical processes.

Institutionalization

When we develop, review, and implement processes that are repeatable, effective, and long-lasting, we say that we are institutionalizing those process across people, projects, and the organization. What then is institutionalization? Institutionalization involves implementing practices that provide needed infrastructure support, ensuring that processes are defined, documented, and understood, and enabling organizational learning to improve those processes to take place. Effective institutionalization is evidenced by the fact that the processes are used and are updated as a result of that usage.

Without institutionalization:

- Processes will not be executed or managed consistently.
- The processes will not survive staff changes.
- Process improvement may not relate to business goals.
- The organization will find itself continuously "reinventing the wheel."
- There will not be the commitment to provide resources or infrastructure to support or improve the processes.
- There will be no historical basis for cost estimation.

The Continuous Representation of CMMI® defines capability levels and generic model components to help an organization to focus on its ability to pursue process improvement in multiple process areas and institutionalize their use along the way. Institutionalization, in this context, implies that the process is ingrained in the way the work is performed.

While the continuous representation uses generic practices for capability levels 1–5, the staged representation only uses the generic practices from capability levels 2 and 3. This chapter will concentrate on those generic practices pertaining to levels 2 and 3.

Capability level 2 generic practices

Institutionalization for capability level 2 of a process area includes generic practices GP 2.1–GP 2.10.

GP 2.1—Establish an Organizational Policy   Establish and maintain an organizational policy for planning and performing the process. The purpose of this practice is to define the organizational expectations for the process and make these expectations visible to those in the organization who are affected. Policies are expectation-setting documents that are delivered from the senior management team. Policies then are *expectation-setting documents*. They should describe the behavior that the senior management team expects out of the workforce. For example, if a policy existed that stated that every project must carry out formal life-cycle work product inspections on product components that were identified as critical, an outside auditor could expect to interview a project leader and ask him or her, "What product components have been identified as critical for your project?" Show the place in the project plan or project quality plan where it is stated that formal life-cycle work product inspections will be conducted and the requirements for the reviewers that will participate in those inspections. How these inspections will be carried out, how much training is required, who will serve as moderators, how checking rates and logging rates will be determined, and how results will be analyzed are issues that should be covered in the organization's set of standard processes. Proving that the life-cycle work product inspections are planned and carried out on identified critical product components would satisfy this institutionalization requirement.

GP 2.2—Plan the Process   Establish and maintain the requirements, objectives, and plan for performing the process. The purpose of this practice is to determine what is needed to perform the process and achieve the established objectives on the project, prepare a plan for effectively performing the process on the project, and obtaining agreement on this plan from all relevant stakeholders. Planning the process means planning to use the documented process on a project so that its use will be effective. Even the planning process itself should be planned. We may ask ourselves, "What would it take to ensure that a process will be used effectively on a project?" Considerations for planning the process should include:

- The defined and documented process description accessible and in a usable form;
- The product life-cycle models that are approved, documented, trained, and supported;
- The schedule in which the process must be performed;
- The dependencies among the activities, work products, and services;
- The resources needed to perform the process including funding, people, and tools;

- Training needed;
- Work products to be placed under Configuration Management;
- Measurement requirements to provide insight into the performance of the process, its work products, and its services;
- Objective verification activities for the process and work products.

GP 2.3—Provide Resources   Provide adequate resources for performing the planned process, developing the work products, and providing the services of the process. The purpose of this practice is to ensure that the resources needed are available when they are needed. The resources include:

- Adequate funding;
- Appropriate physical facilities;
- Skilled people or training, mentoring, and coaching to help the existing workforce gain the necessary knowledge and skills;
- Appropriate tools.

Remember that in Chapter 4 we stated that adequate or appropriate must be interpreted in light of the organization's business objectives. Of course, business constraints must always be considered. Organizations are encouraged to take a hard look at their business objectives and company capabilities in the resources category when attempting to institutionalize the suggested practices found in CMMI®.

It is better to reduce the scope of the process improvement initiative for a period of time rather than to attempt to accomplish all of the expected specific and generic practices without adequate resources. This can only result in frustration on the part of the process improvement champions and also on the part of those who would like to utilize those improved processes, but can only get half-developed processes and occasional support.

GP 2.4—Assign Responsibility   Assign *responsibility* and *authority* for performing the process, developing the work products, and providing the services of the process. The purpose of this practice is to ensure that there is accountability over the life of the process for performing the planned process and achieving the specified results. The real emphasis here must be on "appropriate" authority. Most management teams to whom I have talked, assessed, or offered consulting support have no trouble assigning responsibility. When it comes down to actually giving individuals, for example, project mangers, true authority to carry out the necessary processes identified for their project, the difficulties arise. The assignment and authority must be assured over the life of the process. However, one should not overlook the point here that although authority and responsibility should be assigned, there must still be a mechanism in place to effectively coordinate the actions and activities that have been developed. In other words, there must be a managing mechanism to ensure that progress is made in the right direction consistent with the efforts of the others.

GP 2.5—Train People   Train the people performing or supporting the planned process as needed. Training must support the successful performing of the process by establishing a common understanding of the process and imparting the knowledge and skills needed to perform the process or support the performing of the process. The training should be developed for the appropriate levels of management and practitioners. The training should also be for other departments or groups or relevant stakeholders who do not require the details, but do need an intermediate depth training to ensure they have an appropriate vocabulary to understand what to expect and what is expected of them. Overview training should be provided to those who interact with those performing the work to set proper behavioral expectations.

This generic practice focuses on training in the defined processes of a given process area needed at the project level and possibly at the organizational level. An example taken from the engineering process area of Requirements Development gives examples of training that might be offered, including:

> ▸ Requirements analysis techniques;
> ▸ Requirements elicitation tools and techniques;
> ▸ Requirements specification;
> ▸ Requirements modeling.

In my opinion, training should be thought of as establishing the necessary knowledge and skills. Establishing the necessary knowledge and skills includes training, mentoring, coaching, and on-the-job experience. Training should also include updating previous experience.

GP 2.6—Manage Configurations   Place designated work products of the process under appropriate levels of Configuration Management. The purpose of this practice is to establish and maintain the integrity of the work products throughout their useful lives. Remember from Chapter 9 that if a system exhibits integrity we can expect to have things happen like:

> ▸ Changes to any configuration item within the system are only made according to an established and maintained process and procedure.
> ▸ Life-cycle work products are kept consistent when requirements change requests (CR) are approved, and the requirements specification is then updated. All related life-cycle work products are reviewed to determine if accompanying changes to them are necessary as well.
> ▸ Periodic audits are made on the contents of the system to ensure that changes made to product components are both complete and correct.

The word "appropriate" in this practice must not be interpreted as only version control or developmental control is required. For example, change requests to requirements should require an organization configuration control board to be involved because the "contract" or agreement with the customer may be changed.

GP 2.7—Identify and Involve Relevant Stakeholders   Identify and involve the relevant stakeholders as planned. The purpose of this practice is to establish and maintain the expected involvement of stakeholders during the execution of the process. Identifying the set of stakeholders that needed to be involved during the project life cycle was discussed in Chapter 7. This practice reminds us for each process to think which subset of the stakeholders or relevant stakeholders should be involved and to what level to ensure that the processes are adequately accomplished.

GP 2.8—Monitor and Control the Process   Monitor and control the process against the plan and take appropriate corrective action. The purpose of this practice is to perform the direct day-to-day monitoring and controlling of the process implementation, including:

> • Collect and analyze measures of actual performance against the plan.
> • Review accomplishments and results of the implemented process against the planned process.
> • Identify and evaluate the effects of significant deviations from the planned process.
> • Identify problems in the planned and implemented process.
> • Take corrective action when requirements and objectives are not being satisfied, when issues are identified, or when progress differs significantly from the plan.
> • Track corrective action to closure.

GP 2.9—Objectively Evaluate Adherence   Objectively evaluate adherence of the process and the work products and services of the process to the applicable requirements, objectives, and standards, and address noncompliance. The purpose of this practice is to provide credible assurance that:

> • The process is implemented as planned.
> • The planned process satisfies the relevant policies, requirements, standards, and objectives.
> • The implemented process satisfies the planned process.
> • The results of following the process satisfy their requirements and standards.

Objective evaluation should provide all levels of management with confidence in the results that are being provided. It should address what processes are being followed on the projects, whether they are efficient and effective and whether they are helping the developers to produce the required product quality.

GP 2.10—Review Status with Higher-Level Management   Review the activities, status, and results of the process with higher-level management and resolve issues. The purpose of this practice is to provide higher-level management with the appropriate visibility into the process as described in GP 2.9. These reviews may be part of the monthly senior management review meetings or may take place as a separate meeting. One Motorola business unit senior manager conducted monthly meetings on process improvement progress. He would ask the process owners to report on what progress had been made on the process improvement areas they were sponsoring. The process owners were middle managers in this Motorola business unit. This monthly process improvement progress check forced them to talk with their SEPG facilitator and even get involved to show their interest in the process improvement effort.

Also in attendance at these meetings were representatives from quality assurance and process, in addition to the project manager(s) to give the senior management team a panorama of what was really taking place on the projects. These meetings with the senior management team to discuss process and product quality improvement should be conducted such that they ensure that data-oriented decisions on the planning and performing of the process can be made.

Capability level 3 generic practices

Institutionalization for capability level 3 of a process area includes generic practices GP 3.1 and GP 3.2.

GP 3.1—Establish Defined Process   Establish and maintain the description of the defined process. The purpose of this practice is to establish a description of the project's process that is tailored from the organization's set of standard processes to address the needs of a specific instantiation on a project.

The descriptions of the project's defined processes provide the basis for planning, performing, and managing the activities, work products, and services associated with the process.

GP 3.2—Collect Improvement Information   Collect work products, measures, measurement results, and improvement information derived from planning and performing the process to support the future use and improvement of the organization's processes and process assets. This generic practice provides a reminder to all organizations and projects to constantly keep improving the process.

Summary

Institutionalization involves implementing practices that provide needed infrastructure support, ensuring processes are defined, documented, and understood, and enabling organizational learning to improve those processes to take place. These practices are defined as generic practices. They are expected model components and are applicable for all process areas. Generic practices 2.1–2.10 define the practices to institutionalize the process areas as capability level 2 and generic practices 3.1 and 3.2 define the practices to institutionalize the process areas as capability level 3. If an organization has institutionalized the process areas defined in CMMI® Maturity Level 2 and wishes to be appraised at CMMI® Maturity Level 3, it must not only institutionalize the process areas defined at CMMI® Maturity Level 3, but must also ensure that the process areas institutionalized at CMMI® Maturity Level 2 are now institutionalized at CMMI® Maturity Level 3 as well.

The Constagedeous Approach to Process Improvement

The principles behind CMMI® and its use in process improvement are the same regardless of the model representation. The motivation behind launching and sustaining process improvement programs should always be backed by sound business goals.

There are many standards and models that have been developed and have evolved over the past decade that have been used to help guide an organization's process improvement initiative. These standards and models include: ISO 9001, TickIT, BOOTSTRAP, SPICE, CMM® for Software, EIA-731, and CMMI®. Not only are there many standards and models available, but they also come in "flavors" sometimes called *representations*. The two most common representations are staged and continuous, which not only offer a way of categorizing process areas, but are also used as the mechanism to guide an organization's process improvement initiative. Today, strong statements are made as to why one approach is more desirable and effective than the other.

Choosing between the staged and continuous CMMI representations

Given the two representations in CMMI®, an organization may feel it has to choose to approach process improvement from either the process area capability approach or the organizational maturity approach. However, after helping to develop CMMI® workshops for the SEI, teaching those CMMI® workshops to thousands of people, conducting CMMI® assessments, and helping organizations to get their CMMI®-based process improvement program going, it is my belief that both the

261

staged representation and the continuous representation not only can but must be used together to provide a realistic approach that results in effective process improvement to support an organization's business objectives.

In this chapter we will look at the similarities and differences between the two representations and suggest ways that the combined continuous *and* staged, or *constagedeous,* approach can provide guidance that will result in an effective process improvement initiative.

CMMI structure: Staged versus continuous

The difference between the staged and continuous representations lays in the way in which CMMI®'s process areas are presented. As you are aware, a process area is a collection of related specific practices that are performed collectively to achieve objectives pertaining to specific goals. In the staged representation, process areas are grouped into maturity levels. Organizations choosing the staged framework implement those process areas at the specified maturity level. These process areas are predetermined. As each maturity level is achieved, the set of related processes is stabilized, and the organization's ability to predict the future performance of its processes increases.

In the continuous representation, process areas are grouped into four process categories (process management, project management, engineering, and support). These process categories are implementcd as determined by thc organization. Process areas achieve capability levels, which reflect the "manner" in which the content of the process areas is performed. The *manner* simply indicates *how* the content of the process area is performed.

For both staged and continuous representations, the content of a process area is reflected in the process area's specific practices and specific goals. In other words, specific practices are indicators of *what is needed* to perform the process area, whereas specific goals are indicators of *what the expected behavior is*. Generic goals and generic practices, on the other hand, are indicators of process institutionalization. They indicate whether the practices behind the process areas have been mastered by the organization and have become part of the normal way people perform these activities. Institutionalization implies there is an infrastructure in place for ensuring the adoption and permanence of best practices.

In both representations, institutionalization occurs via the generic practices. These were defined in detail in Chapter 21. In the staged representation, institutionalization is embedded in the four common features that organize the generic practices. These common features are: commitment to perform, ability to perform, directing implementation, and verifying implementation. In the continuous representation, institutionalization is embedded within the capability levels that categorize the generic practices. The institutionalization practices that are common in both representations are listed in Table 22.1.

Table 22.1 Institutionalization Mapping

Generic Practices—Staged and Continuous	Common Features (Staged Only)
GP 2.1: Establish an Organizational Policy	Commitment to perform
GP 2.2: Plan the Process	Ability to perform
GP 2.3: Provide Resources	Ability to perform
GP 2.4: Assign Responsibility	Ability to perform
GP 2.5: Train People	Ability to perform
GP 2.6: Manage Configurations	Directing implementation
GP 2.7: Identify and Involve Relevant Stakeholders	Directing implementation
GP 2.8: Monitor and Control the Process	Directing implementation
GP 2.9: Objectively Evaluate Adherence	Verifying implementation
GP 2.10: Review Status with Higher-Level Management	Verifying implementation
GP 3.1: Establish a Defined Process	Ability to perform
GP 3.2: Collect Improvement Information	Directing implementation

The first column in Table 22.1 lists the generic practices that make for process institutionalization. These are the same generic practices for both representations. The second column shows the mapping of the generic practices to the staged representation's common features.

GP 2.1 explicitly states what the organization is committed to do or change. In the staged representation, this generic practice is also known as the commitment to perform common feature.

The generic practices GP 2.2 through GP 2.5 represent the preconditions that need to be in place for the organization to be "able" to perform the practices of the process area. That is, the organization has a plan to perform the process, explicit assignment of roles and responsibilities pertaining to the process practices, trained resources, and funding and appropriate technology to perform the practices. In the staged representation, the generic practices GP 2.2 through GP 2.5 are also known as the ability to perform common feature.

The generic practices GP 2.6 through GP 2.8 focus on what happens once the processes are executed. This is the point where organizations get the day-to-day visibility into the processes that they put in place. Thus, it is necessary not only to put processes in place and appropriate resources to execute them, but also to understand how these processes are operating and how effective they are. We obtain this visibility by controlling the processes' work products, ensuring the involvement of the relevant stakeholders during process execution, monitoring the progress of the processes, and taking corrective actions as insight into the process performance is gained. This insight is typically achieved through the measurement and analysis of measurement data. In the staged representation, the generic practices GP 2.6 through GP 2.8 are also known as the directing implementation common feature.

The generic practices GP 2.9 through GP 2.10 ensure that the organization conforms to the applicable processes, procedures, and standards. In the context of process improvement, the organization cares that its processes, associated training, and resources are indeed the right processes that represent the organizational collective knowledge and the current needs of the organization.

In the staged representation the generic practices GP 2.9 and GP 2.10 are also known as the verifying implementation common feature.

In the continuous representation, the manner in which the process area is performed takes on the institutionalization generic practices indicated within the various capability levels. For example: A process area whose content is satisfied has achieved capability level 2 if the manner in which it is performed is supported by a policy, a plan for executing it, resources, funding, and training, explicit identification of all appropriate stakeholders in that process, adherence evaluations, and reviews with high-level management, as well as day-to-day monitoring and controlling of the process and its performance. Additionally, the specific practices themselves are associated with a capability level. Those specific practices whose capability level is 1 are known as base practices, whereas the specific practices whose capability level is higher than 1 are known as advanced practices. Advanced practices are found in the engineering process areas. Thus, when evolving a process area through the capability levels, one has to consider not only the application of the appropriate generic practices at the capability level of interest, but also any advanced practices at that same capability level for the process area.

In the staged representation there is no concept of an advanced practice. The highest capability level specific practice in the continuous representation is the same as the one found in the staged representation. Moreover, if an advanced practice evolves from a lower capability level specific practice, the lower-level specific practice is inserted as informative material in the staged representation, so the difference between the staged and continuous representations are where there are advanced practices is in terms of granularity of information, and not in terms of pure content.

In the staged representation we talk about improving an organization's maturity and we do that by satisfying that process area's specific goals that are prescribed at the maturity level of interest, as well as by satisfying the common features of all appropriate process areas (i.e., the generic practices).

Now it appears that the *similarities* between the two representations are stronger than the differences. Functionally speaking, both representations focus on the best practices that meet the objectives of the various process areas as well as on the practices responsible for institutionalization.

Process improvement is the driving force

Organizations that opt to choose CMMI® SE/SW/IPPD/SS V1.1 as a framework for process improvement do so because they want mature, stable, and predictable processes. Representation is not the driving force. Process improvement is the driving force. Process improvement does not happen just for its own sake. Every organization determines what its business goals are and what its problems are, and, based upon this, they must discern the path to process improvement. When you look at your own business and you know what the model content is, you start thinking about what you need to do to address your business issues. You don't think continuous or staged. You implement process improvement to satisfy your issues.

The question is then: Why has there been such a controversy over the use of the staged or continuous representation of the CMMI®? Certainly the legacy of the use of CMM® for Software is a reason to lean towards the staged representation of CMMI®. Certainly if you were an engineering-oriented company, you might be tempted to choose the continuous representation of the CMMI®, as it has a strong focus on the engineering process areas, and the front-end material of the CMMI® Model—Continuous Representation seems to suggest that a business unit could focus on any set of process areas it wants.

However, is it true that if an organization chooses the Staged Representation, the processes can only be improved if they are associated with the process areas defined at Maturity Level 2? In other words, is an organization allowed to try to improve its Requirements Development processes if the organization has not achieved CMMI® Maturity Level 2 yet? Requirements Development is a CMMI® Maturity Level 3 process area. But how can an organization successfully institutionalize the practices found in Requirements Management at CMMI® Maturity Level 2 if they do not have the proper mechanism to gather and analyze the requirements in the first place? The Staged Representation has no restrictions on doing what makes good business sense and good practical sense.

If an organization chooses to focus on the Engineering process areas brought over from the Systems Engineering CMM®, and it chooses the Continuous Representation, does it have to worry about project management at all, or can that come later after the engineering processes are in place and being implemented? The Staged Representation guided organizations to implement project management practices to support the engineering practices. Does this mean the Continuous Representation is too unstructured?

However, if you are focused on process improvement to support your business objectives with measurable results, you will probably want to use an incremental approach to collect or gather the requirements in an ad hoc manner at first and then evolve to using more effective requirements elicitation techniques described in the Requirements Development process area. You would apply the principles of Requirements Management on the requirements you have gathered regardless of the technique you used. Now you undoubtedly realize that this sounds a lot like the Continuous Representation of the CMMI®. You may therefore ask the obvious questions, "Does that mean that my organization should use the Continuous Representation?" "What representation are you recommending?" The answer to these questions is really what this chapter is all about. In fact, you will want to use both approaches concurrently. How this is accomplished will now be further explained.

Myths and misconceptions

The debates on whether to use the staged representation or the continuous representation have reached fevered pitch at times with level ratings and politics liberally added. We would like to offer a set of myths and misconceptions, negative influences on process improvement, and positive influence on process improvement from the point of view of the staged representation and the continuous representation to make a stronger case for an organization to use "both" as tools to support process improvement.

Staged representation

The staged representation of CMMI® focuses on organizational maturity:

- Represented by the degree of process improvement across a predefined set of process areas;
- Chosen to meet the process improvement needs of an organization;
- Processes ordered and then grouped based upon predefined organizational maturity relationships that address the business needs of many organizations;
- Provides an indicator of the maturity of an organization's processes in order to answer: What will the most likely outcomes be of the next project we undertake?

Myths and misconceptions (staged)

The myths and misconceptions of staged representation are that:

- Requirements Management must be implemented fully before Requirements Development can take place.
- Quality assurance and Configuration Management only apply to projects at CMMI® Maturity Level 2.
- An organization's measurement program must be fully implemented by the time it reaches CMMI® Maturity Level 2.
- Peer reviews should not be implemented until the organization is ready for CMMI® Maturity Level 3 activities.
- Risk Management should not be implemented until the organization is working on CMMI® Maturity Level 3.
- Organizations will not have troubles with suppliers after reaching CMMI® Maturity Level 2.
- Engineering activities are not necessary to achieve CMMI® Maturity Level 2.
- Organizational training is not necessary until an organization is ready to start on CMMI® Maturity Level 3 processes.

Negative influences on process improvement (staged)

Negative influences on process improvement for staged representation are that it:

- Gives organizations the idea that they can only implement process improvement initiatives that focus on process areas that are included in a particular maturity level;
- Does not provide guidance for how to incrementally implement process areas such as Technical Solution;
- Does not provide any guidance for what it would look and feel like to implement an ML 3 process area from a lower maturity level perspective;
- Focuses the organization more on the achievement of a maturity level than on measurable improvement that supports the organization's business objectives;
- Can influence the organization to over focus on management practices and neglect technical practices.

Positive influences on process improvement (staged)

Positive influences on process improvement for staged representation are that it:

- Helps organizations to prioritize their process improvement efforts, especially when:
  - The organization's process improvement initiative is just getting started.
  - The organization is at a low maturity level.
  - The organization has little experience in process deployment.
- Focuses the organization on putting in place project management functions that are needed to support all of the organization's engineering and management activities throughout its process improvement journey.

Continuous representation

The continuous representation of CMMI® focuses on organizational process area capability:

- The extent to which a process is explicitly documented, managed, measured, controlled, and continually improved;
- Represents improvements in the implementation and effectiveness of an individual process area;
- Supports the continuous improvement of individual process areas that are critical to the organization's business needs;

> ▸ Provides an indicator of improvement within a single process area in order to answer: What is a good strategy for implementing improvement of this process area?

Myths and misconceptions (continuous)

The myths and misconceptions of continuous representation are that:

> ▸ An organization can focus its process improvement initiative on any group of process areas it wants without worrying about possible dependencies.
>
> ▸ Capability level 1 for a given process area is easily obtained (e.g., Quantitative Project Management).
>
> ▸ An organization can practically evolve any process area to capability level 5.
>
> ▸ Focusing on the continuous representation and the capability levels will remove the focus on the number that is associated with the staged representation.
>
> ▸ There is a clear evolution path for all process areas that can simply be followed to help an organization evolve to capability level 5 for all or most of its process areas.
>
> ▸ Using the continuous representation will not require prioritization of the implementation of its process areas.
>
> ▸ The engineering process areas are not as useful for software engineering application since they are based primarily on systems engineering needs.

Negative influences on process improvement (continuous)

Negative influences on continuous improvement for continuous representation are that it:

> ▸ Does seem to indicate that an organization is given extreme flexibility of choosing the process areas for implementation in any order desired without regard to dependencies;
>
> ▸ Allows an emphasis on implementing the engineering activities and diminishing the importance of the management activities.

Positive influences on process improvement (continuous)

Positive influences on process improvement for continuous representation are that:

> ▸ Through the use of the engineering process areas and the generic practices, the continuous representation can provide an individual capability improvement path for each process area.

> If the business need demands it, the path to evolve a particular process area or category of process areas to higher levels of capability can be easily identified and measured.

> It assists an organization in constructing a target profile of process areas that collectively will help the organization to solve known business objectives.

The constagedeous approach to process improvement

If your company is truly focused on process improvement to support its business objectives and deliver high-quality products and services, then it should use the *constagedeous* approach to process improvement. In reality many organizations do constagedeous improvements, choosing the continuous representation (whether they realize it or not) in a staged way. They address a couple of process areas at a time before they move to another set of improvements. They may look at their progress by assessing the process area(s) of interest (continuous assessment), or they may put a number of improvements in place and decide to examine the process areas belonging to a certain maturity level (staged assessment).

Less experienced organizations may want to avoid being overwhelmed at the demand of the staged representation to assess progress of all process areas belonging to a maturity level and may thus choose an evolutionary approach to realizing and validating improvements, a couple of process areas at a time, using the constagedeous approach. It is all a matter of how one looks at these possibilities. Process improvement is an evolutionary activity, small steps at a time in an incremental way. No one can address all issues all at once. You conduct interim progress checkups, regardless of the representation, but you could employ the continuous approach to assess the capability of your process areas, or you can still put improvements in place and wait and assess the maturity level of a bunch of process areas at a level, as prescribed by that level. If you want to focus on project management process areas, your organization still needs to gather requirements; design, build components, peer review, and unit test them; and perform integration, conduct systems testing, and eventually produce a product that is delivered. In other words, you still need to perform basic engineering activities. Claiming CMMI® Maturity Level 2 without doing engineering makes absolutely no sense.

If you want to focus your organization on the engineering process areas, you still need enough project planning, project monitoring and control, and risk management. You still need to perform sufficient Configuration Management to control the life-cycle work products that your project produces and you must ensure the more critical processes are followed to guarantee the minimal product quality defined in your requirements. You may even have to manage suppliers who will build subsystems that you will integrate to build the final product. In other words, you still need to perform the basic project management functions and eventually produce a product that is delivered. Claiming CMMI® Maturity Level 2 without doing project management makes absolutely no sense.

Summary

The message is clear. When you choose the continuous approach, the capability of your various process areas has implications on organizational maturity, and when you choose the staged approach, the organizational maturity has implications on the maturity of your process areas. Process improvement is the driving force, and process improvement does not happen for its own sake. Every organization must focus on its own business objectives and vision. It must determine what its problems or process weaknesses are and, based on these, must determine the path to process improvement. When you look at your own business objectives and you know what the model content is, you can start thinking about what you need to do to address your business issues. You do not think continuous or staged. You simply do process improvement to satisfy your business issues, and you do this using a constagedeous approach.

Selected Bibliography

Ahern, D., A. Clouse, and R. Turner, *CMMI Distilled: A Practical Introduction to Integrated Process Improvement*, Reading, MA: Addison-Wesley, 2001.

Bate, R., et al., *Systems Engineering Capability Maturity Model, Version 1.1, (SE-CMM)* Pittsburgh, PA: Software Engineering Institute, (CMU/SEI-95-MM-003), 1995.

Bouldin, B. M., *Agents of Change*, Englewood Cliffs, NJ: Yourdon Press, 1989.

Brassard, M., and D. Ritter, *The Memory Jogger II*, Salem, NH: GOAL/QPC, 1994.

Basili, V. R., *Software Modeling and Measurement: The Goal Question Metric Paradigm*, Computer Science Technical Report Series, CS-TR-2956 (UMIACS-TR-9296), College Park, MD: University of Maryland, September 1992.

Basili, V. R., G. Caldiera, and H. D. Rombach, "Goal Question Metric Paradigm," *Encyclopedia of Software Engineering, Volume 1*, J. J. Marciniak, (ed.), New York: John Wiley & Sons, 1994, pp. 528–532.

Burr, A., and M. Owen, *Statistical Methods for Software Quality*, Boston, MA: International Thomson Computer Press, 1996.

Bush, M., "Modern Software Assurance and a Five-Level Model of Software Assurance Maturity," *High Integrity Systems*, Vol. 1, No. 2, 1994, pp. 157–169.

Charette, R. N., *Software Engineering Risk Analysis and Management*, New York: McGraw-Hill, 1989.

CMMI Product Development Team, Capability Maturity Model Integration (CMMI), *CMMI for Systems Engineering, Software Engineering, Integrated Product and Process Development, and Supplier Sourcing Version 1.1* (CMMI-SE/SW/IPPD/SS, V1.1), *Continuous Representation*, (CMU/SEI-2002-TR-011, ESC-TR-2002-011), Pittsburgh, PA: Software Engineering Institute, Carnegie Mellon University, March 2002.

CMMI Product Development Team, *CMMI for Systems Engineering/Software Engineering/Integrated Product and Process Development/Supplier Sourcing, Version 1.1 Staged Representation* (CMU/SEI-2002-TR-012, ESC-TR-2002-012), Pittsburgh, PA: Software Engineering Institute, Carnegie Mellon University, March 2002.

Crosby, P. B., *Quality Is Free*, New York: McGraw-Hill, 1979.

Curtis, B., W. Hefley, and S. Miller, *People Capability Maturity Model*, Reading, MA: Addison-Wesley, 2001.

Dalziel, M. M., and S. C. Schoonover, *Changing Ways*, New York: AMACOM, 1988.

Daskalantonakis, M., "A Practical View of Software Measurement and Implementation Experience with Motorola," *IEEE Software*, Vol. 18, No. 11, 1992, pp. 998–1010.

Daughtrey, T., *Fundamental Concepts for the Software Quality Engineer*, Milwaukee, WI: American Society for Quality Press, 2002.

Deming, W. E., *Out of the Crisis*, Cambridge, MA: MIT Center for Advanced Engineering Study, 1986.

Dowson, M., *Proceedings of the First International Conference on the Software Process Manufacturing Complex Systems*, IEEE Computer Society Press, October 21–22, 1991.

Electronic Industries Alliance, "EIA Standard: EIA 632 Standard, Processes for Engineering a System," (ANSI /EIA/IS-632-1998), Washington D.C., 1998.

Electronic Industries Alliance, "EIA Interim Standard: National Consensus Standard for Configuration Management," (EIA/IS-649), Washington, D.C., 1995.

Electronic Industries Alliance, "Systems Engineering Capability Model," (EIA/IS-731), Washington, D.C.: 1998.

Evans, M., and J. Marciniak, *Software Quality Assurance & Management*, New York: John Wiley & Sons, 1987.

FAA-ICMM Project Team, *Federal Aviation Administration Integrated Capability Maturity Model (FAA-ICMM) for the Acquisition of Software Intensive Systems*, Federal Aviation Administration, 1997.

Ferguson, J., et al., *Software Acquisition Capability Maturity Model (SA-CMM) Version 1.01*, Pittsburgh, PA: Software Engineering Institute, (CMU/SIE-96-TR-020), December 1996.

Florac, W. A., and A. D. Carleton, *Measuring the Software Process: Statistical Process Control for Software Process Improvement*, Reading, MA: Addison-Wesley, 1999.

Fowler, P., and S. Rifkin, *Software Engineering Process Group Guide*, Pittsburgh, PA: Software Engineering Institute, CMU/SEI-90-TR-24, September 1990.

Gilb, T., *Software Metrics*, Bromley, England: Winthrop, 1977.

Hall, E. M., *Managing Risk: Methods for Software Systems Development*, Reading, MA: Addison-Wesley, 1998.

House, R. S., *The Human Side of Project Management*, Reading, MA: Addison-Wesley, 1988.

Humphrey, W. S., *Managing the Software Process*, Reading, MA: Addison-Wesley, 1989.

IEEE Standard for Industry Implementation of International Standard "ISO/IEC 12207: 1995 (ISO/IEC 12207) Standard for Information Technology," (includes IEEE/EIA Stds 12207.0-1996, 12207.1-1997, and 12207.2-1994).

International Organization for Standardization (ISO) and International Electrotechnical Commission (IEC), "ISO/IEC TR 12207 Information Technology-Software Life Cycle Processes," 1995.

International Organization for Standardization and International Electrotechnical Commission, "ISO/IEC TR 15504 Information Technology-Software Process Assessment," 1998.

International Organization for Standardization, "ISO 9001, Quality Management Systems—Requirements," 2000.

International Organization for Standardization, "ISO 9000, Quality Management ISO Standards Compendium," 1994

International Organization for Standardization and International Electrotechnical Commission, "ISO/IEC TR 15939 Software Engineering-Software Measurement Process," 2002.

Juran, J. M., *Juran on Planning for Quality*, New York: Macmillan, 1988.

Kaplan, R. S., and D. P. Norton, *The Balanced Score Card*, Boston, MA: Harvard Business School Press, 1996.

Kasse, T., *Action Focused Assessment for Software Process Improvement*, Norwood, MA: Artech House, 2002.

Kasse, T., *CMMI Workshop*, Phoenix, AZ: Kasse Initiatives LLC, 2000.

Kasse, T., *Configuration Management Workshop*, Plano, TX: Kasse Initiatives LLC, 2003.

Kasse, T., *Project Management for Systems Engineers Workshop*, Kasse Initiatives LLC, Plano, TX: 2003.

Kasse, T., *Requirements Engineering Workshop*, Phoenix, AZ: Kasse Initiatives LLC, 2001.

Kasse, T., *Risk Management Workshop*, Phoenix, AZ: Kasse Initiatives LLC, 2001.

Kasse, T., *Software Quality Engineering Workshop*, Phoenix, AZ: Kasse Initiatives LLC, 2001.

Kasse, T., *Supplier Management Workshop*, Plano, TX: Kasse Initiatives LLC, 2003.

Kasse, T., *Systems Engineering Workshop*, Phoenix, AZ: Kasse Initiatives LLC, 2001.

Kezsborn, D. S., and K. A. Edward, *The New Dynamic Project Management: Winning Through the Competitive Advantage*, New York: John Wiley & Sons, 2001.

Kotonya, G., and I. Sommerville, *Requirements Engineering: Processes and Techniques*, Chichester, England: John Wiley & Sons, 1998.

Kulpa, M. K., and K. A. Johnson, *Interpreting the CMMI: A Process Improvement Approach*, Boca Raton, FL: Auerbach Publication, a CRC Press Company, 2003.

Military Standard, "Defense System Software Development (DOD-STD2167)," Washington, D.C.: United States Department of Defense, 1985.

Military Standard, "Defense System Software Development (DOD-STD2167A)," Washington, D.C.: United States Department of Defense, 1988.

Military Standard, "Software Development and Documentation (DOD-STD498)" Washington, D.C.: United States Department of Defense, 1994.

Moti, F., "Engineering Systems Thinking and Systems Thinking," *Systems Engineering*, Vol. 3, No. 3, 2000, pp. 163–168.

Mutafelija, B., and H. Stromberg, *Systematic Process Improvements Using ISO 9001:2000 and CMMI*, Norwood, MA: Artech House, 2003.

Oosterlking, Hans, *Software Process Improvement with ING Group Technical Report*, London, England: European Software Engineering Process Group (ESEPG), June 1998.

Paulk, M. C., et al., *The Capability Maturity Model: Guidelines for Improving the Software Process*, Reading, MA: Addison-Wesley, 1995.

Paulk, M. C., et al., *Capability Maturity Model for Software (Version 1.1)*, Pittsburgh, PA: Software Engineering Institute, CMU/SEI-91-TR-24, August 1991.

Paulk, M. C., et al., *Key Practices of the Capability Maturity Model, Version 1.1*, Pittsburgh PA: Software Engineering Institute, CMU/SEI-93-TR-25, February 1993.

Paulk, M. C., M. B. Chrissis, and C. V. Weber, *Capability Maturity Model for Software, Version 1.1*, Pittsburgh, PA: Software Engineering Institute, CMU/SEI-93-TR-24, February 1993.

Radice, R., et al., "A Programming Process Architecture," *IBM Systems Journal*, Vol. 24, No. 2, 1985.

Shaw, M., "Prospects for an Engineering Discipline of Software," *IEEE Software*, Vol. 7, No. 6, November 1990, pp. 15–24.

Shaw, M., et al., *What a Software Engineer Needs to Know*, Pittsburgh, PA: Software Engineering Institute, CMU/SEI-89-TR-30, DTIC Number ADA219064.

Sheard, S., "The Frameworks Quagmire, A Brief Look," *IEEE Software*, Quag 14d SPC, 1998.

Shewhart, W. A., *Economic Control of Quality of Manufactured Product*, New York: Van Nostrand, 1931.

Software Engineering Institute, *The Capability Maturity Model: Guidelines for Improving the Software Process*, Reading, MA: Addison-Wesley, 1995.

Software Engineering Institute, *Integrated Product Development Capability Maturity Model, Draft Version 0.98*, Pittsburgh, PA: Enterprise Process Improvement Collaboration and Software Engineering Institute, Carnegie Mellon University, July 1997.

Software Engineering Institute, *Software CMM, Version 2.0 (Draft C)*, October 1997.

"Trillium: Telecom Software Product Development Process Capability Assessment Model," Draft 2.2, Bell Canada, July 1992.

U.S. Air Force, *Software Development Capability/Capacity Review*, U.S. Air Force, ASD Pamphlet 800-5, September 10, 1987.

Weber, C. V., et al., *Key Practices of the Capability Maturity Model*, Pittsburgh, PA: Software Engineering Institute, CMU/SEI-91-TR-25, August 1991.

About the Author

Tim Kasse is the CEO and principal consultant of Kasse Initiatives LLC. Previously, he was the CEO and principal consultant for the Institute for Software Process Improvement (ISPI), which he cofounded with Jeff Perdue in 1991. His focus is on innovative solutions for process improvement of business, systems, software, people, and lifestyles.

Prior to starting ISPI, Mr. Kasse spent 4 years at the Software Engineering Institute. He was a major contributor to the development of the Capability Maturity Model® for software. He is recognized as the individual most responsible for the evolution of SEI's assessment method, which was commercialized in 1990. Mr. Kasse also led the development of the Software Engineering Institute's Intermediate CMMI® Workshop for Lead Assessors. He has been authorized by the SEI to conduct SCAMPI^{SM} assessments and has participated in more than 80 Process Assessments in North America, South America, Europe, and Asia.

Mr. Kasse is the architect of the Action Focused Assessment, which has been applied in major organizations throughout the world. He is also the author of *Action Focused Assessment for Software Process Improvement* (Artech House, 2002). He is the primary developer of many Kasse Initiatives workshops, including Software/Systems Quality Engineering, Software/Systems Configuration Management, Risk Management, CMMI®, Action Focused Assessment, and Systems Engineering. Mr. Kasse is a recognized speaker at major process improvement and quality management conferences around the world.

In the SEI, Mr. Kasse is a visiting scientist supporting the CMMI® through training and presentations worldwide. He holds the position of visiting fellow at the Institute of Systems Science/National University of Singapore and is instrumental in developing and teaching parts of the ISS Masters of Technology curriculum. He has an M.S. in computer science and a B.S. in systems engineering and has more than 30 years of systems/software-related experience. Mr. Kasse can be reached at kassetc@aol.com.

Index

A Practitioner's Guide to Software Test Design, Lee Copeland

Risk-Based E-Business Testing, Paul Gerrard and Neil Thompson

Secure Messaging with PGP and S/MIME, Rolf Oppliger

Software Fault Tolerance Techniques and Implementation, Laura L. Pullum

Software Verification and Validation for Practitioners and Managers, Second Edition, Steven R. Rakitin

Strategic Software Production with Domain-Oriented Reuse, Paolo Predonzani, Giancarlo Succi, and Tullio Vernazza

Successful Evolution of Software Systems, Hongji Yang and Martin Ward

Systematic Process Improvement Using ISO 9001:2000 and CMMI®, Boris Mutafelija and Harvey Stromberg

Systematic Software Testing, Rick D. Craig and Stefan P. Jaskiel

Systems Modeling for Business Process Improvement, David Bustard, Peter Kawalek, and Mark Norris, editors

Testing and Quality Assurance for Component-Based Software, Jerry Zeyu Gao, H. -S. Jacob Tsao, and Ye Wu

User-Centered Information Design for Improved Software Usability, Pradeep Henry

Workflow Modeling: Tools for Process Improvement and Application Development, Alec Sharp and Patrick McDermott

For further information on these and other Artech House titles, including previously considered out-of-print books now available through our In-Print-Forever® (IPF®) program, contact:

Artech House
685 Canton Street
Norwood, MA 02062
Phone: 781-769-9750
Fax: 781-769-6334
e-mail: artech@artechhouse.com

Artech House
46 Gillingham Street
London SW1V 1AH UK
Phone: +44 (0)20 7596-8750
Fax: +44 (0)20 7630-0166
e-mail: artech-uk@artechhouse.com

Find us on the World Wide Web at: www.artechhouse.com